CW00404849

FOOD FOR THE SOUL

Part 1

FEAST DAY HOMILIES

FOR

YEAR A

BY

FATHER FRANCIS MAPLE O.F.M. Cap

(Seasons of Advent, Lent and Easter)

http://fatherfrancismaple.co.uk/

ABOUT THE AUTHOR

Being told at school that he had a pleasant voice was the encouragement which led to the guitar and, eventually, the title of "The Singing Friar" with concerts at the Liverpool Phil, Preston Guildhall, Derby Assembly Rooms and London's Drury Lane, and the recording of 42 albums and a Gold Disc for his album the "Old Rugged Cross".

This success helped Father Francis raise over one million pounds for charities supporting the poor - for which he was awarded the MBE in the Queen's 1997 Honours List.

Other special moments have been the day of his clothing as a friar when he chose the name of Francis, receiving a very special grace at Mount Alverna where Saint Francis of Assisi was given the five wounds which had been inflicted on Jesus on the Cross, being asked to sing a solo rendering of the "Old Rugged Cross" on the top of Calvary itself and twice shaking hands with Pope Saint John Paul II.

But the musts in daily life continue to be the celebration of the Sacrifice of the Mass, the Divine Office, the Rosary, an hour of mental prayer and, in Lent, the Stations of the Cross.

The three graces prayed for after each Holy Communion are an abundance of God's Holy Spirit, particularly His gifts of wisdom, prayer and final perseverance. And every day he thanks God for creating him, providing the parents he had, giving him the Catholic faith, his vocation as a Capuchin friar and the gift of the priesthood.

Another great love of his is Our Blessed Lady, given by Jesus to us to be our Mother.

Father Francis was born into a Catholic family and blessed with devout parents. They played the greatest part in his vocation to the brotherhood of the Capuchins and the priesthood by giving him the necessary grounding in the faith.

He was inspired when aged nine by a kind and friendly Capuchin, and impressed by his brown habit, white cord, beard and sandals. And he is grateful to a fellow friar, Brother Declan Keogh, who during the noviciate and student days encouraged him with friendship, patience and scholarship to keep going when times were very tough - especially because his public speaking was atrocious.

But from the moment of his ordination the preaching came more easily and became more accomplished.

Today the ardent desire of Father Francis continues to be what it has always been - to get to Heaven.

And one still unfulfilled ambition is that two young men will look at him and say, "I would like to be a Capuchin like Father Francis."

MUSINGS AND ACKNOWLEDGMENTS

Whenever I read a book I ask myself the question "Why did this person write this book and the background behind it?" Now I am in the position of informing you about this book.

Here is the story of my literary beginnings. I was on holiday in Cork and there I met a lady Anne O'Callaghan. She was very bright and full of ideas. One day she said to me, "You have some lovely ideas and you ought to share them with others. Have you ever thought of writing them down and asking an editor of a newspaper to get them printed?"

I came back to my beloved Pantasaph and I followed her suggestion. The Wrexham Evening Leader was literally weeks old and had just started printing for the Wrexham and Chester areas. I put Anne's suggestion before the Editor. He said, "Send me some of your thoughts and if I like them I'll print them." He must have liked them because the Evening Leader employed me for 22 years! So that was my start to literary fame!

Later I approached Joe Kelly, editor of The Universe if I could have a Sunday homily printed each week in his paper and this ran for 13 years.

I never found preaching easy. I remember the day before my ordination walking round the garden with a fellow ordinand and saying to him, "Adrian, do you realise that on Sunday we will be preaching our first homily?" He replied, "Yes, what are we going to say?" If at the time of my ordination I had relied more on the Holy Spirit, and known more about the inspired word of God, I would have found the task much easier. And seeking the help of Mary, our spiritual mother, would have been a definite advantage.

My Mum and Dad also helped me with preaching. My father was a very crafty man. When we came back from Sunday Mass at breakfast he would ask each one of us what the priest spoke about. This was his way of making sure that we listened to the homily. My Mum always used to say, "Son, when preaching try and get a homely story to back up your point and you will get people listening to you. They may not remember your homily but they won't forget the story." So I do have Mum and Dad to thank.

There are several people I have to thank on my preaching journey. I provided my secretary with a computer to help her in her work and I made up my mind that I was never going to learn working that contraption. I was on a parish mission in Heswall in the Wirral, and told the parishioners to consult the beautifully designed newsletter for details about the mission. After Mass the priest's housekeeper, Brenda O'Hare, was not at all pleased with me for what I said about her newsletter. I reiterated and endorsed every word I said. I asked how she did it. She showed me her Amstrad. I said I bought one like that for my secretary and which two other friars use. I told her I did not realise that my computer could produce such a beautiful newsletter. She said, "After I have prepared lunch, I will give you an hour and I will show you how to use one." I wasn't at all pleased. She bullied me into learning it and now I can't thank her enough. When I returned to the friary I tried to retrieve my computer. The two friars said I can't have it back because all their work was on it. I told Brenda this. She offered to order one for me and I would pay for it. It cost £500 in those days. When her parish priest heard this he told Brenda, "Tell Fr. Francis not to send the money he would pay for it. He gave us a good mission and that is our present to him." Wasn't I a lucky man? I tell this tale because I don't how I would have coped in this project without computerization.

However did the patron of our Province, St. Lawrence of Brindisi, who wrote tomes and tomes of homilies cope without a computer?

I have to thank David Williams who recently came to my rescue when the programme I was using just failed. What a patient teacher he is! I could not have managed without him.

I would like to mention Mary Halliwell who was my secretary for years and who gave of her time freely. She must have typed out many hundreds of my homilies over the years and without any doubt helped to better them.

You can imagine how much I owe to my proof-readers - Val Gupta, Lucy Sneddon, Lucia Drycz, Noelle Duffy and Shirley Williams. They have spent many hours poring over the text and punctuation.

Years back my sister Meg Brown and Jean Johnson, both of happy memory, would read them and make sure there weren't any grammatical errors. May they both be now reaping their heavenly reward.

I would like to thank those who have encouraged me to go to print. Every weekend I send the homilies for that Sunday to about fifty people. Two of them are nuns, Sister Christopher OSB, a Benedictine nun in Chester and Sister Sarah McAteer FSM. They very kindly tell me which homily they think I should preach. Sister Sarah even goes so far as to print them out for herself. I find that very encouraging. There are those who tell me that I should share my homilies with a larger audience. One kind lady in our Pantasaph parish, Letitia Shaw, said she has learned so much from the homilies and she would have loved me to have been her RE teacher when she was at school.

Some weekends I have several homilies to preach and I don't know which one to choose. I read them to a friend Anne Johnson in Southport who loves to hear them and she always says, "I hope I don't have to choose because I like them all." Now isn't that praise and encouragement! It is helps like that that have encouraged me to put them in a book.

I must thank Adrian Waddelove for his precise and well thought out words in the book. He has been a treasured friend over the years. If ever I have wanted to discuss delicate preaching matters with him he has always been there for me and has bettered what I intended to write. I would also like to thank his son, another Adrian, for the excellent graphics work on the cover.

Finally, thanks and praise must be given to Victor Moubarak and his son Matthew who coordinated all the homilies and prepared them for the printer. Without them there would have been no book. I am forever in their debt.

I now pray that everyone who reads these homilies will benefit in some way from them and that the book may draw them closer to Our Lord Jesus and help to fulfil His last command to our Church, "Go out to the whole world and spread the Good News." (Mk. 16:15).

ADVENT

(Twenty-seven sermons)

FIRST SUNDAY OF ADVENT

"STAY AWAKE"

Is. 2:1-5, Mt. 24: 37-44, Rom. 13: 11-14

"You must wake up now," St. Paul says to the Christians in Rome. Similarly, Our Lord warns His disciples to "stay awake". Staying awake, fighting off the need to sleep, is not always easy. The exhausted disciples in the Garden of Gethsemane couldn't keep awake even for an hour. Children on Christmas Eve try hard to stay awake, hoping to catch a glimpse of Santa Claus, but inevitably their eyes close long before he arrives. We all need a refreshing sleep at the end of a day's work.

Surely, sleep deprivation is not what Jesus wants for His followers. It is more a matter of being watchful, aware, and ready to respond to what was happening around them and, of course, being good and avoid evil. Those shepherds who were the first witnesses of Christ's birth were watching their flocks at night. It was dark and no doubt they nodded off from time to time, but it was important to keep the sheep under careful surveillance. Because they were alert they were able to receive the angels' announcement, prompting them to go and see the Christ Child.

The Magi in their distant observatories were also on constant watch. They must have been routinely scanning the sky, plotting on their charts the positions of stars and planets. Regular observation made them so familiar with the night sky that they quickly noticed the appearance of an unusual star, large and bright and evidently of great significance. Had they not been vigilant they would have overlooked the star and missed the opportunity to find the Child whose birth it indicated.

During Advent we focus on that birth, the coming of Jesus into our world, but in the Gospel for today Jesus is talking about His second coming. We know He will "come again in glory to judge the living and the dead" but we have no clue to when this will happen, so He urges us to be prepared. "Stand ready, because the Son of Man is coming at an hour you do not expect." How can we maintain a state of readiness? By keeping watch on our behaviour and on what is going on around us. It's a bit like driving a car: we need to be aware always of what is happening behind and in front of us, how we interact with other road users, and what dangers there might be. We watch the road ahead so that we can anticipate any problems and react promptly; knowing that carelessness or inattention could result in disaster. On our spiritual journey we need to be alert, keeping careful watch over what we say and do and the situations in which we may find ourselves.

St. Paul says, "Let us live decent lives: no drunken orgies, licentiousness, wrangling or jealousy." I wonder whether he was thinking about those office Christmas parties! Sadly, for some people the purpose of the four weeks leading up to Christmas is to get drunk as often as possible. Celebrations and parties are fine, but we must be alert ready to leave when the liquor is flowing too abundantly. There is prudence in moderation.

Wrangling and jealousy? Surely not! But in fact the weeks of preparation for Christmas can often be a time of tension and arguments within families. Amidst all the baking, shopping, card-writing and planning, tempers can fray. Who is being invited for Christmas dinner? Who had the in-laws last year? Whose turn is it to have Auntie Elsie? Have you ordered the Christmas tree? Why do I have to do everything? It can all become very competitive, as children demand more and more expensive presents, envying their friends who are getting something bigger and better. We can start to feel like St. Martha, overwhelmed with chores, becoming indignant about it and losing sight of the "one thing necessary", a spirit of prayer. We need to be aware of this danger and be on our guard.

One of our best preparations we can all make at Christmas is to make a fervent Advent Confession. Admitting to God that we are sinners and in so much need of His mercy and help for the future.

Lord Jesus, may we heed Your clarion call to stay awake and be prepared for Your coming this Christmas. Just as little children are full of happy expectation at the presents their parents plan to give them for Christmas we are going to be even happier at the thought of the best gift our heavenly Father is going to give us, His own dear Son. Come Lord Jesus, like Mary and Joseph, we can't wait to receive you into our hearts this Christmas.

THE CANCER OF COMPLANCENCY

Mt. 24: 37-44

In October 1973 the State of Israel was nearly destroyed. The Arab armies joined forces to attack the Israelis on a day they least expected. It was on the day of Yon Kippur, the holiest feast in the Jewish Year, the Day of Atonement. They knew that most of their serving soldiers would be sent back from the frontier positions to pray in their synagogues. Their generals thought that the danger from across the borders was slight. Besides they were so used to defeating the Arabs that they let their guard slip. This was to be the cause of the trouble. They suffered from the cancer of complacency.

Our Faith can be like that. We practise our faith week by week and we think that all is well and there can be a tendency to get in a rut. The Lord offers us challenges to face and crosses to bear and we avoid them. These challenges and crosses are there to be accepted and for us to grow spiritually and we don't. This is why we need the season of Advent when once again we can take a fresh look at ourselves, our Faith, and our life and so be in a better position to prepare for the Birth of our Saviour at Christmas.

Do you remember the cowboy films we used to see when the Indians chased families who were heading for the west? Their defence was to get the wagons into a tight circle, and hope they could defend themselves against their attackers. Very often this spelt disaster. The Indians surrounded them and were victorious. They never seemed to beat the Indians from that defensive position.

Is this how we behave when our beliefs are challenged? Are we always on the defensive? Why don't we mount an attacking offensive against what we know to be wrong? Curling up and hoping for the best in our dark world is unlikely to win many converts for Christ. Advent is a time for us to rethink our attitude to Christ, and the call to faith that we accepted at Baptism and Confirmation.

St. Paul in the Second Reading has good advice to give us. He tells us that we have very little time and we must act now. We can be so busy with the events of daily life and the material preparations for our Christmas that we forget to prepare for this feast spiritually. We need to slow down, to stop and to think. What is Christmas really all about? Is it just to have a good time? That we fail to see how well our hearts are prepared, like those of Mary and Joseph, for the Birth of our Saviour? There is much more to Christmas than enjoying the material side of it. Jesus would most certainly want us to celebrate His Birth by having a good time, but He would first want us to prepare our hearts for Him. Could it be that we haven't been to Confession for a long time and Jesus is asking us to prepare for His Birth by making a sincere and humble Confession?

The night that the "Titanic" headed for the iceberg in April 1912 an officer on the bridge was engrossed in plotting the speed of the ship as it travelled towards America. While he was doing this the phone rang. He ignored it as he was deep in calculations. It rang again he ignored it. Eventually the officer had finished his calculations. The phone rang for the third time and this time he answered it. It was from the look-out in the crow's nest. The sailor shouted, "Iceberg straight ahead! Reverse engines immediately." But it was too late. As the officer tried to respond to the cry, the ship hit the iceberg. If the officer had left his interesting, trivial, unimportant work to answer that call the first time the "Titanic" may well have sailed safely past the iceberg. Two thousand people would have enjoyed their trip of a lifetime. Instead, they died.

There is a tendency to think that everything in our lives will turn out right in the end. We can be so wrapped up in ourselves that we fail to forget the real priorities. This Advent is a time to put things right now. Now is the only time that we have got.

Lord Jesus our life is made up of a million 'nows'. Let us not waste too many of them. Let us prepare like Mary and Joseph for Your coming now.

HOW ARE WE INTENDING TO PREPARE FOR CHRISTMAS?

Is. 2:1-5; Romans 13:11-14 & Mt. 24:37-44

The world insists on telling us how many shopping days there are to Christmas. It prepares well for Christmas. How well are we preparing?

We can prepare for Advent by trying to relive how Mary and Joseph spent their time before the birth of their Son. Mary was well over eight months pregnant and she knew, through scriptures, that the Saviour was to be born in Bethlehem. Yet here she was in Nazareth! She waited patiently for the time when God would reveal to Joseph and herself when they were to travel to Bethlehem. Then the news came to them indirectly through the census of the world ordered by Augustus Caesar: everyone was to record their name in their place of origin. Since they were of the line of King David they would now have to travel to Bethlehem because that was the city of David.

Before this news arrived she would be getting together all the clothes and necessary things a new born baby would need. She would also have to do her everyday chores, like shopping for food for Joseph and herself, cooking the meals, the weekly wash, keeping their home tidy and clean. There would be times when she and Joseph prayed together and spoke about the birth of her child, and when God would reveal to them when they should make their way to Bethlehem.

Joseph would be working hard to get the extra money he would need for their trip to Bethlehem and their stay in the area for the 40 days after the birth of Mary's child so they could present Him in the Temple. There would have to be purchases of wood to make doors, tables and chairs. His tools would need sharpening every now and then. He may even have gone from door to door looking for much needed extra work.

Throughout all these various activities they looked forward eagerly to the time of the birth of Jesus. As with every new mother Mary longed to be able to hold Him in her arms and to see to His every need. We can follow their example, going about our work whatever it may be as best we can, as we look forward to the birth of Jesus in our lives at Christmas. They would be preparing their hearts to receive Him - and so must we.

One of the best forms of preparation is the Sacrament of Reconciliation. How many Catholics sadly neglect this Sacrament! Am I right in saying that a good many people have given up on this Sacrament? They will receive Our Lord in Communion whenever they come to Mass on Sundays, but they will tell you they do not need to go to Confession. They say their act of contrition at the start of Mass is sufficient preparation for their reception of Jesus in Holy Communion.

If you rarely go to Confession and you receive Jesus in Holy Communion, here is something to think about. Suppose a special guest is coming to your home for a visit. What do you do? Even though your home is very presentable you will still hoover the carpets, dust the furniture and fluff up the cushions. That is the equivalent of going to Confession to receive Jesus in Holy Communion.

This must be said that those who neglect Mass for no reason on some Sundays but then receive Our Lord in Holy Communion whenever they come to Mass are committing a sacrilege. To miss Mass deliberately on Sundays and Holydays of Obligations is a serious offence. What did Saint Paul write about receiving Our Lord in mortal sin? "He who eats and drinks unworthily eats and drinks damnation to himself."

And this is what Saint Pope John Paul has to say, "If we do not go to Confession once a month you are not taking your spiritual life seriously." I can think of three reasons why he said that. First, in this sacrament, as in all the sacraments, we meet Jesus - so that is a good reason for going. Second, we never know what is round the corner and we need to build up a strong friendship with Jesus, which we do in Confession, to provide us with loads of graces for the future. Then whatever crisis we may have to face we will never turn our backs on Christ. Third, it is our ticket to Heaven. When someone dies, who goes to Confession every month, I can imagine God saying, 'Come on, Heaven is for you. Every month you wanted to put yourself right with Me and your neighbour.'

Lord Jesus in preparing for Your coming at Christmas we can do no better than prepare our hearts like Mary and Joseph did, and making sure we include time for the Sacrament of Reconciliation in our busy schedules.

CHRIST COMES EVERY DAY

- BUT DO WE RECOGNIZE HIM?

Mt. 24:37-44

What does Jesus mean when He tells us that His coming will be a repeat of what happened in Noah's time? The people then went about their daily lives, failing to repent and never suspecting that a flood would come and sweep them away.

By this Jesus is telling us He will come to us in the midst of everyday living when we least expect Him. He summed up this passage by saying, "Therefore, you must stand ready because the Son of Man is coming at an hour you do not expect." What is the moment we least expect Jesus?

We believe that He came long ago as the Babe of Bethlehem. We believe that He will come again at the end of the world. But we do not expect Him to come today, most certainly not to our house nor our place of work. But since Jesus says He will come when we least expect Him, this must be the most likely time and place for us to find Him - right here and right now!

We have to admit that most of our lives are ordinary. It is only in films, on television and in novels that people are always involved in some kind of excitement. They survive plane and car crashes, experience dramatic court scenes or rescue people from burning buildings. These kinds of exciting things do happen, but not to us. We work, eat, sleep and then get up and start all over again.

At weekends there may be a change from the ordinary. Perhaps we visit the hairdresser, do the laundry that has piled up during the week or shop in the supermarket. We may even treat ourselves to a meal. And on Saturday evening or Sunday we go to Mass … before Monday comes again. This is the routine of living. It was called 'blessed monotony' by some man of wisdom.

That is an apt description of most of our days and, if Christ is to be a real part of our lives, this is where we must find Him. When you come to think of it, that is where most people met Him in the New Testament: Saint Paul's blinding vision on the road to Damascus was the exception. Peter, Andrew, James and John met Jesus while mending their nets beside the Sea of Galilee, something they did every day. Christ came to them and they followed Him. The rest is history. The woman of Samaria met Him while she was at the well drawing water. Matthew met Him at work in his tax collecting office. These were their everyday activities.

This is how people met Jesus when He walked this Earth. Why do we expect to meet Him in a dramatic way? If we do we are going to be disappointed. We must look for Him in the ordinary and learn to recognise Him. If I understand the New Testament correctly, it teaches us that Jesus travels with His true identity concealed. He will not appear in a middle-eastern robe, with sandals on His feet and wearing a beard, as artists portray Him. If He did, we would not recognise Him - we might take Him to be someone in fancy dress!

Jesus is the master of many disguises. One day He will be an old woman in a wheelchair in a nursing home. Another day, He will be a child wanting someone to read him a book. Or a patient in hospital needing a visitor, a teenager desperate for encouragement, a single mother needing of a baby sitter. Tomorrow, He might be a wife, wanting a hug.

It is good for us to anticipate the coming of Jesus at the end of the world. But in the meantime, if we find Him at all, it will be in the midst of ordinary living. This has to be one of the messages of the Advent season.

Lord Jesus, the people in Noah's time were not prepared when You visited them. Let us be ready every day to welcome You in one of Your many clever disguises.

THE UNANNOUNCED CHRIST

Mt. 24:37-44

The whole purpose of the Old Testament was God preparing the world for the coming of His Son. Through the sin of disobedience we had rejected God's offer of Paradise. But God Who loved us so much could not lose us forever so He formed a Chosen People. He would guide and prepare them for the coming of His Son. The prophets had spoken about His coming for centuries, and there was a strong hope in Israel that some day God would send a Redeemer. Certainly they did not expect it to happen the way it did. God must have surprised every one when He allowed His Son to be born in a stable. After all those long years of preparation His Coming was overlooked by most people.

They were certainly not looking for a carpenter leading a donkey on which sat his very tired and very pregnant young wife. Who would have expected Christ to come that way? He slipped into the world unnoticed except for Mary and Joseph, Elizabeth and Zachary, a few shepherds and some Wise Men who came from the east.

Before we become too critical of the Chosen People what about ourselves? How aware are we of the presence of Christ in our lives? Does He often go unnoticed? I hope all of us are aware of His loving presence with us in the Mass and in the tabernacle. What about all the other times He comes to us?

I love that story about a shopkeeper who dreamed that Jesus would visit him the next day. It was one of those vivid dreams that he was absolutely certain would come true. As soon as he got up from bed he wondered whether Jesus would visit him in his shop. So as soon as he arrived at work he and his woman assistant got to work to make sure that in the short time he had everything would look spic and span ready for his important Guest. While they were dusting his assistant told him that her mother, who was very frail and elderly, had had a very poor night and she wondered if after work he would drop her off at her mother's house as it was on his way home. He said he would willingly take her.

The bell above the entrance door would ring every now and then and one of them would briefly stop spring cleaning to attend to the customer. In fact the shopkeeper, every time the door opened, would look to see if it was His special guest, but each time he was disappointed. Around noon a down and out came into the shop and begged for some small change to buy a drink. The shopkeeper took pity on him and made him and his assistant a drink.

The afternoon passed as uneventfully as the morning. Shoppers came and went. One of his regular customers, a widow, stayed long enough to tell him how her wayward son had again got into trouble with the law and was now in jail in the next town. She was so upset. He showed his care and concern by giving her his phone number and told her to ring him when next she wanted to visit her son. He would take her.

The working day was drawing to a close and the shop had never looked so neat and tidy. Jesus had not come and the shopkeeper felt a little disappointed. He dropped his assistant at her mother's home. It was his custom after his evening meal to read at random a passage of the Gospels. That evening he read the parable of the sheep and the goats on Judgement Day. "I was thirsty and you gave Me drink;....I was a stranger and you made Me welcome....sick and you visited Me, in prison and you came to see Me." After reading that, he knew that his dream had come true. Jesus had visited him in many guises.

Lord Jesus You came on earth 2000 years ago and You come to us in the most unexpected ways every day, the time of Advent tells us You will come again to us this Christmas. So let us not while away the time looking for Your final coming and miss Your daily visits in our lives. Yes, "The Son of Man is coming at an hour we do not expect."

PREPARING FOR CHRISTMAS AND OUR LAST END

Mt. 24: 37-44

The clarion call of Jesus on this the first Sunday of Advent is "Stay awake and be ready." Ready for what? Ready for Christ's birth at Christmas. A good question to ask ourselves on this the first Sunday of Advent is, if Jesus was to call me at this moment would I be able to say, "Yes, Lord. I am ready"? It would be a tragedy if the answer is "No".

The secular world can teach us a lot when preparing for Jesus' coming at Christmas. Christmas is four weeks away and yet for months the commercial world has been carefully planning for the event. Advertisements, Promotions, Full Sale Preparations for the most expensive period of the year have begun months before the event. Has the spiritual aspect of Christmas occurred to them, the true message of the celebration? I doubt it. So busy and involved are they with the purpose of making profits that Our Lord has been relegated to the background. However, we could learn from these people, we could adopt their enthusiasm, diligence and hard work in making our spiritual preparation for Christmas.

At the beginning of each day a prayer I love to say is, "Give me the strength Holy Spirit to do the work of this day and grant that at its close I may be found worthy of your trust in me." And so today at the beginning of the liturgical year of the Church our prayer could be, "Give us the strength Holy Spirit to do the work of this year and grant that at its close we may be found worthy of your trust in us." In our preparation for the birth of Jesus we should also invoke the help of Our Lady, who more than any other person made the perfect preparation for His coming. Her approach was loving, humble, reverent and full of joyful expectation. In this she was supported by Joseph, her husband, who was full of concern, devotion and great humility. Together they made ready to welcome God's Son.

What about asking our Guardian Angels to help us prepare for Jesus this Christmas? Is it true that many of us never or seldom think about their daily presence with us? If what I say is true, then we are losing the benefit of such great help that the Lord has given us. I am sure as I write these words our Guardian Angels are smiling at each other and saying, "Isn't it good that someone is bringing to people's notice the valuable help that we can give those we look after?" So in our individual preparations we should seek the help of our Guardian Angels too, to direct our thoughts and actions in a practical way to pray fervently, and respond with joy and love to the service of others.

Lord Jesus, may we heed Your clarion call to stay awake and be prepared for Your coming. Let us resolve earnestly that after having welcomed You into our hearts we shall enter the New Year full of good intentions to follow Him, and to work for the establishment of Your Kingdom here on earth.

WHAT DOES ADVENT MEAN TO YOU?

Mk. 13:33-37

The first Sunday of Advent has arrived. The word "advent" simply means "coming". We use it in this context to refer to the coming of Christ into the world. Jesus comes in three ways.

First, we think of Advent in terms of the Christmas story, when the Son of God came into this world as a little baby, born of the Virgin Mary. Second, we think of Jesus coming again at the end of the world. We refer to this as the "Second Coming" of Christ. Thirdly, we also need to recognise that Jesus not only came in the past and will come again in the future, but that He will also come in the present.

Jesus told a story about a man who was getting ready to travel abroad. Before leaving, he gave specific instructions to his servants, "You do not know when the master of the house is coming. Do not let him come suddenly and catch you asleep." Then Jesus added this comment, "What I say to you, I say to all: Be on guard."

Now, what is the message of this parable? At first glance, it would appear that Jesus is talking about His final coming at the end of time; and we don't want to discount that possibility. But if this is all it means, then it seems to me that we have two problems with the parable. One, it implies that we are like irresponsible children who stop fighting and tidy the home only because they think their parents are soon to return. I hope our commitment to Jesus goes a bit deeper than that!

If this parable speaks exclusively of the final advent of Christ, then it is almost a mockery of every Christian generation but the last one. It is as if Jesus instructed His friends to live in expectation of His coming, and then disappointed that expectation by failing to show up. It seems to me that we have to give this parable a broader meaning than that. I think the Lord is trying to open our minds to the truth of His coming in the events and experiences of our daily lives. Surely, He is never far from us; and we should look for Him, not just in the clouds of tomorrow, but in the streets of today.

Another thing we must do is to teach ourselves to think of His coming, not as a threat, but as a promise. His exhortation to alertness does not mean that we should be feverishly anxious, but rather that we should be joyfully expectant. After all, the one whose arrival we anticipate is not a policeman with a search warrant but our Brother and Friend Who has come to take us to Heaven.

How can we ever think of His coming as something to dread or to fear? We must see Jesus as a faithful Friend who has taught us the meaning of love and forgiveness. If we ever learn that, then we will see His coming as a promise, not a threat.

Next, we should look for Jesus, not just in the big events of life, but in the small things as well. In the parable, the master gave each of his servants a job to do, and then told them while doing it to expect His coming at any time. The two seemed to go together - the work and the return. An old family doctor who had practised medicine for fifty years said, "I do not see how anyone can witness the birth of a baby and not believe in God." There was a man who had learned to see the coming of the Lord in doing his daily work.

There are some who say my work is too drab. How can I find Jesus anywhere in it? If only they would be aware for Whom they work, the Lord, then whatever they do is worthwhile and precious.

Lord Jesus, if all we do is for You, then we will find You in many places - in the face of a child, in the need of other people, in our joys, and even in our sorrows. This is the Advent season, a very special time of the year. It speaks to us of You who came as the Son of Mary. It speaks to us of You who will come as the King of Kings. Finally, it speaks to us of You who comes as a Friend, to walk with us in the midst of all the pain and gladness of our daily lives.

SECOND SUNDAY OF ADVENT

DON'T GIVE UP

Is. 11:1-10; Romans 15:4-9 & Mt. 3:1-12

The prophet Isaiah has a vision. He foresees a time in the distant future when the world around us will have changed completely, in ways we find hard to imagine. Animals which have traditionally been enemies will lie down peacefully together and share food. Former predators will cease to kill their fellow creatures and the lion will take to eating straw alongside the ox. The cow and the bear form an unexpected friendship. Even poisonous snakes are no longer dangerous - a small child can put his hand into the viper's lair without fear of injury. "No hurt, no harm on all my holy mountain." This vision can be compared with last week's reading from Isaiah in which he looks forward to an end to human conflict, "Nation will not lift sword against nation, there will be no more training for war."

All living creatures cohabiting peacefully - it sounds wonderful, doesn't it? Cynics may ask whether it's all a fantasy, a beautiful but impossible dream. All creatures, animal and human, tend to compete with each other for power, for territory, for food, for a mate. That seems to be the pattern of life. Nature being as it is, it looks unlikely that such state of harmony and peace could ever be achieved. But suppose what we call 'Nature' is not really natural at all.

When God created the world and all its inhabitants, was it His intention that they should immediately be at each other's throats? Evidently not, for we read in Genesis that God looked at everything He had made and "saw that it was good." Being good, all creatures, including mankind, co-existed happily. The present troubled state of our world, in which animals kill other species and human beings kill their own, is a consequence of the Fall. Rejection of God's intentions resulted in damage to the whole world, bringing into it rivalry, hatred and death. Our nature is deformed, no longer perfect as it was when God first called us into being.

13

Prior to the Fall, there was no discord, no enmity, but when Satan in the form of a snake deceived our first parents God said He would "put enmity" between snakes and humans. How amazing, then, is Isaiah's picture of a child playing safely with a cobra. Yet in God's perfect creation that is how it should be and will be again one day, Isaiah tells us.

It may seem that there is very little we can do to improve our world, to put an end to cruelty, criminality and war. The transformation Isaiah describes will only come about through Christ, the Lord and Saviour of the world. We should not be discouraged, however. St. Paul tells us that the Scriptures were written to teach us about hope. People who did not despair have been helped by God and He will help us "when we refuse to give up."

In this season of Advent there are small things we can do to help straighten the crooked paths for Our Lord. Making an effort to say an extra prayer or perhaps attend an extra Mass will give us strength. What about our relationships with other people? St. Paul wants us to try to be more tolerant of each other, treating each other "in the friendly way that Christ has treated us." That means being patient and resisting the urge to retaliate. It includes the sarcastic colleague, the irritating neighbour, even that annoying so-and-so who jumps the queue at the supermarket checkout. No-one said this would be easy, but we need to keep trying. As G. K. Chesterton observed, "The Christian ideal has not been tried and found wanting; it has been found difficult and left untried."

Lord Jesus, the fulfilment of Isaiah's lovely vision may still be a long way off, but we continue to pray every day that God's kingdom will come on earth. Advent is surely a time for us to renew our hope and to encourage each other not to give up.

MESSAGE OF JOHN THE BAPTIST

Is. 11:1-10 & Mt. 3:1-12

The Church puts before us today the figure of John the Baptist and his Advent message heralding the Lord's coming, "Repent, for the Kingdom of heaven is close at hand." It was John whom the prophet Isaiah had described six centuries earlier as "a voice crying in the wilderness". John was the immediate precursor of the Lord, and called his contemporary society to repentance as a preparation to welcome the Messiah. Those who heeded this call to repentance were given a symbolic baptism in the waters of the Jordan as a prelude to the real baptism which the Lord Jesus was going to administer in the Holy Spirit. John was gentle with those who were genuinely repentant; but he confronted harshly those whose repentance was a mere pretence or who came to him out of empty curiosity, such as possibly some of the Pharisees and Sadducees. The Lord, in baptising with the Holy Spirit and with fire, would sort out the genuinely repentant from the rest.

Genuine repentance will always produce visible fruits in a person's life, just as a healthy tree produces a good crop of fruit. The main symbol which emerges from today's scripture readings is that of a fruit bearing tree. St. John the Baptist warns us that any tree that does not produce good fruit will be cut down and thrown on the fire. We, too, cannot produce the fruits of repentance unless we are part of the spiritual tree whose root is Jesus, and conversely we cannot be a part of Jesus unless we show fruits of repentance in our lives. The prophet Isaiah, in the First Reading, describes the Messiah Jesus as a tree which grew from the stump of Jesse. Now Jesse was the father of King David, in whose line Jesus was born, thus showing us that Jesus is the long-awaited King, not only of Israel, but of the whole world. Jesus is also the Messiah and the Christ. Both the Hebrew word Messiah and the Greek word Christos from which Christ is derived, mean the same thing, namely the anointed one. Whereas earthly kings were anointed by an oil, Jesus the Heavenly King is the One anointed by the Holy Spirit. So, Isaiah prophesies that on Him the Spirit of the Lord rests with all His gifts: wisdom, counsel, power, knowledge and the fear of the Lord. The Holy Spirit then, is the sap which flows from the root, which is Jesus, into every branch of the spiritual tree, filling it with the nutrients which are the gifts of the Holy Spirit mentioned above. The spiritual nutrients, in turn produce two special fruits which are the hallmarks of the messianic tree, namely: Justice and Peace. And so, the psalmist says, "In His days, justice shall flourish and peace till the moon fails." If, therefore, we too are part of the Jesus tree and are nourished by the same Holy Spirit, then the fruits of justice and peace should be evident in our own lives. Let us examine these in turn.

Justice is the virtue whereby we give God and others what is, respectively, their due. Conversely, injustice involves taking for ourselves what is due to others. The scriptural image which represents injustice is that of hills and valleys. Valleys do not exist without hills. Similarly, if there is a deficiency in one place, it is because there is an excess in another. Pride takes away the glory and credit due to God and attributes them to us. Theft takes away their material possessions; slander takes away their good name. Lust takes away their sexual integrity and dignity; accumulation of wealth takes away the necessities of life from poorer people. We do all this to boost our ego. It is selfishness. If we are to show forth the fruit called justice, then we must level the hills of selfishness and fill up the valleys which we have created in other people's lives. Restitution and voluntary almsgiving are two excellent ways of restoring justice. When we do so, we are levelling the hills and the valleys, and preparing a straight, smooth path by which the Lord can enter our hearts.

The second important fruit of the Messianic tree is peace, and peace is synonymous with integrity which means an undivided wholeness. Sin leads to division and war, whereas grace brings about reconciliation, unity and peace. The reason why there is war is that individuals and societies are being unjust to others, and the reason for this injustice is that individuals are not at peace within themselves. The war which goes on outside is a magnified version of the war which goes on in our individual hearts. When the Kingdom of Christ is established in our hearts in its fullness, then we should be at perfect peace within ourselves. This is the state which is symbolically described by Isaiah as a paradise where animals no longer terrorise the tame. The animals are symbolic of our raw emotion, our sexuality and indeed everything that goes to make up our personality. Due to the effects of our fallen nature and subsequent nature, these elements of our personality are not always at peace with each other. For example, there is in us a capacity for both powerful assertiveness and gentleness. Sometimes we are overpowered by anger and thus assertiveness deteriorates into cowardice. Likewise we are not at ease with our sexuality. Sometimes our sexual urges control us and our capacity for love and affection is torn apart by lust and promiscuity. At other times, we are overcome by fear and gentleness deteriorates into cowardice. Likewise, we are often not at ease with our sexuality. We may not have committed murder or rape in our lives, but none of us can deny that the elements which caused them namely, anger and lust, are present in small quantities within us. The effect of grace which comes to us with the coming of Christ is to re-integrate, at a deep level, the fragmented parts of our personality; so that power and gentleness can live in harmony, as can sexual urges and chastity. In this paradoxical state, we will use our raw emotions in a healthy and challenged way to build, rather than break, relationships.

Lord Jesus, as we heed the Baptist's call to repentance, let us pray that our repentance will be genuine and show forth in the fruits of justice and peace. Let us pray for peace and harmony in the depths of our hearts like the animals in nature. May this inner peace lead us to justice in the way we relate to God and to others, levelling hills and filling up the valleys. Finally, may this justice in turn lead to peace and harmony in our society and in our world. May the reign of Christ truly come so that justice shall flourish and peace till the moon fails.

JESUS CAME TO MAKE OUR WORLD A BETTER PLACE

Mt. 3:1-12

The preaching of Saint John the Baptist can be summarised in the words, "Repent for the Kingdom of Heaven is close at hand." It was with these words that John announced the public ministry of Christ and proclaimed the dawning of a new age. With the coming of Christ, the world could never be the same again. Change was inevitable.

Jesus came to make the world a better place. He never carried a sword or a placard. He never marched in a demonstration to overthrow a government. He simply lived, taught and loved. His ideas were so revolutionary that it frightened and angered some, and they finally nailed Him to a cross. That did not stop His work.

The Kingdom of Heaven is still among us. The revolutionary Christ is still working among us and we are confronted by Him every day. Let us look at just two of His ideas which started a revolution which is still going on today.

The first one concerns the worth of the individual. In Jesus' eyes every single person is important to God and loved by Him. In the first century Roman world this was never the case. Not everyone was treated the same. Some people were important; others were expendable. A few people had supreme rights, others had a few rights - and many had no rights at all.

Some people were masters; others were slaves. The master owned the slave. He had supreme rights over the slave who had no rights at all. A master could do anything he liked with his slave. He could sell him, beat him and even kill him. Human rights just did not apply because slaves were not important.

To a lesser extent the same was true between men and women, and parents and children. Men were more important than women and had more rights. Parents were the owners of children, and could do with and to their children just about anything they pleased.

It was into this society that Jesus entered our world. He wanted to tell people that every person is supremely important to God and was to be treated with respect. It is not surprising that in a few years His Apostle Paul would be writing, "In Christ there is neither Jew nor Greek, bond nor free, male nor female. We are all one in Christ." Those were bold words … even explosive. A revolution was on its way. That message is still being preached today. But even to this day there are some people who think they are superior to others. They still haven't put into effect the message begun by Jesus.

Another revolutionary thought of Jesus was His belief in the power of love. For centuries people had believed in both power and love, but they were two totally different things. Power was might and muscle. Love was something warm and gentle shared with family and friends. Jesus came along and brought the two ideas together.

He taught that love was not reserved for family and friends. It was for everyone, even for enemies. It was more than just a warm and friendly feeling. It was a deliberate act of the will. It was power and strength. It was a deep resolve and a commitment. We are inclined to think of love in terms of something soft, sweet and even sentimental. Jesus thought of it as the most irresistible force in the all the world.

His thinking was so revolutionary and many of us have still not understood it. We still keep believing and behaving as if hatred is strong and love is weak. Let us look at our own experience. Who has touched our lives more deeply – the people who have loved us or the people who have not? What has been the most powerful influence in our lives? If the answer is hate, then we are in trouble. If the answer is love, then there is hope. Love is constructive; hate is destructive. Love is a winner's game; hate is for losers.

When countries go to war they do not heed Jesus' words, "Love your enemies." Why do governments and people not try it? We can only wonder what would happen if we ever learned to turn the other cheek, to repay back good for evil. This is how Jesus behaved. He has given us a great lead and we are so far behind. When will we catch up with Him?

Lord Jesus, if only we would think like You and see the importance of the individual and the power of love, then what a better world would be ours.

REPENTANCE AND ALL IT MEANS

Mt. 3:1-12

What is it that stops me giving Christ a warm welcome into my heart this Christmas? It is my sins and my attachment to them. This is why the Church before Christmas presents us with the simple and direct message of John the Baptist, "Repent." "Repent" was the word he used when he wanted to prepare his hearers for the coming of Christ.

What does the word 'repent' mean? It means to feel remorse, sorrow, self-reproach for what we have done or failed to do. It means I have to say, "I am a sinner." The proud person is unable to say that. Our sorrow is directed to God. If I do not believe in God, how can I say sorry to Him?

Repentance follows certain steps. First, I must recognise my sins. The prayer of the Publican in the temple must be often on my lips, "O God, be merciful to me. I am a sinner." If I don't do this I cannot repent. This is the big hurdle I must jump if I am going to have a relationship with Christ. If I am an alcoholic and do not take the first step of admitting it there is no hope of a cure and getting better.

The second step is I must be sorry for my sins. In addition to recognising my sin I must have sincere sorrow for what I have done. It means I have to let go of what I have done or failed to do. What I have done is not right, even terrible, and so I want to unload and abandon my sins. This I can do by confessing them to the Lord in Confession and telling Him I am sorry.

The thought of what my sins did to Christ on the cross and hurting Him, the best Friend I have, can help me to be truly sorry.

The third step is I am going to make a firm purpose of amendment, that is, to try not to do the same sin again. So if I gossiped, I am going to try not to gossip. If I got angry, I am going to try not to get angry. If I lied, I am going to try not to lie. This indicates how sincere our sorrow is.

The next step is that I must confess my sin to the Lord and for us Catholics it is through the Sacrament of Reconciliation. Granted venial sins are forgiven by privately telling God we are sorry or when we are absolved from them at the beginning of Mass at the Penitential Rite. A monthly habit of going to Confession is strongly recommended by St. Pope John Paul II. He maintains if we do not go once a month we are not taking our spiritual life seriously.

The next step for repentance for some sins is making restitution. That means in so far as we are able we must make right the wrong we have done. For example, a thief should give back what he has stolen. A liar should make the truth known. A gossip who has slandered the character of a person should work to restore the good name of the person he has harmed. If we do these things, God will not mention our sins to us when we are judged as we read in Ezekiel 33:15-16. If a sinner does this God says, "All his previous sins will no longer be remembered."

The next step in repentance is we must forgive others. A vital part of repentance is to forgive those who have sinned against us. The Lord will not forgive us unless our hearts are fully cleansed of all hate, bitterness, and bad feelings against other people.

Repentance isn't about being perfect. It is a practice of making continual improvements, continually carrying our cross and forever dying to self. It is about being continually more alive to God.

So if we want to welcome Christ into our hearts this Christmas we must repent and all that it means. Why did great saints like St. Paul and St. Francis of Assisi call themselves the 'greatest sinners'? It was because the nearer they came to God the more they saw themselves unworthy of His love.

Lord Jesus, as we long for You to come to us this Christmas let us realise we are unworthy of Your love, that we are sinners. We want to repent of all our sins and so be ready to welcome You into our hearts.

A BETTER WORLD STARTS WITH ME

Mt. 3:1-12.

One of the most famous speeches of the last century was made on 28 August, 1963, in Washington D.C. The speaker was Dr. Martin Luther King Jnr. Standing in front of the Lincoln Memorial, the black civil rights leader told an assembled crowd of a quarter of a million people, "I have a dream that one day this nation will rise up and live out the true meaning of its creed....I have a dream that one day....the sons of former slaves and sons of former slave owners will be able to sit down together at the table of brotherhood...I have a dream that my four little children will one day live in a nation where they will not be judged by the colour of their skin but by the content of their character."

He spoke for approximately eight minutes, and when he had finished, the crowd sat for a few moments in stunned silence. That speech rallied the spirits of millions of black Americans and pumped new life into the civil rights movement. It expressed the hopes of the human race. People of all nations have always dreamed of a better world, a world without war and strife, a world where people of all colours and creeds could live together in peace.

We all share this dream. We are sick of the insanity of war. We are exhausted by man's inhumanity to man. We are tired of crime and violence. We are fed up with greed and injustice. We long for a world of peace and righteousness, where people and nations settle their differences through cooperation instead of conflict. Some people have stopped believing that such a world is even possible and many more are deeply discouraged. Though still believing in a better world, they feel helpless to do anything about it. The problems are too big, and the circumstances are too far out of control. All we can do, it seems, is wait, and wish and hope.

Today's Gospel reading has a message for that very mood. It proclaims the imminent arrival of the reign of God. The messenger was John the Baptist. Suddenly, he appeared in the desert of Judea, telling the people, "Reform your lives. The reign of God is at hand." His sermon was short and simple, but it contained a logical sequence. First, reformed lives; and second, the reign of God. First, better people and then a better world.

Doesn't that make sense? We get a better world by becoming better people. How else could it happen? So the message of our reading is plain and direct; if you want a better world, start with yourself, reform your own life.

John is reminding us that the first responsibility of every person is himself or herself. In other words, my primary mission in life is not to change the world, or to save the world, or even to serve the world. My primary mission is to become the best "me" that I possibly can, and yours is the same. Until we tackle the challenge of ourselves, we are ill equipped to tackle the many challenges of society. It is sheer hypocrisy to think that we can change the world unless, first of all, we are willing to change our own lives.

Our Scripture reading tells of certain men who were drawn to the ministry of John. They heard his preaching. They saw the great crowds of people. They felt the excitement in the air, and thought perhaps the reign of God might really be at hand. They decided to jump on the bandwagon, but John would have no part of their scheme. He detected their insincerity and challenged them, "You brood of vipers, give some evidence that you intend to reform." That message is intended for you and me. We deceive ourselves if we think that God is going to hand us a better world on a silver platter. The only way we will ever get a better world is for each of us to become better people. John's message is clear. The first responsibility of every person is himself or herself.

He is also reminding us that all the moral problems of the world are the moral failures of people. We sometimes blame the world and forget that the world is made up of individuals. The world is nothing other than a group of people living together in some kind of relationship. Whatever is wrong with the world is the accumulated result of whatever is wrong with the people who compose it. If we live in a cruel, greedy and violent world, it is only because there are cruel, greedy and violent people. If we ever hope to change the world we are going to have to start with ourselves.

It would be comforting to settle back into some sort of fatalism and blame the world for all our problems. The world does not pollute its own air and water; people do. The world does not fight senseless wars; people do. The world does not cause poverty; people do. The world does not foster prejudice and hatred; people do. You and I are not the pawns of some kind of impersonal fate. Most of the problems of this world don't just happen. They are caused. And each of us must shoulder our part of the blame.

Lord Jesus, we say we want a better world. In some vague sense, we expect a better world. But while we are waiting, we should go to work on our own lives. The only way to get a better world is to build it out of better people. John said it centuries ago, but it still applies today, "Reform your lives. The reign of God is at hand."

ADMITTING OUR SINS

Mk. 1:1-12

John the Baptist had one burning mission in life, and that was to prepare the people of his time for the coming of the Messiah. Part of that preparation was to turn the spotlight of truth on the ugly reality of their sins. Some faced up to that reality. They confessed their sins and repented of them. They recognized that any real relationship with the Messiah was going to require some cleansing of heart and changing of life.

The message that John proclaimed centuries ago is as valid today as it was then. If Christ is to enter our world and our hearts, then we must face up to and deal with the awful fact of our sins. Recognising our sinfulness is a painfully unpleasant experience, and we may go to almost any limit to avoid the pain. The sin of our day is to deny the existence of sin. Some people say, "No one has a right to tell me how I am to conduct my life. I am a free agent. I can do as I please." To think like that is sheer madness and denial of the truth of sin is a fact of life. Sin is not just a word in the Bible. It is not a morbid idea that some gloomy prophets invented. It is not something the Church has dreamed up to spoil life. Sin is a reality.

If we have any doubts about that, then forget the Bible, forget religion and look at life. Read the newspapers. It is full of the sins of mankind, murders, rapes and cruelty of all sorts. Take a walk into town and there you will discover every shopkeeper believes in the reality of sin. They all have locks on their doors. Some of them have bars on their windows. If you drive a car, at this moment where are your car keys? Safe in your pocket or handbag. Why? Precisely because people who manufacture cars and people who buy them believe in the reality of sin.

Most of us could feel smug about these more obvious forms of sin. After all, we've never stolen a car. We've never broken into a shop and don't plan to. We've never committed any of those violent crimes that get reported in the newspapers. We may be inclined to dissociate ourselves from the sin problem as though we were spectators looking on from afar. But when Jesus comes we can't get by with that. Jesus takes us on a tour of our hearts and minds and shows us the seed beds where sin gets started. Jesus knows the problem is a deep-seated wrongness in the human heart.

All of this may sound depressing, but in reality once we recognize it, it is the beginning of hope. This is what the coming of Jesus is all about. To make us face the reality of our problem of sin, and then with His help to find a cure. We can only be cured once we acknowledge that we need a cure.

Why do we shy away from the thought of being saved when we seek salvation so readily in other areas of life? We go to the doctor to be saved from sickness. We go to school in order to be saved from ignorance. We go to work in order to be saved from poverty. We go to friends and family to be saved from loneliness. Why then do we not go to Christ in order to be saved from our sins? All we need is to face up to our sins and commit them to the forgiving grace of God. Only Christ can help us do this.

Lord Jesus, You are saying to each one of us, "Make sure you recognize the sin that is in you. Confess it and be sorry for it in the Sacrament of Reconciliation." It is only then that we will give birth to You in our lives. We ask Mary, our sinless Mother, to help us give birth to You in our lives just as she did in hers. 'O Mary conceived without sin, pray for us who have recourse to thee.'

JESUS WAS A REVOLUTIONARY

Mt. 3: 1-12

John the Baptist knew that his preaching was so much inferior to that of Jesus'. His words were to prepare people for what Jesus had to say. He summarised his message in the words, "Repent, for the Kingdom of Heaven is close at hand." This had to mean, "Change your sinful ways and be ready for the Good News of God's Kingdom which will soon be preached to you by the One whose sandals I am not fit to carry." This Person will baptise you with the Holy Spirit and fire. I wonder what those last words meant to John's hearers. Then John goes on to say that once people know about Jesus they will have to make a decision about their lives. They cannot remain the same. That is indicated by the words, "The winnowing fan is in His hand; He will clear the threshing floor and gather the wheat into the barn; but the chaff He will burn in the fire that will never go out."

By these words John is indicating that Jesus is a revolutionary. His presence precipitates change. Jesus never carried a sword or banner. He never marched in a demonstration nor agitated for the overthrow of the government. He simply lived, taught and loved. His ideas were so revolutionary, but true, that it angered some and they finally nailed Him to a cross. That did not stop His message. The revolutionary Christ is still in our midst and we are confronted by Him every day. Let us look at just two of His ideas which started a revolution that is still going on today.

One is the worth of the individual. Jesus preached the importance and worth of every person. In the first century Roman world, that idea was revolutionary. No one dared to think, let along suggest, such a thing. Their entire social structure and economic system was based on a well-defined discrimination. Some people were important; others were expendable. A few people had supreme rights; others had a few rights. Some people were masters; others were slaves. The master owned the slave. He had supreme rights over him. The slave had no rights at all. The master could do what he liked with his slave. He could sell him, beat him, even kill him. Laws of human decency did not apply because slaves were not important.

To a lesser extent, the same was true between men and women, parents and children. Men were more important than women and had more rights than women. Parents owned their children and could do with their children almost anything they wanted. Into that world Jesus came, treating all people with respect and teaching that every person is supremely important in the eyes of God. This revolutionary idea slowly began to have effect in our world. His Apostle Paul wrote, "In Christ, there is neither Jew nor Greek, slave nor free man, male nor female. We are all one in Christ Jesus." Those were explosive words and a revolution was under way. That message of Jesus has still not got through to every one. Some people are still having to demand their worth and freedom.

One other revolutionary thought of Jesus was His belief in the power of love. People believed in both power and love, but they were two totally different things. Power was might and muscle. Love was something warm and nice to be shared with family members and friends. Then Jesus came along and brought the two ideas together.

He taught love was not reserved for family and friends. It was for every one, even enemies. It was more than just a warm friendly feeling. It was a deep commitment. It was strength and power. The world thinks of love as something soft and sweet. Jesus thought of love as the most irresistible force in the world. His teaching of loving our enemies makes good sense and it works. Surely all sensible people want to live in peace. This can only be achieved if we love our enemies. If we hate our enemies we shall never be at peace. This revolutionary idea of loving our neighbours and our enemies after all these centuries has not taken hold in people's lives. They still believe that hatred is strong and love is weak. When will we learn?

Our own experience tells us the truth of this idea. Who are the people who have touched our lives more deeply? Aren't they the people who have loved us, not the people who have hated us? Love is constructive; hate is destructive. Love is for winners; hate is for losers.

Lord Jesus You said, "Love your enemies." The world at large has not yet dared to try it. What a peaceful and beautiful world ours would be if only we learned to turn the other cheek and repay evil with good. Jesus You are streaks ahead of us and we have a lot to do in catching up with You. May we all take on board Your revolutionary ideas and our world will be a much better place to live in.

THE FUTURE IS BRIGHT

Mt. 3: 1-12

Are you are one of those people who looks at our world today and has a pessimistic attitude to life? You say, "Be realistic. Things are never going to change? There will always be wars. The poor will get poorer and the rich will get richer. There will always be hunger." That is a defeatist attitude!

Alternatively, we could strive to bring peace, to work for greater equality among the rich and poor, and promote positive action to feed the hungry.

Our scripture readings today are there to teach us to rise from a position of doom and gloom and fill us with hope and bright promises for the future. Let us look at what they say. Isaiah tells us, "The wolf shall be a guest of the lamb, and the leopard shall lie down with the kid;

the calf and the young lion shall browse together, with a child to guide them….the boy shall play by the cobra's den, and the child lay his hand on the adder's lair. There shall be no harm or ruin on all my holy mountain."

Isaiah's prophecy of the coming of Christ, the Messiah is one of calm, peace and joy – an idyllic picture. Unfortunately we know Jesus' life on this earth was quite the opposite. You may say that Isaiah's prophecy is an idyllic picture of what the world should be when Christ, the Messiah will come. Christ has come and the world is nothing like that, in fact it is just the opposite. So we might ask, "What has come of the great promises?"

Promises play a great part in our lives. We need them if we hope to make strides for a better world. God promised His people that He would lead them to the Holy Land and even though they were unfaithful to Him, time and time again He did lead them to the Promised Land.

Parents make promises as incentives to get the best from their children.

On one's wedding day bride and groom promise each other lifelong love and fidelity.

Promises encourage us to look for a brighter future. However, we are mature enough to know that in attempting to achieve our goals the road is not always going to be easy and that there will be hard times ahead. There is always the possibility that our goals can be achieved. God has always been faithful to His promises. If the idyllic picture of Isaiah is not achieved God is not to be blamed, it is we who have not cooperated with His help.

Advent is a time when we remember and celebrate the faithfulness of God. Repeatedly His people have been unfaithful to Him. The Israelites broke the covenant that He made with their father Abraham, but God was faithful and kept His promise that He would send His Son to be our Saviour.

Advent is not about the past but the present and the future. It reminds us of our Saviour's presence with us. He has established the Kingdom of God among us and each one of us must play our part in making His reign a reality in our part of the world. How committed are we to bringing this about?

Each year we celebrate the birth of our Saviour to remind us that God kept His promise. What does God expect of us? That we keep the promise we made to Him when we were baptised, that we would lead good and holy lives. This will mean making a humble Confession in preparation for His coming. That can be our best starting point. Then there must be love and gratitude to God for sending us His Son, literally saying to the Lord Jesus, "I love you and thank you for coming to us this Christmas." This acknowledgement must be backed up with good deeds, being forgetful of self and thinking how we can please others and making them happy in our families and our places of work.

Lord Jesus, every Advent we prepare for the second coming of Christ. Each day of Advent may we live alongside Mary and Joseph, and long for Jesus to be born anew in our lives. The greater our longing the greater will be our welcome of You in our hearts. In this way the festival of Christmas will be a period of spiritual renewal, peace, hope and happiness and we can look forward to a bright future for your reign among us.

THIRD SUNDAY OF ADVENT

REJOICE

Is. 61:1-2, 10-11, Thess. 5:16-24 & Jn.1:6-8, 19-28

Today is called Guadete Sunday, a Latin word meaning 'rejoice' taken from the first words of today's Mass. The Church is telling us to rejoice because we are exactly half way through Advent in our preparation for Christmas. The big question at this moment is, "Are you and I full of joy?"

Experience bears it out that rejoicing is not always the hallmark of every Christian. All too often Christianity has been associated with sadness. Many of us are more familiar with the Gospel message of carrying the cross than the abiding characteristic of joy. We tend to think of Jesus as the Man of Sorrows and acquainted with grief, yet as He concluded His ministry and was about to leave for Heaven, He said, "These things I have spoken to you that My joy might be in you and your joy complete." While there is hardship and suffering in the life of Jesus there is a joy which is compatible with pain.

If you attend daily Mass during Advent you will see that the joy of Advent shines forth throughout the readings and prayers with an inspiring message of hope and encouragement urging us to rejoice and be happy because the Lord is near. What is more it tells us that joy is basic to being a Christian and our vocation is to radiate this joy.

We were created for happiness – to be happy in this world and to be happy with God forever in the next. Joy is to be the purpose of our whole being and we should spend our lives searching and striving to attain it. Somehow this happiness seems to escape us as we go searching after it in the wrong places.

Our greatest mistake is to equate joy with pleasure and to look for it in material things. We can buy pleasure and it will cost us dearly, but all the money in the world cannot purchase Christian joy. Christian joy is something deeper and richer than the smile and laughter upon a happy face. It comes from an awareness that God is with us and produces a contentment and an inner peace that cannot be taken from us. Friendship with God is the source of Christian joy. No trials can drown this joy since it is born of faith. Sometimes this joy is hard to describe but it is evident in the life of a believer.

On the first Christmas when God came down in the person of Jesus, He filled the world with glad tidings of great joy. His life pointed towards God His Father in joy, prayer and thanksgiving. He invites us to unite ourselves in joy with Him but we are so caught up with our daily problems that we fail to reflect His marvellous joy.

This joy that we receive from Jesus we will want to give to others.

There is no greater proof that we possess this joy than our desire to give it to others. Our Christmas joy cannot be complete unless we show generosity to those who have nothing to give us in return. We cannot reflect the light who is Christ if we live by values that do not, even remotely, resemble those of the Gospel. The happiest people are those who are doing the most for others. They know from experience that it is in giving that we receive. Their joy will be crowned and be complete when one day they hear from the Master Himself, "Well done good and faithful servant, come and join in your Master's happiness".

One of our best preparations for Christmas is to make a sincere Confession. When did you last go to Confession? Listen to the words of Saint John Paul II, "If you don't go to Confession once a month you are not taking your spiritual life seriously." I can think of three reasons why he said this. First, in Confession we meet Jesus and that's a good reason for going. Second, it strengthens our relationship with Jesus. We never know what is ahead of us. Should we have to face some crisis we will remain close to Jesus and not turn our backs on Him. Third, it is our ticket to Heaven. I can't see when we die the Lord saying, "Who are you?" He will say, "I know you. Every month you wanted to put yourself right with me and your neighbour. Come on Heaven is waiting for you.

Not long left now for Christmas. Spend every day from now until Christmas thinking how Mary and Joseph prepared for the coming of Jesus. They will help us prepare well for Christmas.

Mother Mary, how well you and Joseph prepared for the birth of your Son Jesus. By longing for His birth may we give birth to Jesus in our hearts this Christmas day. If we have prepared spiritually for Christ, it will be the happiest Christmas we have ever had.

JOHN THE BAPTIST STILL PREPARES US FOR THE LORD

Mt. 2: 1-11

God had mapped out the life of John the Baptist. He was to be the forerunner of Jesus. He was born to elderly parents. A prophetic figure who lived a solitary and ascetic life. He attracted a circle of disciples. He proclaimed that God's Kingdom was near and that men and women should repent, receive baptism and do good works. The climax of his life was when Jesus came to him for baptism. John did not want this. He said, "I need to be baptised by You, and do You come to me?" But Jesus insisted that John should baptise Him. John realised what a sacred moment Jesus' baptism was for as soon as Jesus came from the water he saw the heavens opened and a dove descend over Jesus and he heard a voice say, "This is my beloved Son, with whom I am well pleased."

At some point after baptising Jesus, John was imprisoned by Herod Antipas, ruler of Galilee. The reason was that John had denounced Herod's illegal marriage to Herodias, the divorced wife of his half-brother Philip. Prison is never easy for any man and was certainly not for John who had spent his days in the wide open spaces of the desert. In the dark, damp dungeon he found himself in, he now had time to think about his past life and what the future had in store for him. There are some who think that John had doubts and began to wonder if he had wasted his life, and if Jesus really was the one who was to come. This could be so, for Satan has ways of sowing doubts and negative thoughts in our minds. I like to think that John was firm in his belief that Jesus was the Messiah.

While John was in prison he thought about his disciples who were missing him. He knew his work for them was done. Now he had to wean them away from following him and lead them in the direction of Jesus. When they came to visit him in prison he sent them to Jesus with the question, "Are you the Messiah, the one we are waiting for?" He knew that listening to Jesus, and witnessing His works, would make them realise that He was the long awaited Messiah. He was right, for Jesus said, "Go and tell John all the miracles you have seen which only the promised Messiah could perform." When they returned to tell John this he was pleased, for now surely they would leave him to follow Jesus, the Messiah. He could be assured that his work was done. He could now face death which he knew was sure to come soon.

In Jesus' answer to John's disciples He had words which were intended for both John and his disciples, "Blessed is the man who does not lose faith in Me." To John, Jesus was saying, "You have known all along that I am the Messiah and that you are the prophet to proclaim My coming.

Now when your future looks bleak don't give up, hang in there and trust that God will give you all the help you will need to face your future." To John's disciples, Jesus was saying, "You've seen the works of a Messiah, give your allegiance to all that I have to offer."

Once again in our run up to Christmas John the Baptist is doing the work for which he is best known, preparing us for the coming of Jesus. He is telling us to repent as he told the Jews of his time? For us it will mean making a humble and sincere Confession.

Lord Jesus, each day like Mary let us look forward to Your birthday. May we welcome You afresh in our hearts. As we prepare our gifts for our loved ones let us not fail to thank our heavenly Father for the best gift we shall receive this Christmas, namely, You His Son. Come Lord Jesus.

FOCUS ON JESUS

Jn. 1:6-8, 19-28

John the Baptist was a man whose whole life was focused on Jesus. All he wanted was to build a strong relationship with Him that would grow and grow. He also wanted others to know and follow Jesus.

God had called him for one purpose and that was to prepare the people of Israel for the coming of His Son. He was aware that this was his task and he gave himself totally to what God asked of him. By leading an ascetic life in the wilderness he prepared himself for the task in hand. When the time was right he made his way to the river Jordan to preach repentance and baptise the people who were ready to repent.

From his sayings we can see how focused he was on Jesus. Let me quote some of them. "I am not fit to undo His sandal strap." "He must increase. I must decrease." "I baptise you in water for repentance but the One who follows me is more powerful than I am."

He attracted many Jews who came to listen to him and be baptised. Some of them, who were waiting for the Messiah, sensed John was a holy man and was worth following and so they became his disciples. They were men like James and John, Peter and Andrew. When eventually Jesus, the Messiah, appeared on the scene John pointed Him out to his disciples as the Messiah. He now knew his work was nearing completion. When Jesus came to John to be baptised he pointed them in the direction of Jesus, "Look, there is the Lamb of God who takes away the sins of the world. This is the one I spoke of when I said: a man is coming after me who ranks before me because He existed before me."

As a result some of his disciples left him to follow Jesus. This made John very happy. Now he could retire from the scene but he was still found working for God. Not many months later John was not afraid to reprimand Herod for attempting to marry Herodias, the wife of his brother Philip. His condemnation of Herod's behaviour angered Herodias, and for being outspoken, she was responsible for him being sent to prison.

While in prison some of his disciples visited him and told him about the wonderful things that Jesus was doing. His one desire was that they should leave him and follow Jesus and so he sent them to Him to ask, "Are you the One who is to come or have we got to look for someone else?" By doing this some commentators think that John had doubts whether Jesus was the Messiah. I don't believe this. I feel sure that John believed Jesus was the Messiah. By telling his disciples to go to Jesus he was certain that their meeting Jesus would convince them that He was the Messiah and so they would follow Him. That is what he ardently hoped. All he wanted was attention to be withdrawn from him and focused on Jesus. When they came back with the news of the wonderful things Jesus was doing, signs foretold by Isaiah the coming Messiah would do, John was hoping that now they would leave him and follow Jesus.

A firm relationship with Jesus is the principle concern of all the saints. We are all sinners but we want to lead holy lives and so a firm relationship with Jesus should also be our chief concern. We see this in holy men like Pope Benedict XVI. He strived to know the Lord Jesus better and to grow daily in His love. When he resigned he sensed that people thought he had forsaken the cross. "Far from it", he said, "I have not come down from the cross of Christ." He knew that in his mental and physical state he had done all he could for the Lord and someone younger than he would be better suited to lead God's people.

Lord Jesus, Christmas is very near and our chief concern, like John, should be our relationship to You. This, too, was all that mattered to Your mother Mary and Joseph. We are busy preparing for Christmas to make our family and friends have a happy and memorable one. I know You would want that of us, but first and foremost You would not want us to lose sight of the fact that we are doing this precisely because You became a man for us. It is because You loved us so much that we love others.

THE HEALING MINISTRY OF JESUS

Is. 35:1-6,10; James 5:7-10 & Mt. 11:2-11

The prophecy of Isaiah, which we have just heard, must have come like a breath of fresh air, bringing joy to the people of Israel in their despondency. The people of Israel had been taken captive by the Assyrians, and more than a century later, by the Babylonians. Their Temple had been destroyed, the monarchy had been dethroned and a part of the population was now living in exile in a foreign land. The glorious era which Israel had enjoyed under King David and King Solomon seemed to have gone for ever. It is against this background that Isaiah proclaims a message of hope and joy, looking ahead to the coming of the Messiah when God would restore the fortunes of Israel. But how were the people to recognise the Messiah when He eventually came?

Isaiah gives the people a tell-tale sign by which to recognise the Messiah. His coming would be marked by widespread healing among the people. He would make the blind see, the deaf hear, the lame walk and the dumb speak and He would bring His people home from exile. This process of healing and home-coming is described in terms of a wilderness and parched land and suddenly becoming alive and fertile again. A beautiful image of healing!

What God had promised through the prophet Isaiah He fulfilled when He sent His Son, Jesus, into the world. We know well from the Gospel account that a substantial part of Jesus' ministry was devoted to healing people's illnesses, bringing lifeless limbs and bodies back to life. He healed the people not only physically, but also emotionally, and above all spiritually, leading them home to God after their exile of sin. That is why, we read in today's Gospel, when John the Baptist sent messengers to Jesus to ask if He was the Messiah, Jesus, instead of simply replying "yes", gave an indirect "yes" as an answer. He points out all the works of healing He has performed, leaving it to them to deduce from the prophecy of Isaiah that He indeed is the Messiah.

The healing ministry of Jesus is carried out today by the Church through the Sacraments. As Pope St. Leo the Great said, "The visible presence of Jesus has passed over into the Sacraments." To use the imagery of Isaiah, the Sacraments are like a stream gushing forth from Christ, bringing the life-giving waters of the Holy Spirit to the arid land which represents God's people parched with sin and death. In the waters of Baptism we were cleansed of the spiritual leprosy called "Original Sin". In Confirmation, the Holy Spirit came down to strengthen our weary hands and to steady our trembling knees, giving us courage to bear witness to the Lord. In the Eucharist we receive the nutrients for our spiritual growth – the Body and Blood of Christ. In the Sacrament of Reconciliation we receive ongoing healing of our spiritual illness, namely our sins. Finally, in the Sacrament of Anointing the Lord gives us the grace, either to heal us of our illness altogether, or, if it be not His will, then we bear the illness with patience and courage. The Sacraments, therefore, are the primary channels through which we encounter the healing power of Jesus today.

Before we ask Our Lord to heal us, we must first humbly acknowledge the particular illness and want to be healed and second, have an unwavering faith in the Lord's power to heal us. If we are too proud to admit our illness, or if we are doubtful about the Lord's capacity to heal us, then we place an obstacle in the path of His healing grace. A helpful starting point is to look in our lives and identify those areas where we need healing. Physical illnesses or disabilities are obvious enough, and we do not have much difficulty in praying to be healed of them. However, psychological and spiritual illnesses may be more hidden, and we may either be unaware of them, or else feel too ashamed to admit to them. For example, is our life consumed by the cancer or resentment and vindictiveness? Are we crippled by guilt or worry? Guilt keeps us trapped in the past, while worry makes us obsessed with the future, and neither of them helps us to live the present moment to the full, with joy and trust in the Lord. Are our eyes blind to the light of truth which God has taught us through Sacred Scripture and the Church's magisterium? Are our ears deaf to the cry of the poor, to the needs of those who suffer? Or, having heard their cry, are our hands too paralysed by meanness to reach out and help them? Are we tongue-tied by fear and so unable to proclaim the Gospel and to stand up for it even in the face of ridicule or suffering? The list is endless. And if we are honest with ourselves, each of us will definitely identity one or more areas where we need healing.

No matter what our illnesses are, the Church invites us today to be joyful because the Lord is at hand to heal us. The fact that we experience pain in our illness should be no obstacle to joy. Pain and joy can coexist with each other. We only have to look at some people who are terminally ill who, despite the pain they suffer, are able to radiate peace and joy to others. Even though they may not have been physically healed, they are nevertheless emotionally healed and at peace. They have united themselves to the Passion of Christ for the salvation of the world.

Lord Jesus, let us, too, be joyful and patient as we wait for You to come and heal us.

ALL IN GOD'S GOOD TIME

James 5:7-10 & Mt. 11:2-11.

Waiting can sometimes be one of the hardest things in life. If we are expecting something bad to happen, we want it to be over and done with quickly. If we're expecting something good, we are impatient for it to happen.

A classic example of the latter is a small child anxiously awaiting Christmas. How eager and impatient he is. Every hour seems like a day, every day like a week. We who are older are pleasantly amused by the impatience of the young. What about ourselves? We have to learn to wait. Life, to a certain extent, unfolds at its own pace, for some things cannot be hurried.

In our First Reading from the letter of Saint James, we find this very pointed and practical advice, "Be patient, brothers, until the Lord's coming." Then he proceeds to use the farmer as an example of what he means. Farming is a combination of working and waiting - and it takes both to make a crop. A farmer who did nothing but wait would be a miserable failure. The ground has to be prepared and ploughed; seeds must be sown; and the field must be regularly weeded. Nature must play her part as the farmer waits for the rain to fall, the sun to shine, the seed to germinate, and the crop to grow and ripen. Only then will the harvest be ready for him to gather.

Working and waiting - that is what life is all about. Some things we work for, like preparing the ground; other things we wait for, like the harvest. We need to know when to work and when to wait! And waiting demands patience.

Let's see how this applies to our own lives. The person who is impatient with himself is like a farmer who sows the seed today and expects a crop tomorrow. Life doesn't work that way on the farm or in the human heart. Becoming a whole and healthy person requires working and waiting. Strength of character does not happen overnight. The Bible tells us that even Jesus grew in wisdom and grace before God and man. Our Lord spent approximately 30 years in Nazareth preparing Himself for His public mission. That demanded patience because He must have longed to begin telling people that the Kingdom of God was at hand. We too have to practice patience, knowing when to work and when to wait.

We must also be patient with others. What right have we to demand that people move at the speed we dictate? We, most certainly, would not like that demand to be made of us. We also have to learn to be patient with other people's faults. Again, what right have we to demand that they change their way of life immediately? God is patient with our faults and gives us time to rectify them, so we should give others time. So let us be patient with ourselves and patient with all those around us.

Finally, we must learn to be patient with God. This has to be said because we tend to be impatient with Him. We look at our world and see the mess that it is in. We see people who have more than they need, while others starve. We see crime and corruption. We see war and violence. Although we may not say it out loud, nevertheless, we wonder 'Why doesn't God do something?'

Lord Jesus, our heavenly Father is at work in our world, but not to our standards nor our timetable. We can be sure that things are unfolding according to His plan. His purposes will be accomplished. Our part is to join in His work, do what we can, and patiently leave the rest to God.

THE REAL TESTS OF CHRISTIANITY THEN AND NOW

Mt. 11:2-11

For telling King Herod that it was wrong for him to live with his brother's wife, Saint John the Baptist was clapped into prison. To be confined in a prison cell is difficult for anyone, but even more so for John who was an outdoor person.

Some commentators maintain that during that time of enforced idleness, John began to have doubts about Jesus. Was He the promised Messiah, or must the people of Israel continue their long wait for a Redeemer? I cannot accept this. Surely when Jesus was baptised and John witnessed the heavens open and the Spirit of God descend on Jesus and the voice of the Father say, "You are My Son, the Beloved; My favour rests on You?" was enough to convince John that here before Him was the long promised Messiah.

How then are we to explain John sending his disciples to ask Jesus, "Are you the One who is to come or have we got to wait for someone else?" John's work was done. He had prepared and proclaimed to the people of Israel that Jesus was the Messiah, and now he could fade quietly away. I reckon the reason why John sent his disciples to Jesus was for the sole purpose of encouraging them to leave him and join Jesus. If they saw what Jesus was doing that should be enough evidence to convince them that Jesus was the Messiah.

So they went to Jesus and what did Jesus tell them, "Go back and tell John what you hear and see; the blind see again, and the lame walk, lepers are cleansed, and the deaf hear again, and the dead are raised to life and the Good News is proclaimed to the poor; and happy is the man who has not lost faith in Me." Those were all the things expected of the Messiah. Surely that would be enough to convince them that Jesus was no other than the Messiah?

Notice in Jesus' response to John He appealed to the present, not to the past. He cited works, not words. He identified His cause with the most disadvantaged members of society. To this day those are the real tests of real Christianity.

Jesus could have pointed John to Old Testament prophecies that had been fulfilled in His birth. He could have reminded Him of what took place at His Baptism, but Jesus did neither of those. Instead, He calls attention to more immediate events, the things that were occurring there and then. "Go back and tell John what you hear and see." Jesus insisted that the validity of His cause was there for people to witness.

There is no doubt, of course, that Christianity has a glorious past. We could try to validate our faith by pointing out that it was powerful in the first century and has been for 2,000 years since. But how much better it is when we demonstrate its power in the present century. It will do no good, in this modern world, for us to show people our Christian museums. If our faith is real, it will produce evidence that is current and up to date. That is what Jesus offered John.

Another test of real Christianity is works, and not mere words. Jesus said, "The blind see again, and the lame walk, the deaf hear." Surely, that was proof enough that God was at work in the life and ministry of Jesus. But this appeal to miraculous events seems to leave us at a decided disadvantage. We cannot open blind eyes and unblock deaf ears by the touch of our hands. There are some who claim to perform miracles, but few observers are convinced that their religion is real.

There are others who offer no miraculous evidence for their faith. They simply care and try to help. Their efforts often include a great deal of personal sacrifice. They give their money and time, their tears and their prayers, to real human needs. They may not have many words to say but their works are eloquent. The things they do make the Christian faith more persuasive than the most gifted of orators. What made the healings of Jesus convincing was not so much their miraculous nature, as their merciful quality. That is what we can copy. We cannot perform miracles, but we can show mercy. We can be compassionate with people who are hurting. That is the vital test of real Christianity.

One other test is a commitment to the most disadvantaged people in society. Jesus said, "The Gospel is proclaimed to the poor." This was not a new message. It was the renewal of an old message. One of the distinguishing characteristics of the ancient prophets was their burning zeal for the poor. With the passing of years, those voices faded out. The religious leaders had become wealthy, and the poor were virtually forgotten. This was not so with Jesus. He deliberately sought out the poor to tell them the Good News.

No worse fate can befall the Catholic religion than for it to become the lapdog of the privileged. Jesus always gave His attention first to the disadvantaged. That note rings throughout His parables. The Good Samaritan, the rich man and Lazarus, the Final Judgement, all those stories carry the same theme: God's concern is for the poor. Any religion that loses that message ceases to be the religion of Jesus. How much do we care for the most disadvantaged members of society?

I hope when John's disciples went back to tell John the news they were convinced, as we are, that Jesus was the promised Messiah.

Lord Jesus, for the validity of Your cause, You appealed to the present, not the past; to works, not to words; and Your primary concern was for the poor. May we follow Your example.

FOURTH SUNDAY OF ADVENT

TRUSTING GOD

Is. 7:10-14 & Mt. 1:18-24

Trust is an important element of any relationship. Indeed, a relationship cannot grow without trust. It requires confidence in the other person's capacity to be with me and support me and not to let me down. Such a trust can only be tested and proved in times of crisis. It is one thing to say, "I trust you," and another thing actually to trust that person, especially when the odds seem stacked heavily against such a trust. If the relationship is genuine and committed, then the trust will be vindicated, and the crisis will have helped to strengthen the relationship.

On this final Sunday of Advent, we reflect on the virtue of hope which is closely allied to trust in our relationship with God. Trust is founded on God's promises to us and on His capacity to deliver on His promises, the two go together. Time and time again, in salvation history, people have been called to trust God in the midst of confusing and even seemingly hopeless situations. Today's readings provide us with two such examples. In each, God gives the person concerned a sign to help the person trust in Him. It is a sign that assures the person that God is with him in the predicament. That is the meaning of the word "Emmanuel" – God-is-with-us.

In the First Reading, we heard the story of King Ahaz, King of Judah. Ahaz, who was a descendant of King David, occupied the throne at a critical time in Judah's political history. The country was threatened by invasion from the formidable Assyrian army. To make matters worse, Ahaz did not have an heir to the throne. The situation must have been very worrying and puzzling. After all, God had long ago promised King David through the prophet Nathan that He would make the House of David secure and that the throne of Judah would always be occupied by a descendent of David. What, then, had become of God's promises? It was at this point that God intervened and gave a sign to boost Ahaz's flagging trust. God announced through the prophet Isaiah that a maiden would be the sign that God was with him, Emmanuel. In the immediate context, this referred to the imminent birth of an heir to the Judean throne, namely Ahaz's son Hezekiah. However, the prophecy also looked ahead to the day, some 700 years later, when Jesus, the Son of God would be born of the Virgin Mary. Born of the line of David, Jesus would be the real King, not only of Judah and Israel, but indeed of the whole world. He would also be the true Emmanuel in whom God would definitely be with His people.

The second example of trust in God concerns Joseph, the foster-father of Jesus. Joseph was blissfully unaware of the role which God was asking him to play in the plan of salvation. We can, therefore, imagine how Joseph's life was turned upside down when he learnt that his fiancée, Mary, was pregnant even before they came to live together. Whatever the emotions and confusion that passed through his mind, we are told that Joseph was a righteous man and that he acted honourably in the circumstances. He could not understand why God had allowed this to happen to him, and yet, he put his trust in the Lord and acted with the utmost consideration towards Mary. He decided to take the course of action which would be least damaging to Mary's reputation and decided to divorce her informally. Again, God intervened at this point to reassure Joseph with a special sign. The angel of the Lord was sent to inform Joseph that Mary had conceived, not through any human agency, but by a direct action of the Holy Spirit and that, therefore, Mary was still a virgin. In this way, the age-old prophecy of Isaiah came to fulfilment. Joseph's mind was now at ease, and he took Mary as his wife, as originally planned.

In our lives, too, God expects us to show the same trust in Him as Joseph did. This trust will be put to the test in moments of crisis which we are bound to experience at various stages of our lives, whether individually or collectively. One such moment occurred on 11 September 2001. We may be tempted to ask where was God in all of this, and why didn't He do something about it. Some even questioned whether God exists. However, in the midst of all the suffering and confusion, God was there to comfort us in the acts of love which people performed during this crisis: those who risked their lives to save others, those who ministered to the sick and the dying, those who counselled the bereaved and the distressed, and those who, in whatever way brought a ray of light into the darkness of people's lives. All these are signs to us that God is very much with us, right in the thick of suffering. Christ, who is truly God and Man, suffers in the suffering, and ministers to the suffering through those who reach out to help them. Paradoxically, therefore, times of suffering and confusion are also the very times we experience God's presence in a powerful and intimate way.

As we come to the end of Advent, let us pray for a renewal of hope and a deepening of our trust in God. In times of crisis, whether individual or collective, we would do well to imitate the trust which Joseph displayed in God in the following ways: acknowledge the pain and the confusion that we experience; stay with the pain and the confusion, praying patiently and acting honourably as Joseph did, and resisting the temptation to aggression and rash behaviour; watch out for the signs of love and goodness around us, these are the Emmanuel signs which God gives us to show that He is with us.

Heavenly Father, the Kingdom of God has already come among us in the person of Christ. However, as long as this earthly life lasts, the Kingdom of God coexists with the Kingdom of Satan. Hope is the virtue that looks ahead to the end of time when sin and sadness will finally be defeated and Your Kingdom definitely established. Father, You have promised this, and we believe You will fulfil Your promise.

SALVATION BEGINS WITH A RELATIONSHIP

Mt. 1:18-25

Christmas is so near and what does that day mean to us? For children it is all excitement as they look forward to the presents they will receive. For some adults it will mean a break from work, enjoying a well-earned rest with family and friends and eating and drinking well, perhaps with none or very little spiritual input. Others will dread Christmas. They detest the way the world has commercialised this Feast. For others it will be a lonely time. Their loved ones are no longer with them. For others the spiritual side of Christmas is so rich and they long for the coming of Jesus.

I think the angel who spoke to Joseph in today's Gospel sets the spirit and meaning of Christmas. "You must name Him Jesus, because He is the One Who is to save His people from their sins." The whole purpose of Christmas is for Jesus, the Son of God to become a Man and restore our relationship with His Father. The angel was expressing the hopes and dreams of the entire world. All the rest of the New Testament is a commentary on that statement, applying it to all of life. This salvation that comes to each one of us through Jesus includes the whole person, not just the soul, but the mind, the body, work, home, personal and social life.

The essence of salvation begins with a relationship. The angelic announcement identifies Jesus with those He is coming to save. That possessive pronoun 'His' is a very important word. The people that Jesus will save are 'His' people. He commits Himself to them and He claims them as His own. Throughout His ministry, Jesus established relationships with those whom He would save. He said to Peter, Andrew, James and John, "Follow Me, and I will make you fishers of men." That was the beginning of a relationship. They left their families, boats and nets and followed Him. Later He would say to these men, "I no longer call you servants, but friends." Between Jesus and these four fishermen there had grown a bond of trust that enabled them to become something they could never otherwise have been.

Christian salvation begins with a relationship. That shouldn't surprise us because all the saving experiences of life begin that way. Take a good home, for example. There is no greater redeeming influence in the world than a good home. Children who come from a home where they are loved and experience mutual respect have a greater chance in life than those who do not.

What happens when children do not experience this loving relationship in their homes? They find themselves at war with themselves and at war with others. For them, the future is unhappiness, loneliness and distrust. Some of them in time may find a person who believes in them, loves them and shows them respect. Some respond to this and life will never again be the same for them. Here we see that their salvation began with a relationship.

This experience is true of all of us. Jesus came into the world to save 'His' people. He committed Himself to us and claimed us as His own. His purpose for coming on this earth was to establish and build with each one of us a saving relationship. It all starts with that.

From this relationship there follows redemption. The angel said that Jesus would save 'His people from their sins'. We often think of salvation only in terms of the future – rescued from evil and rewarded with Heaven. That is true but it is not the full picture. The redemptive work of Jesus is not just to lead us to Heaven totally divorced from the present. The promise is that He will not only save His people from Hell but that He will save His people from present evils and misfortunes.

Sin is a present reality. We not only need a Saviour who will deliver us from punishment of sin at the end of life but who can deliver us from the power of sin in the midst of life. This is the kind of Saviour the angel declared Jesus to be. His salvation concerns itself not only with eternity but also with the present time. That is the only salvation that has real meaning for life here and now. We don't want to know that we are saved in some sort of vague way in the future but that we are saved from specific concrete sins that beset our lives today. We need to be saved from pride, greed, selfishness, bad temper, impatience and bitterness. This is the salvation Jesus came to give to the world. You can see it on every page of the Gospels – Jesus saving people from the grip of sin, lifting them above their littleness, giving them hope, making them truly alive and different. He is still doing it today. In every part of the world you will find all sorts of people who are being saved from their sins through a personal relationship with Jesus Christ.

Lord Jesus, there is no need for us to go through life constantly defeated by our sins. There is a way out. The angel spoke of it centuries ago. "You must name Him Jesus, because He is the One Who is to save His people from their sins." That is the Good News You came to give our sinful world and that is why we rejoice and celebrate Christmas. Let us long for Your coming and share the hope and joy Your birth brings us with those who need it this Christmas.

A REAL MAN – AND A GREAT MAN

Mt. 1:18 – 25

The husband of Mary must have been a very kind, loving, gentle and compassionate man, yet strong and decisive. Undoubtedly Saint Joseph was a great man. But the Gospel records tells us so very little about him.

All we know is that he was a descendant of David, and a carpenter by trade who lived in Nazareth. His brief story is told only in two Gospels, and that is because he was engaged to be married to a young woman named Mary, who became the mother of Jesus.

Admittedly, that is not much to go on, but just enough to whet our appetites and make us want to know more. We cannot help but be curious about the man God chose to play such a vital role in the life of His Son; to be nothing less than the husband of Mary and the foster father of God's Son. But we are not left completely in the dark. By reading between the lines, we can gain some meaningful insights into the life of Joseph.

He was a man of deep compassion. When he discovered that Mary was pregnant, he was totally puzzled. He knew in his heart that Mary would never be unfaithful to him, but how had this come about? Being an honest man he could not claim her child as his own. He decided to take a course of action that would least hurt the girl he deeply loved. So he decided to break their engagement quietly. This meant that he was unwilling to expose Mary to public humiliation and the harsh judgement of the law.

His heart was broken, his dreams were shattered. But there was something inside Joseph that would not allow him to be vindictive, to seek revenge, or to be unkind. Even though his feelings were deeply hurt and he had the legal right of a public separation, he was still unwilling to humiliate another human being, especially the one whom he loved.

Is it any wonder that God entrusted the early training of His Son to a man such as that? There can be little doubt that the quality of mercy that is evident in the life and ministry of Jesus was due in part to the influence of Joseph. To the people of Nazareth he was known simply as "the carpenter" but careful examination shows him to be a man of deep compassion.

A second characteristic that can be seen in Joseph is a trusting faith. He was willing to trust God beyond the limits of his own understanding.

Consider for a moment the circumstances in which Joseph found himself. He had just learned that his fiancé was expecting a child, whom he knew could not be his own. He had decided to deal with it compassionately. Then in a dream, he is informed by an angel that Mary had not been unfaithful, but that her pregnancy is a miracle of God.

What would you do with a dream like that? Being asked to believe the unbelievable, something that had never ever happened before. Few of us are inclined to take seriously anything that exceeds the limited reach of our personal experience and understanding! But Joseph was not one to set narrow limits to divine possibilities.

This is not to say that he was gullible, but that he was humble. He was aware that he could not hold the entire mystery of life within the small confines of his own mind. Such a man is unwilling to make arrogant pronouncements on what is and is not possible. Years later Jesus would teach His disciples that "with God all things are possible." Surely He must have learnt part of His faith from the man who helped to rear Him.

Joseph was also a man of action. Our reading says, "When Joseph woke up he did what the angel of the Lord had told him to do." That is the real proof of his faith and his compassion. He acted upon them and took Mary as his wife. And that was not an easy thing to do. All he had to go on was Mary's testimony and a dream. For most of us that would not be enough, but it was for Joseph. With only that little evidence he set the course of his life, and the rest is history.

Joseph always played his part in the background. His name is mentioned only a few times in the Gospels, but he made a priceless contribution to the life of Jesus and through Jesus to the world. I am convinced that you and I are more indebted to this quiet and courageous man than we will ever know this side of Heaven.

Lord Jesus, with Christmas so near we ask Your foster father Saint Joseph to help us prepare our hearts for Your coming, that we might know You, love You and serve You better in this world and to be happy with You in the next.

WHAT ST. JOSEPH CAN TEACH US

Mt. 1:18-25

I owe a debt of gratitude to my parents for many things. One of them is that when I was baptised they gave me three saint's names. Marcel, because I was born on the feast of St. Marcellus, pope and martyr; Benjamin, because that was my Dad's second name and Joseph because my father had a great devotion to him.

My father had great faith in St. Joseph. I was ten in 1948 when we sailed from India to England. We had nowhere to live. My grandmother very kindly offered us a home until my father could find a permanent one. I remember my father saying, "If Joseph could find a dwelling for Mary and her Son in Bethlehem, he will find a place for us." St. Joseph never let him down for within five days, for the twelve of us, he found a four storey house in Bedford for £1400. I have to thank my father for teaching me to love St. Joseph.

Joseph had to be a very special man for he was chosen by God the Father to take care of His Son Jesus and Mary, His mother. From the moment he is mentioned in the Gospels we see Joseph wanting to do the right thing. How fortunate he was to be betrothed to Mary, the loveliest human person our world has ever known, but before they came to live together he discovered Mary to be with child. Joseph could not believe this. He was convinced of

Mary's integrity and purity. He knew she would never be unfaithful to him. So how was it possible for her to conceive a child? There had to be an answer to this problem. Joseph prayed for one. Why didn't he ask Mary how this had come about? He loved and respected her and being the gentle and loving man he was he did not want to put any pressure on her. What was he to do?

Being an honest and just man it would not be right to claim the Child as his own. So he decided he would cause the least possible hurt to Mary and divorce her privately. His heart must have been aching because he could not bear the thought of losing Mary, the love of his life. Now the time was right for God to intervene. He answered Joseph's prayer. In a dream an angel revealed to him how this had happened to Mary. "Joseph do not be afraid to take Mary as your wife because she has conceived by the power of the Holy Spirit." He was now the happiest man in the world! He was not going to lose the girl he loved. God was giving him the honour of loving, cherishing and caring for her, and with God's blessing, he would take the role of being the foster father of her child.

If Joseph had been a jealous man how different things would have been. He could have confronted Mary and demanded who was the father and why had she been unfaithful to him. Instead he acted in a gentle and considerate manner.

Is there anything Joseph has to teach our generation? I could think of several things. There is one virtue that desperately needs mentioning and that is purity. Mary was the most desirable woman a man could ever wish to love. Yet, he respected her virginity. This is the lesson that our engaged and young people of today need to learn. They need to respect each other.

There is a growing trend among young and engaged couples to live together before marriage. Those couples who are living like this are living in sin. They are taking the privilege of marriage without first receiving the blessing of God on their relationship. Some parents say they feel helpless in advising their children how to behave otherwise. This, I think, could have been overcome if parents had taken the care to have had family prayers. In that setting a code of behaviour of how to respect and behave towards the opposite sex before marriage could have been discussed and taught. All this needs to be said because the world today has made its own rules and is leading our young people and not so young people away from the Commandments of God. I have heard Catholics say, "Because everybody is doing it, it is right.' That is not a reason for making behaviour right or wrong. If everyone were to kill, does that make killing right? No, God has made it quite clear in the Scriptures, that living together before marriage is fornication and that fornication is a sin. May Joseph be their model and show them how to love and have respect for their partner.

Lord Jesus, the time of Your birth is so near. In the hours that remain let us live alongside Mary and Joseph and be ready to bring You forth in our lives this Christmas.

SIGNS

Mt. 1: 18-25

The obvious theme of today's Mass could be summed up in one word, 'Signs'. The prophet Isaiah told Ahaz that the Lord would give him a sign that "the maiden is with child and will soon give birth to a son whom she will call Immanuel, a name which means 'God-is-with-us'". St. Paul wrote about the Good News from God that came to us through Jesus. He is the sign of our salvation, of our call to be saints. In the Gospel, Joseph receives a sign through his dream that Mary's Son is the "One to save His people from their sins."

The Old Testament seems to be full of signs – the burning bush, floods and plagues. The New Testament has its share, too, with the voice from the cloud at the Baptism of Jesus, and the miracles themselves. If we give it some thought we can enumerate signs throughout the centuries. If a sign is something that points the way, there are many ways that we might be pointed towards our eternal life. The greatest sign we have is the sign of Jesus in Holy Communion. The Holy Eucharist is a sign of eternal glory. If we can possess Him now on this earth, it is a sign that we shall possess Him in the life to come.

There have been many real signs calling us to follow Christ. Our Blessed Lady used Bernadette in Lourdes as a sign-post for the faithful to draw people to repent and pray for themselves and the conversion of sinners. The prayerful faces of the millions of pilgrims who pray at the Lourdes grotto are a sign that the Kingdom of God is here.

The miracle of the sun at Fatima is a modern sign. In 1917 the three children, Lucy, Jacinta and Francesco had been meeting Our Lady just outside their village on the 13th of each month from May to September. Many people were following them to their visions. They asked for some sign that it was true. So, on October 13th. some 70,000 people witnessed the "Miracle of the Sun", when it spun like a Catherine wheel, danced about the sky, and appeared to be heading straight towards the earth, before settling back to its normal position.

There is a story told of an old Jew, who was confined to his bed. He longed for the coming of the Messiah, and hoped to be living at His arrival. Each morning, when his servant woke him and drew the curtains, he would ask, "Has the Messiah come yet?" The answer he got was always the same, "No, Sir." One day the old man asked, "How do you know that the Messiah has not yet come to us?" "Well, Sir, as I look out of your window I can see all those Catholics coming out of morning Mass. I only have to look at their miserable faces to know that the Messiah has not yet come."

I hope that fictional story is not true of this congregation. But is there some truth in it? How do we leave church? If you were to stand outside and just watch as the congregation left any Catholic church, would you be convinced that they have just come face to face with Jesus?

So, there is a message here for us all today. The greatest sign of all, Jesus Christ, did come to us as the angel predicted to Joseph. He was born, lived, and died. He then came back from the dead and lives on. We have access to Him in many ways. We may receive His Holy Spirit. We may have Him as our constant Companion. We may take Him to ourselves in Holy Communion. In a few days time we will once again celebrate His birth.

Perhaps the best sign of all that Jesus really does enter into our hearts is the way we live in harmony at all times with our neighbours. The joy that comes to our world on Christmas Day is more than just presents, food, drink, and a holiday. For a short time, goodness and peace rules the earth. Fighting ceases and peace reigns. Our special task as Christians is to try and ensure that the peace which rules us this week lives on next week, and well into the New Year. Then, it will be an obvious sign to the world that our Saviour Christ has indeed come into our world.

Heavenly Father, the best sign we have of Your love is the gift of Your Son Jesus who will once again come into our hearts this Christmas. We thank you for this and may we give Him the warm welcome that His mother Mary and Joseph gave Him.

JOSEPH, THE FAMILY MAN.

Mt. 1:18-25.

Today's Gospel focuses our attention on St. Joseph. In every manger scene, it is never Joseph who is in the spotlight. The attention belongs to the Virgin Mary and her child Jesus. But in that familiar scene Joseph demonstrates the true spirit of Christmas. He gives his love completely to his family and asks nothing in return.

Joseph was a man of great compassion, a tremendous faith and a real and personal commitment.

Joseph's name appears fifteen times in the New Testament, mostly in connection with the birth of Jesus. Artists have pictured him leading the donkey, knocking on the door of the inn, and standing by the manger that held the Baby. His was a supporting role. There was once a boy who was given the part of Joseph in a Nativity Play. He felt very honoured. At the first rehearsal, his pride turned to disappointment. He had no lines to learn and no gestures to make. When he tried to give some personal interpretation to the role, the teacher would say, 'No, no, Johnny. Just stand there!' When finally he froze into place, the teacher said, 'There, that's perfect.'

I love that other story about the boy in the Nativity Play. He, too, was given the role of Joseph. He felt very important and showed off in front of the others. So the teacher demoted him and made him the innkeeper. He thought to himself, 'I'll get my own back on her.' In the play when Joseph knocked at the door of the inn and asked if there was any room for them, he was most gracious and said, 'Yes, there's plenty. Do come in!'

The gospel records do not report a single word that Joseph ever spoke. But for all his silence, he demonstrates the true spirit of Christmas. Joseph was facing a personal crisis. He began to notice that his bride-to-be was carrying a child which he knew was not his own. He knew that his Mary had not been unfaithful to him. Can you imagine how perplexed and confused he was, yet all his concern was for Mary. He loved her deeply and he didn't want her to be hurt. He demonstrated a compassion rarely seen in human history.

Being a just and upright man it wouldn't have been honest for him to claim the child as his own. So he planned to divorce her quietly. He was betrothed to Mary. This was a serious commitment which could only be broken off by divorce. Joseph realised he had the best reason for a divorce, namely, adultery. He could simply tell the community what Mary had done. The engagement would be officially broken. No one would have blamed him for his action. In fact everyone would sympathize with him. People would applaud him for upholding the law. Joseph knew all that. He also knew what would happen to Mary. She would have been shamed and humiliated.

To spare her that suffering, Joseph intended to break off the relationship quietly and discreetly. This was more than an act of kindness. It would involve personal sacrifice. Rumours were sure to arise about Joseph's own responsibility for the baby. His reputation would suffer, and probably his livelihood as well. This course of action would most likely damage his future chances of marriage and a family. He was prepared to do all this because of the deep love and concern he had for Mary. Is it any wonder that God entrusted the rearing of His Son to Joseph? By his compassion for Mary, this village carpenter demonstrated the true spirit of Christmas.

Now we shall see the tremendous faith that Joseph was to demonstrate. In a dream he was told by an angel, 'Joseph, son of David, do not be afraid to take Mary home as your wife, because she has conceived what is in her by the Holy Spirit.' He could have, very reasonably, reacted with the words, 'I just don't believe it.' Only a person with a great faith could have believed this. He was willing to let God be God and he knew that nothing is impossible to God.

None of us wants to be gullible, deceiving ourselves or allowing others to deceive us. Neither do we want to be cynical, believing only that which our eyes can see and our minds can grasp. Faith helps to accept what our minds cannot grasp. This is the faith Joseph had and by leaving his future in God's hands he opened himself to all kinds of possibilities. If like Joseph we have this deep faith and put our future in God's hands we never know the good things that God can achieve in our lives. It is not surprising that God entrusted the care of His Son to that kind of man. Can there be any doubt that Jesus gained a better understanding of His father in heaven, from the kind of foster-father that He had on earth?

Once he had been told what he had to do, Joseph demonstrated a real and personal commitment. 'He received Mary into his home as his wife.' His story did not end with simply believing. He committed himself to be a father to the child in every way he could. He took the risks and joys of rearing a child that was not his own. It was not an easy assignment, but I am sure Joseph would tell us that the rewards far outweighed the demands.

Joseph's commitment involved him being chaste. We live in a promiscuous world, where free love is encouraged, a world where God does not exist and so neither does His law. Joseph teaches us to think and act differently. Was there any woman more desirable to man than was Mary? Yet, Joseph respected her virginity. He was chaste. Today it would be Joseph who would have the answer to the problem of AIDS.

Lord Jesus, Your foster father Joseph's heart was gentle and kind and his mind open to new ideas. He wanted to do what God expected of him. It comes as no surprise that You came to possess those same qualities. You had a good model in Joseph. May St. Joseph, husband of Mary and Your foster-father help us to prepare for Your coming this Christmas.

CHRISTMAS

(Five sermons)

JOY TO THE WORLD

Somewhere today the carol 'Joy to the World' will be sung. Do we know what "Joy" can stand for? J stands for Jesus, O for others and Y for yourself.

On Christmas Day, let us welcome Jesus as the greatest gift our heavenly Father can give us for Christmas. We could ask for nothing more and receive nothing better. There is no thought better than holding Jesus to our heart and loving Him. He makes us feel so loved and secure.

Others – Forget ourselves for this one day. Let us give ourselves to others. To share ourselves is to enjoy life to the full. Jesus gives Himself to us on Christmas Day. He lived with and for us and gave us the greatest gift of all – His very life. His was a life of giving, never taking. If we imitated Him this day how much richer our life would be!

Yourself – Give yourself to Jesus today. If we try it just for one day, we will find it easier to try it on the days that follow.

What joy there is in heaven on this beautiful day! What joy there should be on earth!

When any expectant mother awaits the birth of her baby, what preparation she and her husband make for it. Everything, if possible, must be new, attractive and guarded well before the precious day. In any normal home, nothing is left until the last minute. It's the parents' way of showing how much they want to welcome their beautiful baby and how perfect everything must be for it. Surely this was the manner in which Mary and Joseph prepared for the birth of Baby Jesus?

How do we prepare for the birth of the most perfect Baby of all time? Have we cleansed our souls and made them shining to receive Jesus in Holy Communion? Will we share our day with Him, or will He be dismissed from our minds even before we leave Church? Is Christmas Day really what it should be, a day of rejoicing, love, gratitude and happiness? If we put Christ back into Christmas, it can only spell "Joy" and happiness for us. If peace is in our hearts, it will be in our homes. The Life of Our Lord is the greatest love story of all time. It is all about love from beginning to end. Let us share Jesus' first day on earth with Him. No one rejects a new baby. We all want to love and cherish it. May we take this beautiful Baby to our hearts?

Heavenly Father, thank you for our best Christmas gift, Your Son. May we show our gratitude by loving Him above all else and to love our neighbour as You love us. Thank you Mary, our Mother, and St. Joseph for playing your part in bringing Jesus to us. Our hearts are bursting with joy and we can't thank you enough.

GOD SPEAKS TO US TODAY

It is especially at Christmas that God speaks to us. Some people say, "Wouldn't it be grand if God spoke to us directly. For example, if we could see on a clear day a banner being pulled by a plane giving God's message. In America they go in for that sort of thing. On the road side you will see bill boards saying, "Tell the kids I love them," or "That part about 'love your neighbour' I meant that," or "If you don't behave, I'll make the rush hour longer." God doesn't work that way. His Son told us that even if one were to return from the dead and give us a message people wouldn't listen. How then does He speak to us?

God is in fact giving us constant signs. Christmas is one of God's signs. We get ready for the birthday of Christ for weeks. For many it represents a holiday from work, a time to exchange gifts, a trip to see relatives and consume excessive amounts of food and drink. Anyone can see Christmas is here, but do they realise the true meaning behind Christmas?

The Gospel recalls the familiar story of the shepherds on that first Christmas day. Let's see how God reveals His signs. Let us once again listen to the announcement of the Christmas angel, "Do not be afraid. Listen, I bring you news of great joy, a joy to be shared by the whole people. Today in the town of David a Saviour has been born to you; He is Christ the Lord. And here is a sign for you: you will find a Baby wrapped in swaddling clothes and lying in a manger." What can we learn from this angel's words?

First, it tells us that this extraordinary God makes Himself known to ordinary people. Could there be any people more ordinary than the shepherds of the first century? Although Jacob, Moses and King David were the great men of the Old Testament they were shepherds. The people of the time of Our Lord considered shepherding a task for commoners. In fact, the religious authorities of the day treated shepherds as outcasts and the scum of society. They were treated as lost souls beyond redemption.

God did not think so for it was to the shepherds He sent His angel with the message that the Saviour had been born. He could have revealed His message to anyone He liked. God is making a statement here. If shepherds can be honoured with the inaugural announcement of Christmas, then Jesus really has come for everyone. What did the angel say? "I bring you news of great joy, a joy to be shared by the whole people."

God's good news is that Christmas is for everyone. If you are not treated like royalty by the world, if you feel treated as an outcast, if your job makes the bulk of your life seem menial and drab, you are today's shepherds. Christmas is for you.

God wants the word 'today' to have a special significance for us. Again notice what the angel said, "Today in the town of David a Saviour has been born for you." "Today" was an important word. Sometimes we miss the signs of God because we think God works best in the past, or in the distant future. God is also at work in the present. If you cannot see Him here and now, you may never see Him at work anywhere or at anytime.

The problem for many of us with "today" is that it seems so plain, so ordinary. Today is the day my bunions are hurting. Today is the day I have too many chores to see to. Today I am bored. God seems to see every day as special. In St. Luke's gospel we see Jesus using that word several times. In the first sermon He preached He said, "This text is being fulfilled today even as you listen" (Lk. 4:21). In the middle of His ministry, He answered His critics, "Learn that today and tomorrow I cast out devils and on the third day attain my end" (Lk. 13:32). Jesus said to Zachaeus, "Zachaeus come down. Hurry, because I must stay at your house today" (Lk. 19:5). On the cross He told the repentant thief, "Indeed, I promise you, today you will be with Me in Paradise" (Lk. 23:43). God does move in the present. He loves today.

If you have to wait for everything to be just right before you are open to God's signs, you may see nothing at all. When God gave the sign of Christmas to the shepherds, it was an ordinary day.

Finally, an extraordinary sign is hidden in an ordinary sight. What did the angel send the shepherds to see? It was nothing as spectacular as the parting of the Red Sea, or a cosmic arrangement of the stars. It was a baby wrapped in swaddling clothes and lying in a manger. This was the way all first century mothers wrapped their newborn children. Many a shepherd would have used a manger as a cradle.

The shepherds now had a choice. They could either believe this message or doubt it. The moment of faith was exercised after the angels left. The sight of all these angels, the bright light and the heavenly music was enough to convince that they had to go in search of this Baby. If they had not gone, they would have missed their first Christmas.

Let us thank God that every Christmas day we are able to celebrate the birthday of Jesus. If we are feeling ordinary, if life seems plain let's be happy because on Christmas day God our Father has the best Christmas gift for us, His beloved Son. All we can say is, "Thank you Heavenly Father, thank you Jesus, thank you Mary and Joseph."

THE ONE DAY WE ARE INCLINED

TO SHARE THE PEACE OF CHRIST

Christmas day is the only day in the year when we can put aside any animosity we may have with our enemies and be a true neighbour.

It was Christmas day 1914, the first Christmas of World War 1. The British and German armies had fought themselves to a standstill in northern France. Thousands of soldiers on both sides stood in muddy trenches, glaring at each other across the narrow strip of land that separated them. For the first time their guns were silent, and in the eerie silence of that grey dawn, everyone was wondering what that day would bring.

When daylight had fully come, the British soldiers saw three men rise out of the German trenches. Slowly and cautiously, they inched forward. Their hands were stretched out with open palms, to show that they carried no weapons. They moved past the barbed wire barriers and stood unprotected in 'No man's land.' Suddenly, hundreds of soldiers began pouring out of both trenches, and rushed out to meet their enemies. Their hands were clasped in friendly greetings. In broken English and in broken German, they wished one another a Merry Christmas.

Yesterday these men were killing each other, today they were exchanging gifts of cigarettes or anything else they could find. The British boys were singing, 'O Little Town of Bethlehem.' The Germans were singing, 'Stille Nacht.' They sat in groups and shared their canned rations. They showed pictures of their families and sweethearts and carried on conversations with few words and many gestures. Not a single shot was fired that day. Then, as the sun began to set, they went back to their trenches, and once again started trying to kill each other.

What brought about this strange peaceful lull in the midst of war? Why did two armies lay aside their weapons for one day and treat each other as friends? That brief armistice wasn't planned. It was a spontaneous reaction to the fact that today was Christmas Day, the day when God our heavenly Father gave us the greatest gift that our world has ever received. That gift was a Baby, His only Son, who became our Saviour.

Why did God give us this wonderful gift? He wanted to express His love in the most understandable and most convincing way. He wrapped His love in human flesh and gave It to the world. Now, we find it is easier to hear God's message of love, and to understand its meaning. He has poured it into a life. There is no more touching way of doing this than by pouring His love in the life of a new born baby. The writer of the Letter to the Hebrews put it this way, 'In times past, God spoke in fragmentary and varied ways to our fathers through the prophets. But in this final age, He has spoken to us through His Son.' That has to be the greatest gift of all.

Many of the gifts we get at Christmas can be received in a rather casual manner. All we have to do is put them on, or hang them in a wardrobe, or eat or drink them, or deposit them in a bank. Sometimes we are less than enthusiastic about the presents we are given. For example, we priests are always receiving socks and handkerchiefs. I tell you, we receive so many that we could have a stall in the market.

How should we receive God's gift, the greatest gift we shall ever receive? There is only one way - with our whole hearts, because this is the one gift that we all want and most definitely need. God wants us to use this gift not just today but every moment of our lives. Those soldiers in the trenches exchanged gifts and showed friendship to each other on Christmas Day, but then went back to fighting each other the following day. This must not be so with us. We receive the Child Jesus into our hearts on Christmas day, and show goodwill to all we meet, but what about tomorrow and the day after that? Will Our Lord see us showing the same goodwill to all we meet? If He doesn't, just how much have we appreciated God the Father's Christmas gift? Is it of no more value than another pair of socks? Christmas day and every day we should show our gratitude by taking Jesus into our hearts and making Him the centre of our lives. This is what Mary and Joseph did and we must follow their example.

Heavenly Father, we thank You for the best gift You give us on Christmas day. We thank Mary and Joseph for the part they played in us receiving this Gift. May Christ the Prince of Peace give us the grace to share His peace to all we meet not only on this day but every day of our lives.

GOD'S LOVE FOR US IS AMAZING AND AWESOME

There are two words that our young people use to describe the 'wow factor'. They have cheapened those words. The words are 'awesome' and 'amazing'. Those words describe the unconditional love God has for His children. God knowing how people will treat His Son, nailing Him to a cross, never deterred Him from sending His Son into our world. Why should this be? It is because it has always been the will of God the Father, God the Son and God the Holy Spirit, the Three Persons in One God, to be loved perfectly by one of His creatures. Most people think that God's Son became Man to save us from our sins and take us to Heaven. That is true for that is what is stressed when we talk about the Incarnation, God becoming Man, but there is more to it than that. What should be stressed is the fact that God from the very beginning, always wanted to be loved perfectly by one of His creatures.

Jesus expressed this thought perfectly when He said, "God so loved the world that He sent His only Son into the world."

God the Father, if He wanted, could have sent His Son into our world as a Man of 30, for all things are possible to God. Instead, He wanted Him to be born of a virgin and begin His human existence like the rest of us. He needed a mother for His Son and the virgin He chose was Mary from the town of Nazareth. He prepared her for the coming of His Son by ensuring that from the first moment of her existence, from her conception, she was to be sinless. He also gave her the unique grace to remain sinless all her life. Joseph, the carpenter, who was betrothed to Mary, was to be His Son's foster father. He was to be the one to provide a home and protection for his wife and her Son.

You would have thought that Jesus should be born in splendour. This was not God's way. Instead He was born in poverty like the majority of people. In this way He wanted to identify Himself with the majority of us. His birth as our Saviour was announced by angels to poor shepherds, who were regarded as the scum of society. He came not only for the poor, but also for everyone, the poor as well as the rich, the unlettered as well as the lettered. By the guidance of a star He led wise men, also known as kings, from the east to acknowledge and worship Him.

Friday is a day of abstinence, but St. Francis maintained that if Christmas fell on a Friday we should not hesitate to feed the walls with meat. In other words we should rightly celebrate the birthday of God's Son as Man, but we should not let our material celebrations distract us from the true meaning of Christmas, namely, God's tremendous love for us.

Christmas is a time of giving and receiving. It is summed up beautifully in a verse of a carol,

"We receive gifts at Christmas and give gifts in return,

But God's gift is best of all in giving us His Son."

Our world lurches from one disaster to another. There is so much evil in our world, but let us not be afraid to emphasise that there is also so much good in our world that goes unnoticed. When I see governments wanting answers to all their problems I would love to shout from the rooftops, "Our hope is to be found in the Baby that Mary bore. It is He, our God and our Brother, who has the answers to all our problems. We shall never solve them if we ignore Him or deny His existence. Jesus, is the Lamb of God, who takes away the sins of the world."

The shepherds said, "Let us go to Bethlehem and see this thing that has happened which the Lord has made known to us". At Christmas, let us kneel at the Crib and love and thank our God for His thoughtfulness towards us. We should all say "Father, Son and Holy Spirit, we love you and we thank you." We should also express our love and thanks to Mary and Joseph. The joy, love and peace we experience on Christmas should be expressed in our lives not only on that day but every day.

It is true the love of God for each one of us is awesome and amazing.

JESUS IS THE ANSWER

Mary knew the Scriptures. She pondered on them. She knew the Messiah she was carrying was to be born in Bethlehem and here she was in Nazareth eighty miles away. She trusted that God, who was responsible for the conception of her child, would bring about how the Messiah would be born in Bethlehem. All was made clear when Augustus Caesar decided to make a census of the known world. Everyone was to register at their place of origin. Since both Joseph and Mary were from the line of David, they had to travel to Bethlehem, the city of David.

The time for Mary to give birth to Jesus was very near. This journey to Bethlehem for Mary was going to be arduous in the condition she was in. Joseph and Mary got their necessary belongings together and set off for the four day journey. Mary would not be able to walk twenty miles a day. Joseph would have provided a donkey to carry Mary and their belongings. If, as tradition has it, the birth of Jesus took place in the winter, the journey would be harsher and more tiring. Joseph would have shielded Mary from the cold blast of wind coming from the Mediterranean. As they made their way a host of angels would have surrounded them as they worshipped their God Mary was carrying.

Eventually, they reached Bethlehem and the little town would be crowded with visitors like themselves who had come to register their names. The Inn which not only housed people but their animals too was bursting at the seams, and was no place for Mary to give birth to her Son. Joseph would want Mary to enjoy the privacy she deserved for such a wonderful occasion. My guess is that the innkeeper's wife could see the delicate condition Mary was in and suggested to Joseph that not far from the Inn was a cave which could be made comfortable for the birth of the Child. It was in that humble dwelling Mary gave birth to her Son, Jesus.

That is the event God our Father wants us to celebrate this Christmas. Sadly, many children in our country would not be able to tell us that Christmas is the birthday of Jesus. For them Christmas is the day Santa Claus brings them presents. God the Father gave us Jesus, His Son, to love. He is the One to lead us back to the Father and so many people do not know about this. Our world is in such a mess because so many people fail to see that Jesus is the answer to all our problems.

God the Father gave us 10 Commandments to be our Rules of Happiness. So many in our world regard them as restrictive. They want to be free. Besides they will tell you that so many of them have been couched in negative terms: do not steal, do not kill, do not commit adultery. Yes, they may be couched in negative terms but when observed they have very positive results. Take the Commandment, "Do not steal." Supposing no one ever stole, there would be no fear of people being robbed or burgled. There would be no need for keys to lock our houses or cars. They would be kept safe because no one stole. This principle of showing respect for God's commands and for people could also be applied to all the Commandments. They really are there to be observed and make us happy.

What I would love to do, and I am sure you would too, is to stand in Parliament and tell our politicians that the reason why there is so much unhappiness in our world today is because we have forgotten that God our Father gave us His Son to lead us to Heaven and that we should take our lead from Him; that the immoral laws they pass are not the answer to our problems, laws such as the right to abortions, divorce and gay marriages, to mention just a few. All these laws they pass are against the Commandments of God. Let us live our lives God's way, which have been taught to us by His Son Jesus. It is today that the Father says to each person in the world, "This is my beloved Son, listen to Him."

Lord Jesus, we thank our heavenly Father and Mary for giving us their Son and we promise that we will do all in our power to listen to Jesus and follow His example.

EPIPHANY

(Ten sermons)

WHAT CAN WE BRING HIM?

What gift can you give a person who has everything? Many of us will have pondered on that problem during the weeks before Christmas. Some fortunate people seem to have everything they need and so whatever you buy them is going to be superfluous. Those first visitors to the new-born baby Jesus may have asked themselves the same question. The shepherds in the fields outside Bethlehem had been told by an angel that a Saviour had just been born in a stable in the town. Three wise men from the East, guided by their study of astronomy, came to look for an infant king. Clearly, this child was someone very special. He must have everything he needed. What gifts could they bring him?

Tradition tells us that the shepherds gave Him a lamb and the wise men presented Him with gold, frankincense and myrrh. Each brought whatever they could, the very best they had to offer. We would all love to give Jesus something special. In the words of the Christmas carol,

"What can I give him, poor as I am?

If I were a shepherd, I would bring a lamb.

If I were a wise man I would do my part.

Yet what can I give Him? Give my heart."

But is my heart worth offering? Some people have happy and contented lives. They have a strong marriage, loving children, a stable job, a roof over their head, and they try to live a good moral life. They can bring to Jesus a heart full of joy and gratitude. But what about those people whose hearts are deeply attached to sin? What about those whose hearts are filled with sadness, loneliness, anger, doubt? Their heart is damaged and they are convinced that it is not worth giving to anyone. What can I bring Jesus if the best I can offer is my pain and despair? It would be like bringing a child a broken toy. Jesus wouldn't want that kind of gift, would He?

Jesus does want our hearts, whatever condition they may be in. He loves us at every stage of our lives, whether we are near to Him like Our Lady and the saints, or far away because of our sins. If all we are able to offer Him at this moment is a heart that is broken through pain and suffering, He still wants it so that He can heal it. If all we have to offer is a sinful heart He wants that, too, so that He can forgive us and fill us with His love.

The child born in Bethlehem does have everything, because He is God. There is nothing He needs from us. But there is just one thing He may not have and wants, and that is your heart and mine. We may think that it is too poor and imperfect a gift, but it is the only gift Jesus wants from us. He wants it desperately, because He came into our world for the sole purpose of rescuing us from Satan's clutches. So today let us give Him ourselves and our love, because He is our Saviour.

THE WORTH OF EVERY PERSON & THE POWER OF LOVE

Mt. 1:1-12

Matthew says of the Wise Men, "they returned to their own country a different way." They had gone to Bethlehem by one road, and, no doubt, intended to return the same way. A dream changed their plan for God warned them to avoid any further contact with King Herod. So they went back home by a different route.

These men were not the same men who had left home. Their lives had been profoundly affected by what they had seen and heard. My guess is that their return journey was not filled with light-hearted chatter. Their minds were flooded with thoughts too deep for words. What did it all mean? They had been guided by a strange star. In Jerusalem they had reached their destination by the help of a scriptural prophecy. Their journey ended in the presence of a little baby Boy with his mother and father. Their whole journey had to do with that Child.

Bethlehem confronted them and it also confronts us with two fundamental facts of life. The first is the worth of a human person. The Wise Men were probably astrologers. They studied the stars, hoping to find there some hint of life's meaning. The eternal truth they were seeking was not in the distant reaches of space, but right here on earth in the person of a little Child. The Child did not bow to the star. It was the star that went on its way to make deference to the Child.

When we compare ourselves to the countless billions of heavenly bodies, we seem rather insignificant. On a clear night when we look into the sky who are we compared to that brilliant sight? The psalmist too on this matter had a question to ask of God, "When I behold your heavens, the moon and the stars which you set in place, what is man that you should be mindful of him?" That question was wrung from a man who was feeling his own smallness. He was wondering how God could be aware of him in such a vast universe. Imagine how he would feel today with the aid of astrologers modern equipment?

It is not easy to believe in our worth. When I see the way some people regard abortions and euthanasia it tells me that they don't realise the worth of a human person. If they did, they would have the greatest respect for the life of every individual. I hope they would come to believe that every person is especially created by God in His own image. Again, when we hear of the natural disasters that claim so many human lives we wonder what worth there is in the loss of those many lives. We could ask the question, "Who cares about these lives that are lost?" The answer is God cares. He cared so much that He sent His Son to be one of us and live with us. His name is "Emmanuel" – "God is with us". That Child in Bethlehem affirms the worth of every person.

The second fact of life, Bethlehem confronts us with, is the power of love. Are we really sure of this? We know love can be beautiful and nice, but what has it got to do with power? Some people would say a gun is a powerful tool, it can intimidate and control people's lives, but that is all it can do. It cannot change minds and win hearts like love can. Love is a far more effective tool.

A mother with a little baby does not look like a picture of power. In fact it seems like the very essence of weakness. But look again. That baby will take complete charge over loving parents' lives. For him, they will change their plans. For him, they will get up in the middle of the night to see to his needs, no matter how desperately they may want to sleep. For him, they will rewrite their budget. They will do without in order to meet his needs. No law requires them to do any of this, but the power of love makes them do this. They will suffer and even die to protect the life of their baby.

God knew what He was doing when He sent His Son in the form of a little Baby. Of course that Baby did not stay a Baby. He became a Man who was the embodiment of love. He went to a Cross, had nails driven through His hands and feet to attach Him to that Cross because He just could not stop loving us. That Man has a grip on our world that nothing can ever loosen.

So the story of the visit of the Wise Men in search of the Messiah teaches us this Christ Child is the One who shows us the worth of every human person and the power of love.

Now let us look at the ones who came to Bethlehem.

WHO CAME TO BETHLEHEM?

Mt. 2:1-12

We know, of course, what individuals belong in a nativity scene: the baby Jesus, Mary, Joseph, three wise men, and some shepherds. The Gospels of Matthew and Luke tell us that these are the people who came to Bethlehem to see the Christ Child. But are they too familiar to us? Were the visitors merely wise men and shepherds? Who really came to Bethlehem?

The socially unacceptable came to Bethlehem. The Bible, in general, and Jesus, in particular, have helped us idealise shepherds. The Psalm 23, "the Lord is my Shepherd," is universally known and loved. Jesus identifies himself as the "Good Shepherd" who lays down His life for the sheep. It is little wonder that we in the West have an exalted view of shepherds. But in biblical times, as well as throughout the Middle East today, shepherds were anything but sentimental figures.

The significance of the shepherds in the Christmas story is that they epitomized the socially despised and the economically deprived of their day. Shepherds belonged to the "people of the land," that group of common people who were considered outside the realm of religious respectability. The manner of life required of shepherds made it impossible for them to participate in the religious rituals that rendered people ceremonially clean. Shepherding was literally a full time occupation. Night and day they tended their sheep, which means they essentially lived out of doors, with all the problems of sanitation and inconvenience associated with such an existence. Who came to Bethlehem? To whom did the angelic chorus sing of the Saviour's birth? Not the powerful and the prominent. Not the wealthy and the respected. The unacceptable in first-century society received the good news first.

The religiously unacceptable came to Bethlehem. The Gospel of Luke tells us of the lowly shepherds, but the Gospel of Matthew tells us of those at the other end of respectability who came to Bethlehem. The wise men were prominent sages from the East. They were wealthy enough to make such a long journey and to bring extravagant gifts of gold, frankincense, and myrrh. Do these, then, represent the opposite end of the socio-economic spectrum from the shepherds? Hardly. The magi may have known privilege and prestige in their own homeland, but in Palestine they were Gentiles!

The Jewish leaders of Jesus' time had made Israel's divine "election" a matter of racial supremacy. While God had chosen Israel to be a light of witness to the other nations of the world, the danger from the beginning was that the people would emphasize the privilege aspect of their chosenness and overlook the responsibility that was involved. The word "Gentile" means all non-Hebrews, all non-Jews, and it was widely held that Gentiles were beyond the pale of God's concern. The first great controversy in the early church was over whether Gentiles could become Christians without first becoming Jews. Jesus offended His own people by visiting Gentile regions, but He realized He was fulfilling Isaiah's prophecy that Gentiles would ultimately trust in His name. The Apostle Paul understood the unique aspect of his own calling was as the "Apostle to the Gentiles," but at the time of Jesus' birth, Gentiles were openly discriminated against.

In the most segregated years of the deep South in the United States, blacks were openly, blatantly, and officially discriminated against. Signs were posted everywhere to exclude African-Americans. It was unthinkable that they would show up for a city council meeting or attend a white church. This is the level of discrimination that existed towards Gentiles when Jesus was born. The wise men were Gentiles, religiously unacceptable in Bethlehem.

Anyone can come to Bethlehem. Ironically, today Bethlehem is predominantly a Gentile town. Most of its citizens are Arabs, many are Arab Christians. Much has changed since Mary and Joseph sought lodging in an overly crowded Bethlehem. Yet, spiritually, it has always been true that anyone can come to Bethlehem. The Apostle Paul argued for missionary expeditions to the Gentiles, while the mother Church in Jerusalem insisted that Christ had come only for Israel, Christianity was in danger of becoming nothing more than a little sect within Judaism. But when the early church embraced the vision of Christ as the Saviour of the whole world, the way to Bethlehem was opened to all – the shepherds, who were the outcasts of society and the wise men, who were Gentiles. Are you different from those who celebrate Christmas? Remember the wise men, foreigners from the East, aliens to the faith of Israel, and hardly knowing who they were looking for. Anyone can come to Bethlehem - even you. Why? Because God in Christ has come to everyone - even to me, even to you.

The story of the Epiphany can help us to take stock of where we are in life.

TAKING STOCK IN THE NEW YEAR

Mt. 2:1-12

Some astrologers from the East came to Jerusalem in search of the Infant King of the Jews. Led by a mysterious star they found Him in Bethlehem. They stayed long enough to worship and present their gifts. The story concludes with the words they "returned to their own country by a different way."

It is those final words of the story I wish to concentrate on because they have a message for us. This New Year presents us with an opportunity to stop, take stock and start over again. It is a good time to look where we have been, and to ask where we are going, and, if necessary to alter the course and change the direction of our life.

Let's start by taking a brief look at where we have been. We shouldn't live in the past, but it is a good thing to take an occasional glance in the rear-view mirror. We can never know where we are unless we have some understanding of the way by which we've come. What do we see when we look over our shoulder? I hope we see some good things, some successes and some happy times. We should see them because they are there. Sometimes in the midst of problems we tend to lose sight of those good things that have been a real part of our lives. They are there to encourage us on our journey through life. To forget them would be both dishonest and destructive. Any accurate inventory of life will always include a liberal sprinkling of the good we have achieved. I like the attitude of the old man who had a positive outlook on life. He said, "When everything is considered, it still comes out a beautiful world. There is something good about most things. Even some of the thorn bushes have roses on them." So as we move from the old year into the new, let's not forget to carry with us a grateful memory of the good times.

What else do we see as we look at the road behind us? No doubt we see some failures, hurts, disappointments and missed opportunities. Because we are imperfect people living in an imperfect world they are an inevitable part of life. The important thing is how we handle the bad times. I hope we will not carry into the New Year a lot of excess baggage packed with bitterness and resentment. That is such a self-defeating thing to do. Also we must make up our minds that we will not succumb to the temptation of cynicism. We have all been hurt to some degree, but we must use those hurts as means of spiritual growth. We must leave them in the past where they belong. If we don't, they only drag us down and make us bitter and miserable, and harder for us to move on in life.

Our next consideration is where do we go from here? The inescapable fact is that we are going somewhere. In life we cannot remain static. Life is like being on a boat in a river. Despite our indecisiveness and lethargy, the river carries us along. So it is with living. The plain truth is that the years are taking us somewhere. I always remember the conversation of Alice in Wonderland with the cat. Alice asked the cat, "Would you tell me please, which way I ought to go from here?" The cat replied, "That depends a good deal on where you want to go." Alice said, "Oh, I don't much care." "Well," said the cat, "it doesn't matter much which way you go." "But," insisted Alice, "I want to get somewhere. "Oh," the cat answered, "you are sure to do that."

One of the most useful things we could do at the outset of a new year is take an honest, hard look at where we are going with our lives – what we are doing, what we are becoming.

How true are the words of Socrates, "The unexamined life is not worth living." It can so easily happen. The days can melt into weeks, the weeks into years. We just drift along in life without any purpose or planning. It doesn't have to be that way. We are endowed with the capacity to choose a destination and to chart our course towards it.

This gets us to our central thought, namely, that getting to where we want to go may require a change of direction in life. It is so easy to make a wish, set our hearts on something, deeply resolve to be something, and then fool ourselves into believing that is our destination. There is no use choosing a particular goal unless we also choose the day-by-day road that leads to that goal. It is what we are doing, not what we are dreaming that determines our destination. If we have made up our mind that our destination is Heaven, we must examine the daily acts we do to see that we are on the road leading us to Heaven. Any actions or thoughts that veer us from the path to Heaven have to be discarded. That is why our Morning Offering and our daily Examination of Conscience is so important. We use them to keep us on the road to Heaven. I find a very useful prayer to say at the beginning of every day is, "Give me the strength, Holy Spirit, to do the work of this day and grant that at its close to be found worthy of Your trust in me." Then at the end of the day to ask, "Holy Spirit, how did we get on today?" Notice I did not say, "How did I get on, but how did we, the Holy Spirit and I?" We will find that when we left Him out it was then we probably sinned.

As we look towards a New Year, our lives may need some redirecting. Somewhere along the way we may have drifted off course. The road we are now travelling may not be consistent with the place we want to go. Like the astrologers of old, let us make a deliberate decision to travel by another route.

The story of the Epiphany tells us that Jesus is the Saviour of the world.

JESUS, THE SAVIOUR OF THE WORLD

Mt. 2:1-12

Matthew's Gospel is the most distinctively Jewish of the four Gospels. More than any of the others, it seeks to establish that Jesus is the true Messiah of the Jews. At the beginning of his book is a genealogy that traces His ancestry from Abraham, to David, to Joseph, "the husband of Mary". The list contains the names of some forty men, all of them the ancestors of Jesus, and every one of them a Jew. After tracing His genealogy, he then tells the story of His birth. Then follows a strange incident. Some foreigners from the east came to Bethlehem and worshipped this Jewish Messiah.

Why should Matthew, who wrote his Gospel to present the Jewish Messiah to the Jews, wish to bring foreigners into the picture? I think the answer must be that he wanted to tell His fellow Jews that Jesus, their Messiah, is not the exclusive possession of the Jews. Jesus doesn't belong to one nation, He belongs to the world.

If that truth was needed to be known by the Jews in the first century, it is no less needed to be known by Christians in the twenty first century. There is a dangerous tendency to monopolise Christ and make Him the representative of our personal interests. Strangely, we do this out of a sense of devotion. He is ours and He is our ideal. If we are capitalists, we make Him a capitalist. If we are socialists, we make Him a socialist. If we have enemies, He is on our side and we forget that He not only loves us, but also our enemies. This misguided concept of devotion has produced tragic consequences throughout history. Wars have been fought on both sides in the name of the Lord.

Jesus was a Jew. His birth fulfilled the Jewish hope for a Messiah. Matthew believed this and wanted others to know it, but a mystical star guided foreigners to Bethlehem. There they found the Child and bowed down to worship Him. Who were these strangers? No one knows. The only thing we know is that they came from the east outside Israel. This happened to tell the world that this Jewish Messiah was bigger than the nation of Israel. He belonged to all nations and to all peoples. He was not the exclusive possession of the Jews, neither is He the exclusive possession of the Catholic or other Christian Churches.

Our faith tells us that Jesus is not only a great Person, but He is God and the greatest Person who ever walked our earth. He was born in a manger and died on a cross. He had no wealth and held no political position. All He had to influence the world was the quality of His own character. Yet He stands not only among the giants of history, but the greatest of them all. Someone has written of Him, "Of all the armies that ever marched, of all the navies that ever sailed, and of all the parliaments that ever sat not one has ever influenced the world like that one solitary Life."

Jesus like other great personalities belongs to the world. Take people like Pasteur. He was a Frenchman, but because he was the father of medicine he belongs to the world. Then there is Ghandi. He was Hindu and an Indian. In his lifetime, he was claimed by most of the world great religions. A Christian called him a great Christian. A Buddhist called him a great Buddhist, and a Moslem called him a great Moslem. Because of this Ghandi belongs to the world.

Recall to mind many of Jesus' sayings and you will find that they are eternal. They apply to the lives of everyone. "You shall love the Lord your God with all your heart and your neighbour as yourself." "Treat others as you would have them treat you." "Whoever would be the greatest among you, must be your servant." This is just to mention a few. The things that He taught are so universally true that they can never be the private possession of any one nation or even a Church. Jesus is like the sun. The sun and He belong to everyone.

To conclude, we thank Matthew for proclaiming that Jesus, the Jewish Messiah, belongs not only to the Jews but also to the whole world. We acknowledge and love Him as the Saviour of the whole world.

The Epiphany prompts us to ask what gift can we bring to Jesus.

MAKE A GOOD START TO THE NEW YEAR

Mt. 2:1-12

Nutritionists tell us that the most important meal of the day is breakfast. The reason is because it gets the day off to a good start. What is the most crucial moment in a 100 metres race? It is the first step after the starting gun has fired. The reason is because the race is often won by the runner who can correctly anticipate the start. Begin too soon and the runner is disqualified. Begin too late and the runner loses the race. What is the most delicate sentence to speak in a sales presentation? It is the opening line. Why? Because this sentence will be the 'hook' that determines whether your audience will take the journey with you. So it is worth taking time over that first sentence. So it is always important to get off to a good start.

A good start. Isn't that what we all want to do at the beginning of this New Year? We are in the season of good resolutions, of bettering our character, shaping up our waistlines and controlling our budget.

The Christian Church every year celebrates the Epiphany. We hear once again the story of God's great love for the entire world – a love so great that He gave His only Son to save the whole world. The Magi were drawn by a star they saw in the east to visit a tiny Child. They brought their gifts to celebrate the arrival of the Baby. They wanted this Child to get off to a good start. Since Matthew chose to begin his gospel with the story of these wise men, he must have considered their example a fitting sign of a good start. For those of us who want to make a good start at the beginning of a year perhaps the Magi can give us two pointers.

The first is to pay attention to mystery. If you want to start the New Year right, ask God for the wisdom to notice the mystery of holiness all around you. Try to see the small miracles in your life, and to be grateful for them. Pray for openness to see the goodness in unexpected places, and unexpected people. Learn to look for signs of God at work in the world. Train your mind to believe the best about people, and look for evidence to confirm this premise.

To do this it means that you have to slow down and not rush through life. You must have a positive outlook on life. You must develop a sense of humour, a sense of trust and a sense of wonder. This will involve three things, praying, listening and observing. Soon you will begin to see God everywhere and you will begin to see more good in people. The daily newspapers seem to specialise in reporting bad news and spreading stories of gloom, crime and tragedy. That isn't the full story. It is only part of the real human story going on around you. Even in the newspapers, with their bias for feeding our morbid curiosity for the tragic, see if you cannot find stories that tell of the goodness in people. Who emerged with heroism in the face of tragedy? Who had the courage to stand up for justice in a sad situation? Who upheld the truth and goodness in the midst of crime? At least we can thank God for that.

Soon we will begin to notice the presence of goodness in people all around us. Catch someone red-handed in the act of doing good, and bless them for it. Look in the face of a baby, and see if you can find something mysterious and wondrous. Notice the old couple holding hands and supporting each other in the street and thank God for their continued love. See the teenager holding the door open for an adult and stranger and thank God for parents who still teach their children the small courtesies in life.

If you can make goodness surround you, you will make God surround you. The rare and beautiful thing about the Wise Men in Matthew's story is that they had the sense of wonder to look up in the sky and see a sign, a new star, placed in the sky for the whole earth to see. Either the rest of humanity failed to see the star at all, or they failed to believe the possibility that such a sight might be a sign from God. Does God still communicate with our world today? Of course He does. Just look how He controls the seasons, day and night, to mention just two ways. The problem is not that God is not speaking and communicating with us, the problem is that we are not observing and listening. So at the beginning of a year we have to pray, observe and listen.

The next thing the Magi teach is that we must be generous. Once we begin to recognise goodness in people, and the presence of God in the world we have to respond with generosity. Christians do not hover at a safe distance over the world's tragedy like a helicopter to report bad news. Christians respond like the hospital helicopter bringing rescue and showing courage. In like manner Christians do not sense the mystery and presence of God in the world without responding.

If you believe that all you have is a gift from God, you will begin to see your purpose in God's plan. So when you see human need, or the chance to make a difference in the world, using the resources God has given you, you will help wherever you can. This will bring joy and fulfilment in your life.

This year look for the signs of God's work in the world around you and work alongside Him. When you arrive at the presence of God, as the Wise Men did in Bethlehem, open your heart and your treasures with gladness. Then you will find yourself giving away your gold, frankincense and myrrh, instead of hoarding it. You will be like the Magi. You will become a shining star, a sign of God at work in the world, for someone else who is looking for God's presence. You will have become an epiphany, a manifestation of God's love in the world. You will most certainly have made a good start to the New Year.

Matthew told us the story of the Epiphany to convince us that Jesus is the God of all nations.

THE GOD OF ALL NATIONS

Mt. 2:1-12.

People who write biographies like to find in the childhood of their subject some event that symbolizes what that person ultimately became. Today's Gospel reading tells of such an event in the early life of Jesus. A group of astrologers came from somewhere in the east in search of a newborn king. With the help of a guiding star, they made their way to the little village of Bethlehem and bowed down before the Christ child. Their presence in the Nativity story is a clear prophesy that the ministry and message of Jesus would not be confined to the Jewish nation.

Let us never forget that Jesus was a Jew. Yet today He belongs to the world. People of every nation on earth bow before Him, just as those astrologers did long ago in Bethlehem. How do we account for this? That a Man who spent most of His life working as a village carpenter should become the leading citizen of the world? The answer to that question, as I see it, is that Jesus showed Himself to be the Son of God.

The Jewish religion in which Jesus was reared was monotheistic, that is, they believed in only one God who was Creator and Sustainer of the world. They looked upon God as belonging primarily, if not exclusively, to the Jews. The scribes and Pharisees were convinced that God lived in the Temple in Jerusalem, and they were determined to keep Him there.

Jesus knew that God could never be confined to one place. Yes, He was in the Temple alright, but He was also out in the open countryside, decorating the flowers and feeding the birds. Yes, He was the God of Israel, but He was also the God who 'so loved the world that He gave His only Son that whoever believes in Him may not die but have eternal life.' Jesus came to tell the whole world that both He and His Father loved everyone with an everlasting love.

More than anything else on the face of the earth the human person was sacred to Jesus. He valued people above everything else. To all religions, something is sacred. To the scribes and Pharisees of the first century, the Law was sacred, especially the Law pertaining to Sabbath observance. Nothing should be done on the Sabbath that would in any way violate that sacred day. Jesus was of a different mind. He respected the ancient laws of His nation, but saw them as means to an end, not an end in themselves. In His scheme of things, the purpose of the laws was to benefit the lives of people and He always applied them with that thought in mind.

One day the scribes and Pharisees brought to Him a woman who had been guilty of committing adultery. They reminded Him that according to the Mosaic Law she should be stoned. Their concern was protecting the sacredness of the Law. But Jesus was more concerned with the sacredness of her life and the chance for that woman to reform her evil way. In a brief but brilliant discussion, He confounded the woman's accusers. Then He sent her on her way with a new lease of life.

No wonder that the religious leaders hated Him. They loved the Law in all its details. He loved people, and regarded the Law as a guideline to help people live happy and decent lives. Every person was sacred in His sight, rich and poor, young and old, men and women, priests and prostitutes. It made no difference to Him. Because of that attitude He became known as a 'friend of sinners.' His enemies intended this title to be an insult, but Jesus was happy with it, for He had come precisely to call sinners to repentance.

Across the centuries people of every nation on earth have been drawn to Jesus. They have found it easy to love Him, because they have believed that He is the Son of God and that He loves them.

Matthew wrote his gospel to convince his fellow Jews that all the prophecies concerning the Messiah were fulfilled in Jesus. Yet, he was the only evangelist who records this visit of the astrologers. He did this to make the Jews realise that Jesus was not just the Messiah for the Jews but for all peoples. The gifts these foreign visitors brought were indicative of who this Child was. Gold represented His kingship, frankincense his Godhead and myrrh that He was to be the suffering Messiah. We thank Matthew for revealing to us the truth that Jesus is the God of all peoples.

The story of the Epiphany is a story of the Wise Men searching for the Christ and about our search too.

O GODHEAD HID

Mt. 2:1-12.

One of the most popular games among children has to be hide-and-seek. The rules are very simple. One child closes his eyes and counts to a hundred, while all the others hide. He then shouts, "Are you ready? Here I come." One by one he seeks out those who are hiding. When all have been found, the first to be discovered becomes the new seeker, and the game starts again.

There are several reasons for the enduring popularity of hide-and -seek. It doesn't cost any money and it doesn't require any special athletic skills. Everyone can play it, boys and girls, even adults. I suspect the main reason lies in the fact that the game is somewhat true to life. In a real sense we never stop playing it. As we get older, the rules change; but the basic plot remains the same. We spend a good part of our lives hiding from and looking for other people.

Sometimes we even play this game with God. There are days when we fool ourselves into believing that we can hide from Him, and there are other days when it seems that He is hiding from us. All through the Bible there are testimonies from people who were looking for God and having difficulty in finding Him.

The story of the Epiphany tells of a group of men who made an incredible journey in search of Christ. They finally found Him, but it wasn't easy, not even with the help of a guiding star.

You could say that the experience of these eastern astrologers is not entirely different from ours. We too have those times when Christ seems so far away and so very hard to find. Could it be that we are looking for Him in the wrong places?

The astrologers who came from the east, in search of Christ, went straight to the capital city of Jerusalem, knocked on the door of the royal palace, and enquired about the newborn king. That would seem the logical place to begin. Where else would you look for a king, but in a palace? But He wasn't there. They could have searched the palace from top to bottom, and never found Him. He wasn't very far away. He was just six miles down the road in the little village of Bethlehem and that's where they finally found Him. This could be our problem, that we are looking for Christ in the wrong places.

When the astrologers from the east found the Christ child, He was not in a palace with a king, but in a stable with His mother. If you and I find Him, it will not be among the stars, or back in history, or out in the future, but in the ordinary events of life. When He was on this earth, we may have found Him in the temple teaching people. We could also have found Him at a wedding helping an embarrassed host; in Bethany having dinner with His friends; on a hillside admiring the wild flowers; on the seashore talking to some fishermen or at a graveside weeping with a heartbroken family.

Jesus was very much a part of the everyday lives of people. Why should we suppose that He should be any different today? So let us start searching for Him in the ordinary events of life. If He seems hard to find it could be that we are looking for Him in the wrong places.

Herod the king was also looking for Jesus but he failed to find Him because he sought Him for the wrong reason. He claimed that his purpose was to worship, but it was to destroy. Herod was very proud of his position and power, and feared that this newborn king might become a threat to both. In a sense he was right. Of course Jesus did not want to replace Herod and become the puppet king of a Jewish Province. He was after something much bigger than that. His Kingdom was the human heart. He wanted the voluntary loyalty and devotion of all people everywhere. That is still His purpose today, and only those who seek Him with a surrendered heart will find Him.

A few moments ago we spoke of the game hide-and-seek. Perhaps in closing we should remind ourselves that God is not playing games with us - not hide-and-seek or any game.

He is after something far more important, the redemption of a sad and sin-sick world. That is what the coming of Christ is all about. He is God's way of making Himself known to all those who sincerely want to know Him.

So we can be certain that Jesus is not hiding Himself from any of us. If He sometimes seems hard to find, don't let that bother us. Let us just surrender our hearts to Him and keep on looking for Him in the everyday events of life. We are sure to find Him, because He is there.

The story of the Epiphany is fraught with mystery.

LIVING WITH MYSTERY

No story in the Bible is more fraught with mystery than the story of the Epiphany. It raises a number of questions, but offers few answers. Who were those strange visitors that came to Jerusalem in search of "the newborn king of the Jews"? Matthew does not tell us and he is the only one of the four Gospel writers to relate this story. What was their country of origin? The only thing we are told is that they came from somewhere east of the land of Israel. That could have been any of a dozen different countries, but no one knows which. How many were in the group? Tradition says there were three, but the story itself does not give us a clue.

What started them on their incredible search for this infant King? They explained it to Herod by saying, "We have seen His star as it rose and have come to do Him homage." What does that mean? How did the rising of a star convey the message that a new king had been born in Israel? What happened to them after they had seen the Christ child and gone back home? No one knows. Matthew does not give us so much as a hint. These men glide into the Gospel story and glide out again, leaving nothing behind but a feeling of wonder and awe. We are not even sure what to call them. Some translations call them "astrologers". Others call them "wise men". Some transliterate the Greek word and call them "magi".

Our only sure knowledge of these visitors is that they were not Jews, and that they paid homage to the Christ Child. Beyond that, they remain shrouded in mystery. Matthew tells us just enough to get his point across. His point is that God, through Christ, was making Himself known to the whole world. That is a truth worth contemplating. The moral and ethical implications of it are immense. Today, let us focus our thoughts on three of the mysteries in our lives.

Let us consider, first, the mystery of the universe.

This story introduces us to some of the early scientists. Magi were men who studied the stars. They looked at the vast expanse of a night sky, with its countless sparkling lights, and wondered what it all meant. People have been doing that ever since. The tools of this study have been greatly improved, everything from telescopes to cameras mounted on satellites. These better methods have brought increased knowledge. We understand more about the stars today than those ancient astrologers ever imagined. But our improved knowledge has not cleared up the mystery. It has only done the exact opposite. The more we learn about the universe, the more mysterious it becomes.

No one is more aware of that than the scientists themselves. Sir Isaac Newton was one of the fathers of modern science. He died in 1727, and is buried in Westminster Abbey. His tomb is inscribed with this epitaph, "Nature and nature's laws lay hid in night. God said, 'Let there be Newton', and all was light." Newton would never have said that. He used to compare himself to a boy on the seashore, who had found a few interesting pebbles, while all around him stretched a vast ocean of the unknown.

Two hundred years after Newton another English scientist, Sir James Jeans, published a book entitled "Through Space and Time." In it, he said, "The ultimate realities of the universe are at present quite beyond the reach of science, and may be forever beyond the comprehension of the human mind." He wrote that almost sixty years ago. It is no less true today than it was then. We yearn for answers and seek for truth, but every new discovery enlarges the scope of things that are yet unknown. At least for now, and maybe forever, we must live with the mystery of the universe.

Let us now consider the mystery of ourselves.

We do not know who the magi were. That is not so surprising. There are times when we are not even sure of our own identity. Human nature is such a strange mixture of light and darkness, of good and evil. It has produced saints like Mary and Joseph, and monsters like Herod, who plotted the murder of Mary's baby and others. Looking back on this story, we admire that brave young couple who stood by the cradle of Jesus. We detest that wicked old king who ordered his soldiers to drive a sword through children's hearts. We are more than spectators of that scene. We are a part of it.

All of us are aware of that same light and darkness in our own souls. We are reasonable one day, and utterly unreasonable the next. We are generous today and selfish tomorrow. The beauty of Mary and Joseph and the ugliness of Herod reside within each of us. That is a confusing combination, but it is an accurate description of human nature. A bad man sometimes looks like a good man, as for example, when his baby is sick. And a good man sometimes appears to be a bad man, like when he loses his temper over some petty offence. All of that leaves us wondering who and what we really are. Good or evil, light or darkness, saint or sinner? An honest reading must include both. We say with Edward Sanford Martin, "From much corroding care I would be free, if once I could determine which is me." We must live with the mystery of ourselves.

Finally let us consider the greatest mystery of all - God, Himself.

We are considering the Epiphany. It comes from a Greek word that means the manifestation of God. This is the heart and soul of our Christian faith, not that God has been discovered, but that God has made Himself known. He somehow communicated with the magi. As far as we know, they had never read the Old Testament Scriptures. They had no knowledge of the holy prophets, but without the help of any human voice God was able to talk to them. That is an encouraging note. It tells us that in all places, among all people, God makes Himself known. In a hymn we sing, "This is my Father's world. He shines in all that's fair. In the rustling grass, I hear Him pass. He speaks to me everywhere."

As Christians, we are convinced that God has manifested Himself in Mary's little Child. He was and is the most complete picture of God that the world has ever seen. The more we learn about Him, the more we know about God. It is sheer arrogance for us Christians to think that we are the only people who know God. It is even more arrogant for us to think we know all about God. For all of His manifestation, God remains the ultimate mystery. If we do not understand this vast universe, how can we understand the God who created it? If we do not fully know ourselves, how can we know the God in whose image we are made?

All people who see life as it really is must content themselves to live with mystery. We will always have more questions than answers. But that alone is not the whole story. The magi did find the Christ Child and paid Him homage. The first thing they did after that encounter was to inconvenience themselves for His sake. "They returned to their own country by a different way." People of faith have been doing that ever since. Anyone who truly meets Christ, and bows in His presence, will always travel a different road. What God has given to us in Christ is enough light by which to live, even in the midst of mystery.

SEARCH FOR JESUS AND YOU WILL FIND HIM

Mt. 2:1-12

Today, we are presented with the story of Wise Men from the East who travelled through desert, mountains and valleys, led by a star, to a stable where they find a mother and father adoring a tiny Baby. These men had come to adore this Child. They came with gifts of gold, indicating that this Child is a king; frankincense, that He is also God; and myrrh, that He is One who will suffer and die.

What significance has this story for you and me? The Wise Men represent all of us. It tells us that every life is a pilgrimage; a journey in search of God It also tells us that we can only reach our destination, which is God, if we are led by faith. It was God who, by means of a star, led these Wise Men to their Saviour.

By our manner of living we indicate how committed we are to our pursuit of God. Are we allowing Him to lead us to our Saviour? God will always see to it that people who really search for Him will find Him. Those words you have just read are probably the most important words of this homily!

The Wise Men each brought a gift for the Child Jesus. What gift can we give Him? Clearly this Child is someone very special. He must have everything He needs. Yet there is one thing He does want - and that is our hearts. But are our hearts worth offering?

Some people have happy and contented lives. They have a strong marriage, loving children, a stable job, a roof over their heads, and they try to live a good moral life. They can bring to Jesus a heart full of joy and gratitude.

But what about those people whose hearts are deeply attached to sin? What about those whose hearts are filled with sadness, loneliness, anger, doubt? Their hearts are damaged and they are convinced that they are not worth giving to anyone. What can I bring to Jesus if the best I can offer is my pain and despair? It would be like bringing a child a broken toy. Jesus wouldn't want that kind of gift, would He?

Fortunately for most of us Jesus does want our hearts, whatever their condition. He loves us at every stage of our lives, whether we are near to Him like Our Lady and the saints, or far away because of our sins. If all we are able to offer Him at this moment is a heart that is broken through pain and suffering, He still wants it so that He can heal it. If all we have to offer is a sinful heart He wants that too, if we truly repent of our sins and are determined to change our ways, so that He can forgive us and fill us with His love.

Already the Christmas season is drawing to a close with sagging decorations and curled up, dying holly and mistletoe; but the Epiphany comes at a time which reminds us that we are at the beginning of another year in our journey of searching for God. We must remind ourselves we are never alone, fumbling in the dark in that search.

We will encounter Jesus in various circumstances of our lives, in our sorrows and joys, in the people we will meet. Jesus is in our midst, in situations where previously we were unaware of His presence. He comes in people and places we least expect and at times when we are most unprepared for His company. Once we discover Christ in these situations it lays upon us the responsibility of announcing to the world the Good News of His presence; and to awaken in people that God is very much in us and in our world.

Heavenly Father, lead us by the manner of our lives, to search constantly for Your Son, our Saviour. May we find Him and strive to be a beacon that leads others to Him.

HOLY FAMILY

(Four sermons)

LEARNING TO GROW UP

Lk. 2:41-52

Growing up is never easy for anyone. A happy and stable background helps immeasurably. And at school the understanding and encouragement of teachers is vital. But maturity is not guaranteed by the passing of time. What does it mean to grow up? We can answer that question by observing the maturing process in the life of Jesus.

Growing up means the acceptance of responsibility. Jesus said, "I must be busy with My Father's affairs." We have no way of knowing how much He was aware, at the age of 12, of His special mission. It is not clear just when He came to understand that in a very unique sense He was the Son of God but, already, He was in the process of trading His toys for His tools in life. He knew He had a job to do, and He was preparing Himself for it.

That is one of the signs of a boy becoming a man and a girl becoming a woman. To go through life thinking only of your privileges and little of your responsibilities is to remain forever a child. Growing up starts with little things like learning to pick up the toys and put them away; helping with small chores around the house; trying their best at school.

There is a sense of joy and fulfilment as parents see their efforts come to fruition and their children enter the adult world. If you feel that way about your children, surely our Heavenly Father must feel something like that about us? He longs to see His children shouldering some of the responsibilities of being a Catholic in this troubled world.

We are told that Jesus "increased in wisdom". This is another aspect of growing up and, in His later ministry, Jesus would put a great deal of emphasis on its importance. Wisdom involves spiritual insight, integrity of character, an understanding love of things worth loving, a scale of values that puts first things first. I like to think of wisdom having the eyes of God, seeing everything as He sees them. I once knew a priest I loved and admired, and he told me to pray every day to the Holy Spirit - for the gift of wisdom.

Gaining wisdom is not easy. It requires listening, observing and learning from others. It takes study, thought, searching and prayer. It sometimes involves making mistakes, correcting them and trying again. It is a vital part of growing up and, as Jesus increased in wisdom, so must we.

In growing up we must also develop relationships. The Gospel tells us that Jesus "increased in favour with God and men" as He kept enriching, deepening and expanding His relationship with God and the people around Him. This is something we can never stop doing whatever our age. It is a constant growing up process.

Relationships are absolutely essential. No one can be a whole person without them. Leave God out of your life, and you will remain forever only a small part of the person you were meant to be. Turn your back on people and you are the loser. They need your love and you need to be loved by them.

Holy Spirit, inspire us to be what our Heavenly Father wants us to be, so that every year He finds us growing in wisdom and stature, in favour with Him and those around us.

RAISING A LOVING FAMILY

Ecclesiasticus 3:33-7, 14-17; Col. 3:12-21 & Mt. 2:13-15,19-23

Today the Church draws our attention to the Holy Family of Joseph, Mary and Jesus. The first reading focuses on the love and the respect that parents should have for their children and the children for their parents. It mentions the rewards that will come to children who honour their parents, "Long life will come to him who honours his father…kindness to a father shall not be forgotten but will serve as a reparation for your sins."

In the second reading we are encouraged to practice the virtues that will bond a family together sincere compassion, kindness, humility, gentleness and patience; to bear with one another and forgive each other as soon as a quarrel begins, but above all to love each other.

In the Holy Family there were two people, Mary and Jesus, who were sinless. They practised all those virtues we have mentioned. Because they were sinless that doesn't mean to say that they were not tempted to sin. Temptation to be selfish and uncooperative in relationships would have surfaced for they were human but because they were good, generous and sinless they would not allow themselves to be selfish and uncooperative. How fortunate Joseph was to live with the two best people who ever lived. I am sure that the concerns of each person in the Holy Family were to promote the happiness and welfare of the other members of the family.

I am certain that there were many smiles, hugs and kisses between each member of the family. They would pray together. There were many times when they would sit in each other's company in silence and were just happy to be with each other. I am sure they would tell each other how much they loved each other. They were not afraid to show their emotions. It is here that families could learn so much from this Holy Family.

Do the members of our family smile, hug and kiss each other? I think it is sad when we are afraid to show our emotions. It should all start in childhood. It is the most natural thing for mothers and fathers to play with their babies when they prepare them for their bedtime, to kiss, hug and cuddle them. Obviously the older the children get this child play is toned down, but I still think the kisses and hugs should not stop. I think it is wonderful when a teenager comes from school and meets Mum and Dad at home and the first thing he or she does is to give both Mum and Dad a kiss and a hug and tell them the kind of day they have had at school. Or before they retire to bed to give both parents another kiss and hug and say, "Good night, Dad, good night, Mum." I think it is the most natural thing to do. There is nothing cissy about that.

If parents and children can relate like that to each other imagine the consequences. There will be a loving reaction. The result is each one is concerned about the other. If one is happy the others are happy. If one is sad or hurting the others will want to know what is up and how they can help. Anyone who comes among them will witness the love and bonding there is between them. Selfishness, envy, jealousy will not show their ugly heads in this family.

It will be easier for such a family to pray together. Isn't this lacking in many families today? It is in their prayer times that mothers and fathers can teach their children their faith and how they should behave at all times. One of the sad and tragic things of our society today is that there are more young people living together than are married. It is at these prayer times that parents can point out moral matters like this to their children that this kind of behaviour is not right, is unacceptable and forbidden by God. Parents and grandparents today say they are helpless to advise their children to act morally in this matter because everyone is behaving like this. If they had made the effort to have had family prayers they could have taught their children how to behave correctly.

If there are any young families listening to me perhaps they could put into effect some of the things I am pointing out. It is even not too late for older families to try and model their homes on that of the Holy Family. If they do, the result will be to bring untold happiness and holiness into their homes.

Lord Jesus, on this feast of the Holy Family, we pray for all married couples. Give them the wisdom, understanding, tolerance and all the patience they need to raise their children to be worthy members of Your heavenly kingdom.

HOW MUCH DO WE CARE FOR OUR CHILDREN?

Mt. 2:13-15; 19-23

King Herod was planning to murder Jesus. An angel appeared to Joseph in a dream, warning him of the evil plot. There was no time to waste. The soldiers were already on their way. That very night without waiting for morning, Joseph hurriedly grabbed a few necessities, and under the cover of darkness, he and Mary, with their Baby, began their long journey into Egypt. They remained there until the wicked king had died, and then returned to the land of Israel. But Herod's successor was also an evil man, so Joseph went farther north to Galilee and settled his family in Nazareth.

It is no small matter for a family to pick up sticks, in the middle of the night, and move to another country. Think of it! Put yourself in their place. Where would you go? What would you do? How would you live? Mary and Joseph faced those same daunting questions. Like all refugees, their future was uncertain, bleak and frightening. At that moment, personal comfort and convenience were forgotten. Nothing else mattered except the safety and security of their Child. This episode in the life of the Holy Family confronts us with a question: How much do we care for our children?

It is sad to say that unlike Joseph and Mary, our world has not given the welfare of children top priority. Think of millions that are spent on military equipment, while many children all over the world go hungry. Think of the millions that are spent on luxuries, while many children go without necessities. Think of the neighbourhoods that are no longer fit places for children to live. Think of the mother in a slum tenement, who lives in daily fear that her sleeping baby will be bitten by rats!

Think of the children who are well-housed and well-fed, but emotionally starved. Their childish mistakes are met with impatience. Their longing for love, time and attention are frequently denied. Our hearts go out especially to single parents, who must work long hours, and have little time or energy left over for their little ones. Many of them are doing an heroic and excellent job. We wonder about the priorities of those parents who could invest their hours in teaching, training, and loving their children, but simply choose to do otherwise. If we truly cared for our children, there would be drastic changes in society. There would be some shifting of priorities in many homes. Watch the Holy Family as they head for Egypt with little more than the clothes on their backs. Observe their total commitment to the well-being of their Child.

Let us consider what Jesus teaches us about children. They were definitely a priority in His teaching. Several times He turned the spotlight on children, and measured life by them. Recall that occasion when His disciples were arguing among themselves who would be the greatest in the Kingdom. Jesus entered that debate by placing a child in their midst and saying, "Unless you change and become like children, you will not enter the Kingdom of Heaven. And whoever humbles himself like this little child is the greatest in the Kingdom." (Mt. 18:3-4)

One day Jesus was surrounded by parents, and their children. They wanted Him to touch them and pray for them. The scene must have looked like a Santa Claus grotto in a crowded department store - children everywhere. His disciples became impatient with this waste of their Lord's valuable time. They scolded the parents and told them to take their children away. Jesus rebuked His disciples and said, "Let the children come to Me, for the Kingdom of Heaven belongs to such as these." (Mt. 19:14)

Once He spoke of how to welcome Him into our lives. All we have to do is to welcome a child in His name. He said, "Whoever receives one child in My name receives Me." (Mt. 18:5) Again He spoke of a crime that was so grievous that no punishment for it could be too great. What, you might ask, would such a crime be in the eyes of Jesus? Listen to what He said, "Whoever causes one of these little ones to sin, it would be better for him to have a great millstone hung around his neck, and to be drowned in the depths of the sea." (Mt. 18:6) With our Lord, nothing was more important than children. May God give us the wisdom to share that view.

Surely Jesus is telling us that our children are not only our greatest responsibility, they can also be our greatest inspiration. Do you ever grow weary of this insane world and want to give up on it? At times human nature seems so perverted that we can see no solution to our problems, but we must not give up. We must do all we can for the sake of our children. We must provide a safe and peaceful environment in which they can grow in the love of God and one another.

When life looks like that, where can we turn for renewed courage and strength? To God, of course. He is our primary hope. He will inspire us not to give up, but to fight for the sake of our children for they cannot help themselves. They depend on us. We cannot let them down. They are worth whatever it takes. If we do not have the will to build a better world for ourselves, maybe we can find the decency to build a better world for them.

Lord Jesus, Your mother Mary and Joseph did not undertake that arduous journey for themselves. They did it for You. You had to be safe. Whatever that cost, they were willing to pay it. Today we stand in their place and face a similar challenge. Do we care for our children as they did for You?

JESUS WAS A FAMILY MAN

Col 3:12-21 & Mt. 2:13-15, 19-23

One of the highest compliments that can be paid to a person is to call him or her a family man or woman. It obviously means that they are married and have children. But it also means that they are stable and dependable, that they are faithful to their spouse, devoted to their children and a credit to their community.

I like that compliment. The only problem that I have with it is that we use it in too limited a sense. We need to expand its meaning and apply it to a lot of people, who under the present rules do not qualify.

For example, can't we maintain that Jesus was a family man? We are well aware that He never married and never had children. But we will all agree that in the broader and deeper meaning of the term, Jesus deserved to be called a family man. We can say this for two reasons.

First, He was the product of a family, to which He was deeply devoted, and for which He was genuinely grateful. It is impossible to study the life and work of Jesus without discovering the influence His family had on Him. His concept of God must have been shaped, at least in part by His relationship with Joseph. His high regard for women, which was not characteristic of His culture, was surely rooted in His relationship with Mary, His mother, and in the relationship He observed between Joseph and Mary.

Many of the stories that He told reflect experiences of home life. Since Joseph was a carpenter He must have observed Joseph create furniture and even help in the building of houses. With the passing of time, He saw those houses withstand storms and even floods. Other houses were blown down or washed away. Jesus asked why, and Joseph explained that the difference was the foundation. He built his houses on bedrock. Those other houses were built on sand. And years later Jesus said, "Anyone who hears My words and puts them intro practice is like the wise man who built his house on rock."

He watched His mother making bread. He observed that she took a small amount of yeast and carefully worked it into the dough. Then she covered it with a cloth and put it in a warm place. He saw the dough begin to swell slowly, until it had more than doubled in size. And years later Jesus said, "The kingdom of God is like yeast which a woman kneaded into three measures of flour. Eventually, the whole mass of dough began to rise."

These are just two examples of the influence His family had on His life and work. Much more could be cited. There is no denying that Jesus was the product of a healthy home life. We call it the Holy Family. This does not mean the members wore haloes or that they were not real people. They were just as real as the members of your family and mine. They had problems just as other families do. They were not exempt. Today's Gospel reading tells of the time when they were forced to protect their Child from the wrath of a paranoid king.

Luke's Gospel tells of a time when Jesus was a missing Child. He was only twelve years old. Mary and Joseph searched for Him, and their hearts were filled with fear and foreboding. Gratefully, the story had a happy ending. After three days of searching they found Him. Mary scolded her Son. It was a gentle scolding, but a scolding nonetheless. All families have misunderstanding and disagreements, and the Holy Family was no exception.

We can presume that Joseph died when Jesus was a youth, certainly before He began His public ministry. This idea is based on two things. One, that Joseph is never mentioned after the second chapter of Luke. And the other, that Jesus from the cross, committed His mother to the keeping and care of John. So it seems almost certain that Joseph died an early and untimely death. All families have sorrows, and the Holy Family was no exception.

Jesus was the product of a real family that had problems, disagreements and sorrows just as all families do. Our lives have been influenced by our family. Perhaps our family was not everything that we may have wanted it to be. Very few families are. Some are tragic, but I hope all of us can find somewhere in our hearts some reason to be grateful for that person or persons that we call our family.

A mention must be made of those mothers, and in some cases fathers, who are rearing their children alone? Are they not families? Of course, they are, and many of them are beautiful families.

I would like to note that a husband and wife and their children are not a family, in the best sense of the word, until they are tied together with bonds of love. Listen to Paul's instructions to the Church in Colossi, "Because you are God's chosen ones, clothe yourselves with heartfelt mercy, with kindness and patience. Bear with one another, and forgive whatever grievances you have against one another. Over all these virtues, put on love which binds the rest together and makes them perfect." Those are the elements that bond a family.

Lord Jesus, in some sense we all belong to a family. It could be our own family, or the Church, a school or our place of work. In whatever family we find ourselves may we play our part in modelling our family on that of Yours where love, thoughtfulness, obedience and the presence of God flourishes.

THE BAPTISM OF JESUS

(Three sermons)

JESUS IDENTIFIES HIMSELF WITH US

Mt. 3:13-17

The Baptism of Jesus marked the beginning of His Public Ministry. For thirty years He had lived and worked in a carpenter's shop at Nazareth. But now His life took on a new turn. He came to John, that rugged outdoor preacher, and presented Himself for baptism. John at first refused, but Jesus insisted, and so John baptised Him in the River Jordan. It was a strange scene, the Son of God submitting to a baptism that symbolised repentance. It not only troubled John, it has puzzled Christians ever since. John felt that it was he who needed to be baptised instead of Jesus, and we agree with John. But we bow to the superior wisdom of Jesus and try to understand what His baptism means to us.

For one thing it reminds us that Jesus towers above us. This is what John was feeling when he said, "I am not worthy to loosen His sandal strap." Those words were not an expression of false humility. John was so conscious of the gap between himself and Jesus that in His presence he felt totally unworthy.

It doesn't take much thought for us to realise how unworthy we are in the presence of Jesus. Look at the quality of His character, the depth of His intelligence, the greatness of His spirit. See how he responded to rejection and hostility. This was one of the things about Him that impressed Peter the most. Years later he wrote, "When He was insulted, He returned no insult."

How different that is from us. Locked into our small world of retaliation, we exchange insult upon insult, blow for blow. Simon Peter just couldn't understand this capacity of Jesus to endure suffering without resentment, and neither can we. It goes far beyond our own experience so that all we can do is to say with John, "I am not worthy to loosen His sandal strap." When we compare ourselves to Jesus, He towers above us as the most challenging personality we will ever face.

Jesus accepted John's baptism to tell us that He walks among us, that He identifies Himself with us.

Let me tell you a lovely story. There was once a man on Christmas Eve who told his wife he no longer believed in this incarnation stuff of God becoming man and he was not going to Midnight Mass. He would stay at home while the rest of the family went. This saddened his wife and children, but they said nothing.

Shortly after they drove away in the car, there was a heavy fall of snow. Minutes later the man was startled by a thud on the window, then another and another. At first he thought someone was throwing snowballs at his house. When he went to the front door to investigate, to his surprise he found a flock of birds huddled in the snow. They had been caught in the storm and in a desperate search for shelter had flown towards the light of his large windows. He felt for these birds and couldn't leave these poor creatures to lie there and freeze.

He thought of the barn where his children stabled their pony. That would provide a shelter, that is, if he could direct the birds to it. Quickly he put on his coat and wellingtons, and tramped through the deepening snow to the barn. Opening the doors wide he turned on the light, but the birds would not go in. Thinking food would entice them in, he hurried into the kitchen, fetched a hunk of bread and sprinkled the bread crumbs on the snow, making a trail from where they lay to the door of the barn. To his dismay, the birds ignored the food. He tried catching them. He tried walking round them, waving his arms. That didn't work, it only frightened them and scattered them in every direction. He then realised they were afraid of him. They did not understand that he was trying to help them. He reasoned, "To them I am a strange and terrifying creature. If only I could think of some way to let them know that they can trust me and that I am not their enemy but their friend. But how? If only I could be a bird, speak their language and tell them not to be afraid. I could make them see, hear and understand and show them the way to the safe warm barn."

At that precise moment the church bells began to ring. The sound reached his ear above the sound of the wind. He stood there listening to the bells and the people singing, "Come to the manger." In that instant the truth of Christ becoming man to save us hit him and tears came to his eyes. He now realised that Jesus became a man so that he could identify Himself with us and help us, but he could not become a bird to help those frightened birds. He rushed inside his home to change and join his family in Church.

The baptism of Jesus tells us one more thing, that Jesus had the approval of His Father. When He was baptised, a voice from heaven said, "You are my beloved Son. On you my favour rests." What greater achievement in life is there than to have the approval of God? Deep down inside us that is what we all desire. Yet it seems so elusive. We never lead our lives as we should. Self keeps getting in the way and we keep stumbling and falling.

Lord Jesus, help us to seek the approval of Your Father in all that we do. You showed us what a person ought to be. You became one of us and lived life at its very best. Now if we identify with You through faith, we will share with You the approval and the acceptance of Your Father.

ARE WE TRUE TO OUR BAPTISM?

Mt 3:13-17

For the occasion of my Golden Jubilee to the Priesthood I was given permission to spend a whole month in the Holy Land. I can't blame you if you are envious. One of the places I was able to visit was the River Jordan where John the Baptist baptised Our Lord. Can you imagine my feelings? I sat for some time on the steps leading into the river, my feet in the water being nibbled by hundreds of little fish. My thoughts recalled the great and solemn moment when John the Baptist baptised Our Lord.

Matthew relates the event for us very briefly. We know thousands of people from different walks of life heard about this man John the Baptist, who had lived a very frugal life in the desert and was preaching a baptism of repentance, came to listen to him and repent of their sins and be baptised. One of the many who came was his cousin Jesus. There is so much we would love to know about John and Jesus' previous meetings.

John had been telling his hearers, that if they had been impressed with his message, there was One to come after him who would baptise them, not just with water, but with the Holy Spirit and fire. How would they understand that? Jesus had not yet revealed the Holy Spirit. John would certainly have some knowledge of the Holy Spirit for Mary may have revealed to her cousin Elizabeth how she had become pregnant. She had conceived by the power of the Holy Spirit. John added that the One to follow him was so great that he not even worthy to carry or undo his sandal straps.

When Jesus came to be baptised by John he recognised Jesus as the Messiah, that He was sinless and did not need his baptism. If anything John needed to be baptised by Him. Jesus insisted that John baptise Him. He said, "Leave it like this for the time being; it is fitting that we should, in this way, do all that righteousness demands." I wonder what John made of that. In so many words Jesus was telling John that He wanted to identify Himself with the rest of humankind.

So Jesus stepped into the water and John obediently baptised Him. As soon as He came out of the water three things happened; there was a break in the clouds; a dove appeared and descended on Jesus and a voice spoke from heaven.

What are we to make of this? The ancient Jews thought of God living somewhere above the sky. They believed that if God wanted to speak to them He would have to separate the clouds and speak. The prophet Isaiah believed this and so he wrote, "Oh, that you would tear the heavens and come down." (Is. 64:1). The psalmist too said, "Lower your heavens, come down to us." (Ps.144:5).

Next, a dove flew above Jesus and the water. This takes our mind back to the book of Genesis at the beginning of creation when "God's Spirit hovered over the water". This indicated that with the baptism of Jesus a new creation was being heralded. God was renewing His world.

Finally, a voice from heaven is heard. It is obviously the voice of Jesus' Father for He says, "This is My Son, the Beloved; My favour rests on Him."

Now what are we to make of all this? We can turn to St. Paul to help us understand the significance of this happening. He explains this in 1 Cor. 15:45-49. Jesus is the "new Adam" of the new creation. Paul compares Jesus and Adam this way: "The first man, Adam, was created a living being; but the last Adam (Jesus) is the life-giving spirit…The first Adam…came from the earth; the second Adam came from heaven…" "As the earthly man was, so are we on earth; and as the heavenly man is, so are we in heaven. And we, who have been modelled on the earthly man, will be modelled on the heavenly man."

With St. Paul's help we can summarise the meaning of the baptism of Jesus in these words: Jesus' baptism in the River Jordan marks the start of a "new era" in history. This new era is a "new creation" in which Jesus is the "new Adam".

The baptism of Jesus naturally makes us think of our own baptism. His baptism was not just an isolated event in His own life, it was the beginning of a new era in God's relationship with humankind, and has implications for us all, as it affects each of us at the deepest and most personal level. At baptism the Spirit of God took possession of us in a very special way, to direct and guide us in the footsteps of Christ. Baptism unites us with Jesus in the most intimate manner, bringing us into the family of God with the right to call God our Father.

Heavenly Father, we thank Jesus through His baptism for identifying Himself with us and giving us the example of how we should live our lives.

JESUS NEEDS YOU AND ME

Mt. 3:13-17

We are all conscious of the fact that we need Jesus, but has it ever occurred to you that He also needs us? He needs each one of us if we are to build up the Kingdom of God on this earth.

This is clearly indicated all through the New Testament. The Baptism of Jesus is a very sacred moment in the life of our Lord. Matthew says, "He saw the Spirit of God descending like a dove and coming down on Him." Then a voice from Heaven saying, "This is My Son, the Beloved; My favour rests on Him." Jesus' Baptism was crowned with divine approval. We should not overlook the fact that it was accomplished by human hands. Jesus was baptized by a man, an extraordinary man, but a man none the less. John, at first, was reluctant to do this incredible thing. He said to Jesus, "It is I who need baptism from You and You come to me." Jesus replied, "Leave it like this for the time being; it is fitting that we should in this way, do all that righteousness demands." That sentence strongly suggests that neither man could do the will of God without the cooperation of the other. John needed Jesus, and Jesus needed John.

How often the Son of God needed the help of people. He entered this world as a newborn infant. Like all little babies, He needed someone to take care of Him. He grew from babyhood to manhood, and, like all growing boys, He needed someone to feed, guide and teach Him. He gathered around Him twelve men and He needed them to help Him with His work.

He needed a woman of Samaria to give Him a drink of water; a peasant boy to help Him feed five thousand hungry people; Peter, James and John to pray with Him in the Garden of Gethsemane; a man from Cyrene to help Him carry His cross; Joseph of Arimathea to provide Him with a place of burial and after His resurrection, He needed His friends to share the good news with the world.

John the Baptist clearly understood his need for Christ, but it was hard for him to see that the Christ also needed him. We have the same difficulty. It seems almost irreverent to speak of His need for us. Yet, it is no less true today than it was that day when He was baptised in the Jordan River. All good relationships involve mutual need, and that includes our relationship with Christ.

Consider, for a moment, how something inside of us responds to those who need us. Picture yourself in bed at night, sound asleep. Then suddenly the silence is shattered by a voice crying for help. I doubt that anything would awaken us more quickly and more completely than that. However selfish we may be, there is something within us that is deeply touched by a cry for help. When we are needed and know it, most of us respond. We have an example of this in the life of Chuck Yeager one of the best, and probably the most famous, test pilot in the world. He wrote an autobiography in which he shared some of his experiences. He was testing a plane over the desert. A friend was in another plane, and each was pushing his plane to its limit and beyond. The engineers who designed the planes had calculated their capacity. The test pilot's job is to go beyond that and try to determine the precise endurance.

As Yeager was flying, he realized that his friend in the other plane was in trouble. He appeared to be on the verge of passing out. Apparently, something had gone wrong with his oxygen system. Yeager tried to rouse him, but without success, and time was running out. Then he decided on another tactic. He pretended to be in trouble himself. Over his radio, he said, "I can't make it", and put his plane into a steep dive. His friend heard the message and began to follow him, trying to help. Soon they were both at a lower altitude where the oxygen supply was adequate. When Yeager tried to wake his friend, it did no good, but when the friend thought Yeager was in trouble, he pulled himself together and was ready to help. There is something within us that responds to those who need us.

Often we go through life and are not aware how someone close to us can help us. You have probably had an experience like that in your family. You have a family gathering and everyone has a wonderful time. Then people begin to drift away. Just two of you are left in the room. You begin to talk about the things that are really in your heart - the problems you haven't solved, the hurts that haven't been healed. When the evening finally ends, you feel closer to that person than ever before. You have shared your mutual needs.

None of us will ever get very close to another person who is always strong, always able, always helping and never needing help. That is like a mother's relationship with a small child. The need is all one-sided. If the child grows up and discovers that his mother has needs too, then the two of them have a chance to become real friends. If that never happens, they may never really be close.

That same concept can also apply to our relationship with Christ? There is no doubt that He is the Master and we are the servants. We need Him, but the need is not one-sided. He also needs us. By His own admission, without the help of John the Baptist, He could not have fulfilled all of God's demands. He could not baptise Himself. He needed John. Once we realise that Jesus needs us to spread His love and work, it can make our relationship with Him stronger. There are some things today that He cannot do without our help. I remember a little poem that goes something like this.

"He has no hands but your hands to do his work today.

He has no feet but your feet to guide folk in His way.

He has no lips but your lips to tell them how He died.

He has no love but your love to bring them to His side."

He is the Christ who needs us.

Lord Jesus, we are so conscious that we need You, but thank You for assuring us of the tremendous privilege of knowing that You also need us to spread Your kingdom on this earth.

PRESENTATION OF THE CHILD JESUS IN THE TEMPLE

HAVE WE SEEN GOD IN THIS CHILD?

Lk. 2:22-40

One day in the temple in Jerusalem an old man named Simeon offered a most unusual prayer. "Now Master You can let Your servant go in peace." He was telling God he was now ready to die but what is so unusual about that? Many old people have told God of their wish to die because they felt tired, useless or helpless and death would be a welcome release. But not Simeon. His prayer was not an expression of weakness nor despair. It sprang from a sense of fulfilment. He felt that now his life was complete and he was ready to go.

This feeling, strangely enough, was conveyed to him by a Child, the Baby Jesus Whom he recognised as the long awaited Messiah. This did not surprise Simeon because he had been expecting it. Somehow, God had told him, "he would not see death until he had set eyes on the Christ the Lord." That promise came true when Mary and Joseph brought Jesus into the temple. Simeon looked at that little Baby and saw what God was going to achieve through Him. This Baby was a sign of hope.

You and I can understand that experience, because it is not entirely strange to any of us. There is a sense in which every new-born child is a sign of hope. Babies awaken within us a mood of expectancy. You can never tell what a little one might do. We habitually think of them as needing care, and indeed they do. But we also need them because babies get things started. They blaze trails. They open doors to new eras and new ideas. Think back to the fifteenth century. In Genoa, in Italy, a little boy was born. No one thought much about him although, of course, his family loved him. He was Christopher Columbus. So long as there are babies we will never know what may happen next.

The Child Jesus is the hope of all nations. If we trust Him and follow Him we will be saved. If we reject Him and His way of living, we are doomed. This is what Simeon predicted. "You see this Child; He is destined for the fall and for the rising of many."

It is easy for us to become sentimental about babies, to be touched by their helplessness and charmed by their innocence. They make us feel good. No doubt Simeon had those same feelings when He held the Baby Jesus in his arms but he did not stop there. He looked beyond the Baby to the Man He would become and saw Him as the decisive factor in people's lives.

History confirms the truth of that prophecy. Over and over again, those who chose the way of selfish power and glory have fallen. Those who chose the way of service and love have endured. Nero, along with his empire, is gone and remembered only for his infamy. But Paul, a contemporary of that Caesar, is more influential today than he was when he lived. The difference between those two men was the Baby that Simeon held in his arms.

Lord Jesus, what shall it be for us? We cannot take it for granted that You will necessarily be a redeeming influence in our lives. So much depends on us. Have we, like Simeon, seen God in this Child? If so, are we going to rise by following Him, or fall by rejecting Him?

We can start by embracing the Christ Child today, and at the end of our lives, please God, like Simeon, we shall depart in peace.

FIRST SUNDAY OF LENT YEAR A

(Four sermons)

THE DEVIL - OUR GREATEST ENEMY

Mt. 4:1-11

Someone in this church today is not very happy. He is the Devil. He knows I am going to talk about him and tell the truth about him and he doesn't like that. He likes us to think that he doesn't exist, so that furtively he can do his evil work. People sometimes say that we priests do not preach about the Devil. Well I am going to talk about him today. He is such a powerful force of evil in our lives. He never leaves our side, and he is always there to try and get us in his clutches. He hates God and us. There is no love in him at all. God loves and creates; Satan hates and destroys.

Jesus knows Satan all too well and He wants us to be aware that we are constantly in danger from Him and we must be vigilant. That is why He told His apostles how He was tempted by the Devil in the wilderness and made one of the petitions in His prayer the Our Father deal with Satan. 'Deliver us from the Evil One.'

Satan originally enjoyed the company of God in Heaven, but through his pride and envy he said with other angels, "I will not serve!" He turned his back on God's love and so placed himself in Hell, which is simply a place devoid of love. Now his one ambition is to encourage us, through subtle ways, to follow him there. Satan has a great deal of power and experience, and he knows all our human weaknesses. But we have our weapons. He has a great dread of the crucifix, of the holy Name of Jesus, and especially Our Lady. He is panic-stricken at any mention of Mary and recognises the damage she has done to him. He has never forgotten the words of God," I will put enmity between you and the woman, and between your offspring and hers; He will strike your head....." (Gen. 3:15).

The powers of the devils are limited. They are powerful, but they are "chained dogs." None of us, however, is safely beyond their reach, so we always need to pray for God's help. Let us ask our heavenly Father to protect us from all their evil schemes. We thank God that He has given each of us a Guardian Angel to protect us and keep us safe.

In cartoons and comics, the devil appears as a cute, benign tempter, pushing you to do something that's fun or a little bit wrong. In reality however, Satan is anything but cute. His mission is to kill, destroy or enslave us. St. Peter warns, "...be watchful. Your adversary the devil prowls around like a roaring lion, seeking someone to devour." He has the capacity to ruin a person's life.

His primary tactic is to deceive us. He twists and distorts what is true. He managed to trick Adam and Eve to believe that if they disobey God they could be equal to God. Look at the trouble he caused them and all their children. His greatest desire is to keep all of us far away from God. But God repeatedly affirms His love for us. "I have loved you with an everlasting love.." "For God so loved the world that He gave His only Son, that whoever believes in Him should not perish, but have eternal life."

We all face problems. It's part of life. What Satan neglects to tell us is that if we have a relationship with God and depend on Him, God can lead us through those problems. We do not need to shoulder or solve them on our own. God can give us wisdom and real strength in the midst of those problems. Not only that, but He says while we face difficulties, "...My peace I give to you..."

Satan, not only tells lies, he tempts people towards slavery and addictions. "Go ahead," he says, "One more won't hurt you. No one will find out. You're not really hurting anyone. And you'll feel so much better."

If you decide to begin a relationship with God, you will still be tempted by Satan. But God is faithful. He will not allow the temptation to be more than you can stand. When you are tempted, he will show you a way out so that you can endure.

I love C.S. Lewis's story of the three apprentice devils. It was their final exam before they could roam the world to tempt people and bring them to hell. They had just one question to answer, "What tactics will you use to bring men and women rushing headlong into hell?" The first one said, "I'll tell them there is no hell." "Don't be stupid," cried Satan, "every man has a conscience and he knows there will be a day of reckoning – that there is a hell. You've failed." The next one said, "I'll tell them there is no God." "Will you never learn," said Satan in disgust, "although we hate the Bible, we have to accept what it says, 'That only the fool says in his heart there is no God.' You too have failed." Finally, he asked the third apprentice. Very confidently this little devil said, "I'll tell them they have plenty of time." "Marvellous, marvellous," said Satan, "do that and you'll have them rushing into hell." Yes, Satan is very subtle and we must never underestimate his skill.

Lord Jesus, we saw in the Gospel today how You were tempted by the Devil but he never overcame You. Now he wants to tempt us by his lies and lead us away from You. May we remain close to You and Your mother and never allow him to come close to us. May our Guardian Angel protect us.

SATAN TEMPTS JESUS AS HE TEMPTS YOU AND ME

Mt. 4:1-11

We know that Jesus is God, but there are times we forget that He was also a human like you and me - with the one big difference that He was sinless. In today's Gospel we witness just how human He was, having to face temptation like we do many times a day.

Nobody witnessed what took place in the desert, so Jesus must have made a point of telling His Apostles so that they could tell us that just as He had to struggle with temptations, so must we. His message to us is that temptations are necessary, for they help us to prove our love for God, and it gives God the chance to see our ability for service. 'If I could overcome them - so can you. The road will be difficult, but don't be discouraged. Let Me be your inspiration and help.'

After being baptised by John, Jesus was led by the Spirit into the desert to see if He were up to the demanding task that lay ahead. In the next three hard years He had to choose the right men in whose hearts He would implant the Good News, so that they would carry it throughout the world and continue His work from one generation to the next. He spent 40 days in the desert and at the end of the vigorous fast was physically weak.

It is always when we are at our weakest that Satan comes along to tempt us. Knowing that the Redeemer of the world was imminent but uncertain as to whether it was Jesus or not, Satan was going to make sure by tempting Him. "If You are the Son of God, change these stones into loaves of bread."

Jesus knew it was Satan tempting Him. So quoting Scripture He said, "Man does not live on bread alone, but by every word that comes from the mouth of God." In other words, 'Satan, you have only bread to offer. Man has more than a body, he has a soul as well, and that has to be fed and you can't do that, only God can.' Jesus had won the first of this three round contest!

The second temptation is perhaps the most difficult to understand. Obviously Satan did not physically transport Jesus to the top of the Temple, but must have done this in His imagination. Probably at that time the Temple area was crowded with people. We can see Satan whispering in Jesus' ear, 'Go on, jump. God will not let His Anointed One come to any harm. Just think what an impression You will make among the people! What a spectacular way to begin Your public ministry!' Satan is still wondering if Jesus is the Saviour, and so He says, "If you are the Son of God, throw Yourself down, for it is written, 'He has given His angels charge over You and in their hands they will bear You up, lest You dash Your foot against a stone.'"

Again Jesus quotes Scripture at him. "Thou shalt not tempt the Lord, thy God." In other words Jesus is saying to Satan, 'Life is not lived on the level of the spectacular. I have not come to live on this Earth among people and have my head on the clouds! I want to weep with the broken hearted and mend broken lives. I want to accept the hospitality of despised people and handle the rejection of respected people. I want to love even those who do not love Me. Get it into your head Satan that life is not lived on the dramatic and spectacular level.' Jesus wins round two!

In the third temptation Satan shows himself to be the father of lies. He claims to own the world and he can do with it as he pleases - which he cannot. This time he takes Jesus in His imagination to a high mountain and shows Him the kingdoms of the world and says, "All these will be Yours if You will fall down and worship me." Or in other words 'Why go through the three year slog ahead of You and with a cross at the end? It is ridiculous. Take the easy way out!'

That is one of the subtle ways Satan uses when he tempts us. Life is full of choices. Have you noticed that the wrong choice is always the easy one and the right choice is the more difficult? Good habits are hard to form; bad habits are hard to break. We have to wrestle with that reality all our lives.

Jesus was not going to take the easy way out. He would embrace the Cross in order to win the world for His Father. So He said, "Begone, Satan; for it is written, 'The Lord, thy God shalt thou adore and Him alone shalt thou serve.'" And Satan leaves knowing he has failed to tempt Jesus into sin.

Lord Jesus, these temptations of Yours in the desert were neither Your first nor Your last. Life was a struggle for You and so it will be for us. Temptation is a constant warfare from which there is no escape. But we have the consolation that You blazed the trail before us to conquer temptation and You are with us. Let us fight temptation as You did and so share in Your victory.

JESUS TEACHES US HOW TO RESIST TEMPTATIONS

Mt. 4:1-11

St. Matthew tells us that "Jesus was led by the Spirit out into the wilderness to be tempted by the devil. He fasted for forty days and forty nights." This raises a few questions. Why should Jesus be tempted? How did He spend those 40 days? Why did He tell this episode of His life to His Apostles?

Yes, why was Jesus tempted? It was because He was not only God, but He had taken to Himself a human nature and like us was subjected to temptation. We are tempted so that God can see how much we love Him and how able are we to work in His service. In being tempted we are not meant to sin.

How did Jesus spend those 40 days? 40 days is a long time. Since He did not eat at all there were no meals to prepare. Preparing food and feeding ourselves can take up to at least one to two hours of our waking day. I presume Jesus did drink water. Surely He would have slept, for He could not have gone without sleep for all that time? If He did, let us presume He slept for 7 hours. 7 from 24 leaves 17 hours. What did Jesus do during that time? The desert for most people would be a very boring place – just sand and more sand! We can say for certain that He would have spent most, if not all that time in prayer to His Father. In the wilderness you have to face God and yourself with all your emptiness. In everyday life we have so many things to make us feel good and distract us. We don't have them in the wilderness. We know that Jesus as God enjoyed the Beatific Vision and that must been a tremendous help while being alone. So Jesus was not lonely. He was in constant union with His Father and the Holy Spirit.

Jesus was a man and as a man He had needs. Fasting for 40 days would make Him extremely hungry. A little food would be most welcome. This gave Satan an opportunity to tempt Him. All through Jesus' life Satan didn't like what he saw in the life of Jesus and His Mother Mary. They were different from the rest of human kind. He had been able to tempt all others to sin, but he had never managed this with them. Besides there was an important matter he wanted to know, was Jesus the long awaited Messiah, the Son of God? If He was, He would be the One who would crush his head. Here was his opportunity. He tempted Jesus to change the stones, which looked like loaves, into bread. Jesus chose not to use His Divine power to satisfy His natural desire for food. Jesus was in the wilderness to fast, not to eat. So He would not use His power to change stones into bread.

Jesus was not going to play into Satan's hands. He was not going to let him know who He was. He would have to find that out for himself. Jesus' answer was, "Man does not live on bread alone." It was a subtle way of telling Satan that there are more important things to life than food.

Jesus was able to resist all the devil's temptations because He not only knew Scripture, but He also obeyed it. St. Paul in his letter to the Ephesians tells us that God's word is a sword to use in spiritual combat. Knowing Bible verses is an important step in helping us resist the devil's attacks, but we must also obey the Bible. Yes, Satan had memorised Scripture, but failed to obey it. Knowing and obeying the Bible helps us follow God's desires rather than the devil's.

Next Satan shows the dreadful liar he is. He makes out that he owns the world and if only Jesus worshipped him he would give it to Him. Jesus was being tempted to take the world as a political ruler right then, without carrying out His plan to die on a cross to save the world from sin. Satan was trying to distort Jesus' perspective by making Him focus on worldly power and not on God's plans.

Today the devil offers us the world by trying to entice us with materialism and power. We can resist temptations the same way Jesus did. If we find ourselves craving something that the world offers, we should quote Jesus' words to the devil, "You must worship the Lord your God, and serve Him alone."

Next Satan took Jesus to the parapet of the Temple. Are we to believe that Satan physically transported Jesus? I don't think so. Satan would have done this through Jesus' imagination. He tempted Him to throw Himself down and God's angel would see He came to no harm. God is not our magician in the sky ready to perform on request. Jesus dismisses Satan by telling him not to put God to the test. God wants us to live by faith, not by magic. We must not try to manipulate God by asking for signs.

No one but Satan witnessed these temptations. Jesus deliberately told them to His Apostles so that we could learn how to resist temptation. Jesus' temptations could be summarised under three P's, Power, Possession and Prestige.

Lord Jesus, these are the areas where the devil likes to tempt us as well. What we must remember is that we are not on our own. We have You at our side. With You with us we too can resist all the temptations that Satan can throw at us.

FACING TEMPTATION

Mt. 4:1-11

Jesus was not only divine, He was human. Because He was human, like the rest of us He was tempted.

God allows us to be tempted. He does not want us to fail, but to succeed and so prove our love for Him. Jesus after His baptism was led by the Spirit into the wilderness to be tempted by the devil. There He fasted for forty days. He experienced this as His preparation for His public ministry. The proximity of the two is not unusual. Often our greatest achievements are followed by our greatest times of trial and testing.

Jesus faced three temptations, each directly related to His ministry. What kind of Messiah would Jesus be? How would he proceed in beginning His mission? The tempter's approach was to look for weaknesses in Jesus that might be exploited. Jesus was hungry from fasting, why not turn stones into bread? Jesus would need to reach people, why not do something spectacular that would draw an instant crowd? Jesus would confront a hostile world, why not let the devil give Him control over all worldly powers? The temptations were calculated to appeal directly to Jesus' immediate concerns. How could He possibly resist?

Jesus was prepared for all this, however. First, His priorities were firmly set: complete obedience to God, and love for every person He met. Second, Jesus knew the source of His authority and power. He countered each temptation with appropriate Scripture. Third, Jesus was free of personal concerns and ambitions. He was prepared to face temptation. He was strong in every area where the tempter hoped He would be weak. He was ready to begin His life's work.

Our encounters with temptation are not entirely different from Jesus' experience. Often our temptations seem intensely personal, as if coming from an actual enemy. They strike us when we are weak and where we are vulnerable. Our temptations involve deception, appearing to support us and our worthy intentions, and then enticing us with short cuts and questionable methods. Temptations often appear at first to involve innocent and agreeable opportunities, keeping the truth well hidden. We may even cooperate with the temptation with such thoughts as, "What could possibly be wrong with this?" and "It wouldn't hurt anyone." The human brain is a highly skilled in the art of rationalizing and deception. Sometime later we may find ourselves asking, "How could I have ever imagined that this was a good thing to do?" In short, we need to be smart enough to respect temptation, and not underestimate its persuasive powers. If we are wise we will treat it as a foe, a creative and committed foe. It cannot be trusted. Temptation is inevitable, but not irresistible.

As was true with Jesus, being prepared to face temptation involves keeping our priorities well in mind. One advantage Jesus had in the wilderness was that the issues raised by the devil had already been decided. Nothing was going to deter Jesus from doing the will of God. No argument was going to alter His commitments. He knew who He was, whose He was, and what He was about. He didn't have to decide. He had already decided.

When faced with something tempting, we should ask ourselves several questions. First, would this be pleasing to God? Second, would this violate any of my commitments to myself or to others? Third, would I be ashamed for everyone I love to know about this? These are not fool proof tests, but they help us consider a particular temptation in the light of our highest values and concerns. Remember, Jesus was prepared for facing temptation by having His priorities firmly in place.

The values of resisting temptation are many. The most obvious is that is that it keeps us from error, from harm, and from sin. Perhaps the second greatest value in resisting temptation is that it makes us stronger - morally, emotionally, and spiritually. In so doing, it prepares us to face temptation in the future.

Strength comes from resisting and overcoming temptation with the help of God. Our Lady and the saints all had to face temptation. They know how hard they had to fight to resist. They will want to help us. We can appeal to them and our Guardian Angel for help. We become strong internally by resisting all that would pull us down mentally, emotionally, morally, and spiritually. This requires discipline.

Lord Jesus, we will face temptations of one sort or another today. May we realise You are on our side and with Your help we can overcome all temptations and use them to draw closer to You.

SECOND SUNDAY OF LENT YEAR A

PROOF THAT JESUS IS THE SON OF GOD

Mt. 17:1-9

When I think of the Transfiguration I consider myself a very fortunate person. When I visited Mount Tabor for the first time it was in the evening and words fail me to describe the beautiful red sunset I witnessed. It made it so easy to imagine what happened on that mountain when Jesus was transfigured in all His glory.

The reason why Jesus took Peter, James and John to the top of the mountain was to show them Who He really was – not just a great prophet, but God's own Son. Because Jesus is God He is always surrounded with radiant light, but when He became Man He concealed that light. Today He allowed His three Apostles to see this light. His face "shone like the sun, and His clothes became as white as light" (v. 2). Thus the Lord made that divine glory shine in His person and accompanying Him was Moses and Elijah, "talking with Him" (v. 3).

Jesus wanted to illumine the minds and hearts of His apostles so that they could understand clearly who their Master was. Very soon He was to make His way to Jerusalem, where He would suffer the condemnation to death by crucifixion. Jesus wished to prepare His three close followers for this scandal - the scandal of the Cross, for this scandal was too strong for their faith. At the same time He was announcing ahead of time His Resurrection, manifesting Himself as the Messiah, the Son of God. Jesus prepares them there for that sad moment of so much grief. In fact, Jesus was showing Himself a different Messiah in regard to their expectations. He was not going to be a powerful and glorious king, but a humble and vulnerable Servant; not a lord of great wealth, but a poor man who had no place to lay His head. It was truly a revelation of God turned upside down, and the most disconcerting sign of this scandalous reversal is the cross. But precisely through the cross Jesus will attain His glorious Resurrection, which will be definitive, not like this Transfiguration that lasted a moment, an instant.

Jesus revealed His glory to indicate where the cross leads. One who dies with Christ, will rise with Christ. The cross is the door of the Resurrection. One who fights with Him, will triumph with Him. This is the message of hope contained in Christ's Cross. The Christian Cross is not a furnishing of the home or an ornament to wear, but is an appeal to our love telling us that Jesus sacrificed Himself to save us from sin and hell. In this Lenten Season as we contemplate with devotion the image of the crucifix, we remind ourselves that Jesus died on the cross and rose for us. It also reminds us of the gravity of our sins and the value of the sacrifice with which Christ saved us all.

The Transfiguration has something in common with Jesus' Agony in the Garden. On both occasions Jesus took the same three Apostles so that they could be alone and pray; on both occasions the Apostles fell asleep. There was one great difference. On Mount Tabor He manifested the radiant glory of His Godhead and in the Garden He revealed His Manhood. He showed He was really frightened at the ordeal He was soon to face.

On Mount Tabor Moses and Elijah appeared with Him. Why these two? Moses represented the Law. God gave him the Law on two tablets of stone. Elijah represented the Prophets. Their appearance was to tell us that Jesus was the fulfilment of the Law and the Prophets.

79

Jesus Himself said, "I have not come to abolish the Law and the Prophets, but to fulfil them." (Mt. 5:17) The Father's voice was heard singling out Jesus as the long-awaited Messiah who possessed Divine Authority.

When Peter suggested making three tents he wanted to keep Moses and Elijah with them, but this was not what God wanted. He just didn't want to leave the mountain. All of us at some time have had that joyful mountain top experience. It may be a beautiful friendship or the view of a glorious sunset. We should hold on to them in our memory and recall them in moments of desolation so that we know God is with us and we shall one day share His glory, the glory He displayed on this occasion.

When we enjoy such an inspiring experience we want to stay where we are and never want it to end, away from the reality and problems of our daily lives. Knowing that struggles await us in the valley encourages us to linger on the mountain top, but staying on the mountain prohibits our ministering to others. Instead of becoming spiritual giants, we would soon be dwarfed by our own self-centredness. We need to have that right balance in life, times for retreat and renewal and then with our new gained strength to return to the world and minister to it.

God the Father clearly identified Jesus as His Son. They were to listen to Him for His words have that final authority. If we believe Jesus is God's Son, then we will surely want to listen to Him and seek His guidance and not just rely on human sources.

Lord Jesus, we thank you for sharing this glorious experience with us. In moments of hardship in our lives help us to recognise You as God's Son who can see us through every trial. May we take to heart the words of Your Father to listen to You.

THIRD SUNDAY OF LENT YEAR A

(Five sermons)

A LESSON IN HUMAN RELATIONS

Jn. 4:5-42

Our Gospel setting today was at a water well, nearby a Samaritan village. It was here that Jesus and His followers stopped to replenish their supplies. The disciples had gone into the village to buy food. Jesus, being tired from His journey, sat down on the curb of the well and waited for their return. In the meantime, one of the villagers, a woman, came to the well to draw water. The encounter that followed is a lesson in human relations.

Here were two people, who were about as different as people can be. One was a woman, and the other a man. In that day, women had no status at all. They were owned by their fathers until they got married. After that, they were owned by their husbands. Men were regarded as being far superior to women. It was accepted protocol that men had no public dealings with women, not even to talk with them. This was part of the reason why this woman was startled when Jesus asked her for a drink of water. To do so put Him in a subordinate position. He was acknowledging His dependence upon her. In a male-dominant culture, that was something no self-respecting man would do. You will note that when the disciples returned, they were surprised that Jesus was speaking to a woman. It simply wasn't done.

Another difference that separated Jesus and the woman was race. Jesus was a Jew. The woman was a Samaritan. Between those two nations an ancient antagonism ran bitter and deep. Each side was convinced that the other side was no good. Most Jews hated Samaritans and most Samaritans hated Jews. There was no sensible explanation for it. Racial prejudice never does make sense. That is why it is called "prejudice". The word means "to judge in advance". Without taking the time or making an effort to know an individual, you simply decide, on the basis of race, that a person is no good. Such behaviour is unfair and unintelligent. The prejudiced person is merely advertising his or her own ignorance. It is counter-productive. Nothing, absolutely nothing, useful comes out of it. Even if it were true, what good would it do? What would it accomplish to hate an entire race of people, simply because they were thought to be no good? They are not going to vanish from the earth, merely because we hate them. They would still be here. We would still have to find some way of relating to them. Despite all of its stupidity, racial prejudice endures even to this day. It may well be the greatest curse ever to beset humankind.

Another difference that separated Jews and Samaritans was religion. They both believed in God. That should have been, and could have been, a basis for unity. But both sides got hung-up on the details of religion. It became, instead, a wedge that drove them apart. The focus of their disagreement was where God should be worshipped. The Jews had a temple in Jerusalem. The Samaritans had a temple on Mount Gerizim. Both of them insisted that their place of worship was the proper place. There was no room for compromise. Each side knew themselves to be right. So, they ended up hating one another in the name of God. People who become obsessed with the details of religion will almost always fall into that same trap.

Jesus did not allow any of these differences to separate Him from the Samaritan woman, or from anyone else. He chose, instead, to focus on the similarities that unite all people. This entire story revolves around water. That is an appropriate centrepiece for a lesson on human relations. It strips away all secondary considerations, and confronts us with the basic realities of life. All of us are different in many ways. We are male and female. We are black, and white, and yellow, and brown, and red. We are young and old. We are educated and uneducated. We are married and single. We are rich and poor. When it comes to water, all of us are the same. No human being can survive more than a few days without it. To a lesser degree, the same is true of food. We could live for perhaps a few weeks without eating, but not very long. Our basic physical needs boldly proclaim the essential unity of all people.

Jesus was thirsty. The well was deep. He had no rope or bucket with which to draw water. The woman had both. He needed her help, and she needed His. Here was a woman who shared the story of her life with a total stranger. Why would she do that? The obvious answer is loneliness. The warmth and kindness of Jesus were like living water to her thirsty soul. Can people die of loneliness? I think they can. We all need to be loved. Surely every human heart longs for the sight of a friendly face, the sound of a friendly voice, the touch of a friendly hand? Our common social needs demonstrate that we are all alike.

This woman had not been able to make life work. She looked back on a succession of broken relationships that were forever beyond repair. She remembered missed opportunities that could never be reclaimed. She lived with the pain of failed hopes and shattered dreams. Her life had become a sad litany of things that might have been.

Anyone, who has lived very long at all can understand that. The only difference may be that our failures have not been quite as glaring as hers, but all of us are in the same boat. We all need the kind of help that only God can give.

Human relations have two dimensions. There are the differences that divide us, and the needs that unite us. Jesus chose to emphasize the latter. What about us? When we look at other people which do we see? The differences that tear us apart, or the needs that bind us together?

Lord Jesus, let us concentrate on what binds us together. Then we shall treat all people like You did.

THE MAN WHO REVEALED THE SECRETS OF MY LIFE

Jn. 4:5 -42

I consider myself a very fortunate person for several years ago I stood at Jacob's well in Samaria where Jesus spoke to the woman we read about in today's Gospel. If you were to travel to the Holy Land today I would be very surprised if you would be able to stand at this well as I did. It is now a no go area because of all of the friction there is between the Israelites and the Palestinians. How sad this must make our Blessed Lady who wants all God's children to live in peace.

What lesson can we take away from today's Gospel story? There are many. May I suggest one? It teaches us how each one of us is unique and special to Jesus. He treats each one of us as individuals. It was not politically correct for Jesus, a Jew to speak to a Samaritan let alone a woman. Jesus was above such stupid and petty rules. For Him this woman was a child of God and to Him it made no difference what her sex or nationality was. To Jesus she was unique, like any of God's children. No one in this world had the same personality as she did. I love this thought about ourselves. Because of this you can say no one in this whole world can say to God the words, "I love you" as you can. No one can pray the Our Father as you can. I find that thought very encouraging and comforting when praying.

Jesus' approach to this lonely woman was ever so gentle. He wanted to win her love. There was nothing forceful about His manner. If He had been she may never have opened herself to Him. Jesus began by asking her to give Him a drink. This surprised her and she said, "You a Jew asking me a Samaritan woman to give you a drink." Her reply gave Jesus the opening He wanted. He said, "If only you knew who it is that is asking you for a drink, you would ask Him, and He would give you life-giving water." Eventually Jesus comes round to tell her that whoever drinks the water that He can provide will never be thirsty again. The thought that she would never again have to make the tiresome journey every day from her house to this well was such a pleasant one and unbelievable that she said, "Sir, give me that water."

Now that Jesus had won over her confidence He completely changed the subject of the conversation and said, "Go and call your husband and come back." I wonder what she really thought at that moment. Did she think, "Why do you want to know this and why should I tell you?" So to evade the question she simply said, "I haven't got a husband." What a surprise she must have got when Jesus revealed her dark secret. "You have been married five times and the man you live with now is not really your husband. You were telling the truth. The man you are living with now is not your husband." We may have thought that she would take offence at this instead she exclaimed, "I see you are a prophet, Sir!" What a fortunate woman she was for from that moment, on her own, Jesus gave her the lesson about how and where people will worship the Father. At hearing all this she elicited from Jesus Himself the fact that He was the Messiah.

Jesus had made a conquest. He had completed all that He wanted to say to her and at this moment the Apostles joined Him. He had brought happiness into her life. Without filling her bucket with water she rushed back to the town to tell anyone she could meet of the man who had told her everything about her life. She was so excited that they went with her back to the well to meet this Man.

What can we glean from this story to benefit us? First of all we must believe that like this woman Jesus is interested in each one of us as if we were the only person in the world. He is interested in us and we are special to Him.

This woman was not afraid to open herself to Jesus which is what we do when we go to Confession. Do we get the same benefits from our Confessions as she did from her meeting with Jesus? In Confession are we as honest as this woman? Or are our Confessions just a repeated list of sins and so we make no progress and get no benefit from going? Let us tear up that list and make our Confessions a real heart to heart chat with Jesus. Not being superficial, but going to the root of our failings, our pride, our sloth, our impatience, our anger, our lust.

Lord Jesus, transform our lives like You transformed the life of this Samaritan woman and may we be the means of drawing others to You.

HOW TO EVANGELISE

Exod. 17:3-7; Rom.5:1-2, 5-8 & Jn. 4:5-42

Lent is a time when the Church accompanies catechumens on their journey of faith towards Baptism. It is in Baptism that the catechumen first receives the Holy Spirit for the forgiveness of sins. This work of the Holy Spirit is described in three different ways on the three consecutive Sundays of Lent beginning today. The image of the Holy Spirit which the readings put before us today is that of life-giving water.

Thirst is a limiting human condition with which we are all familiar. It is a signal that the water supply to our body is running low and that we had better do something about it. We are given a gentle reminder of the absolute need for water in order to sustain life. A person may survive for quite a few days without food; but he will not last long without water. Dehydration kills. We have all had the refreshing experience of consuming a cool drink when parched with thirst. That is exactly what happens in our spiritual life at Baptism. When our spiritual lives are parched by the heat of sin and we are on the point of death, the Holy Spirit comes as a fresh draught of life-giving water. St. Paul describes this, in today's reading from the Letter to the Romans, as the love of God being poured into our hearts by the Holy Spirit. Indeed the outward sign of pouring water over the person's head at Baptism affects the inward grace of the Holy Spirit being poured into the person's heart.

This outpouring of the Holy Spirit was already foreshadowed in the Old Testament, as we heard in the First Reading. The people of Israel, having crossed the Red Sea, became parched with thirst as they journeyed through the heat. When they cried out for water, the Lord instructed Moses to strike the rock with the rod, so that water would gush forth for the people to drink. In this story, the rod symbolises the cross and the rock represents Jesus who struck down on the cross and pierced with a lance so that the Holy Spirit could flow into the world parched with sin. By God's plan, Jesus had to die first so that His spirit, which is the Holy Spirit, could be released and then poured out on all mankind, as happened after His resurrection and ascension. This outpouring takes place through the Sacraments, the first of which is, of course, Baptism. The stream of blood and water, which the centurion testified to having seen emerge from the Christ's pierced side, is the source of the Holy Spirit, the agent of the Church's sacramental life.

The Gospel reading about the Samaritan woman's encounter with Jesus brings home to us the same truth, namely, that Jesus is the source of the living water, which is the Holy Spirit. However, the story also gives us some valuable insights into the method of evangelisation, that is, of bringing people to faith in Christ. As a background to this story, it is useful to bear in mind that Jews and Samaritans despised each other. Samaritans were descended from the Jews but they had allowed inter-marriage with pagans and were, therefore, regarded by the Jews as having compromised their religion and therefore "unclean". The Samaritans, for their part, accepted only the first five books of the Jewish Bible, rejecting all the prophets and wisdom books. Moreover, while the Jews worshipped in the Temple in Jerusalem, the Samaritans worshipped on their own mountain, Mount Gerizim. Jews, therefore, had very little to do with the Samaritans. Given such a background, it is wonderful to see the steps which Jesus takes in order to bring the Samaritan woman to faith in Him as the Messiah.

Jesus breaks down the barriers and opens a conversation, despite the fact that she was a Samaritan woman and of questionable morality. Far from despising her, He sees her as a precious human being to be brought to faith and salvation. The first step of evangelisation is to break down the barriers of prejudice and to be willing to reach out to all people.

Jesus takes His starting point the present situation of the woman. She has come to the well seeking water, and so He opened the conversation by asking for a drink. He starts on her wavelength. His unaffected simplicity unnerves the woman and she feels comfortable enough to enter the dialogue. We, too, have to meet people, not where we would want them to be eventually, but where they are at the present, here-and-now, with all their mess. The second step of wavelength is thus to establish a dialogue with the person.

Having opened a dialogue, Jesus then moves her on, step by step, along the journey of faith. His request for water is now followed by an offer of a different type of water which would quench her thirst, not temporarily, but permanently, referring, of course, to the Holy Spirit who was to come. When she expresses interest in this new water, He takes the next step by prophetically revealing her present marital situation, then enabling her to recognise Him as a prophet. Then follows a dialogue on where and how to worship God and Jesus teaches her that true worship depends neither on Samaritan nor Jewish practices, but an altogether new order, namely the worship of the Father in spirit and in truth. Then comes the climactic conclusion of the dialogue when the woman expresses her longing for the Messiah, at which point Jesus intervenes to tell her that He indeed is the Messiah. The woman had finally come to believe in Jesus. Although in this particular story Jesus completes the step-by-step evangelisation of the woman in one simple dialogue, in practice, we may need several conversations and a longer period of time before we complete the evangelisation. We have to meet people where they are and move them gently along at their own pace.

Finally, the woman goes away and brings other people to Christ. Having been evangelised, she herself becomes an evangeliser. Every baptised person, whether man or woman, young or old, cleric or lay, is called to spread the Gospel which he/she has received. The work of evangelisation that needs to be done is enormous. Jesus Himself said that the fields are white and ready for harvest and that the reaping had already begun. His words are timeless. Today there are millions of people thirsting for the living water but look for it in the wrong places. As the Pope reminded us, the potential for evangelisation is enormous indeed. The work of Jesus has now to be done by us. Let us ask today for the grace to be courageous enough to let down our barriers and our shyness and to enter into dialogue with people. Let us meet them wherever they are, and lead them gradually to the joy and belief in Christ.

Lord Jesus, we pray that we may drink anew the living water of the Holy Spirit and so bring others to this spring of salvation.

SHARING CHRIST'S LIFE

Jn. 4:5-42

The poor woman at the well! It seems nothing had gone right for her. Five marriages had come to an end; how they had ended, we are not told. She had apparently given up on her chances of another marriage and was living with a man whom she had not married.

How is it that for some people life seems to work reasonably well, and for others it doesn't seem to work at all? For some life runs smoothly and predictably; they are reasonably happy and have a sense of achievement and fulfilment. Others are restless and discontented with a growing sense of frustration and futility. Why the difference? How do we make life work? This is where Jesus comes in for He is the model of how to live a good life and has the means to make us attain it. What does that involve?

First, there must be a sense of personal responsibility. Unfortunately, in this story we can't hear the tones of voices of Jesus and the woman, nor see the glint in their eyes. They could have embarked on a situation where there was good humoured banter between them as they discussed the drawing of the water. The woman was talking about actual water, whilst Jesus was talking about a spring of spiritual water, namely Himself. She asked to be given it, but Jesus challenged her to see how genuinely she wanted this water.

First, she would have to put her life right. Gently, but pointedly, Jesus confronted the woman with the mess that her life was in. He said, "Go and call your husband." "I have no husband," she replied. Was she being honest with this answer, or was she trying to conceal her private life from a stranger? Jesus, of course, knew the truth. "That's right," He said, "you have had five husbands, and the man with whom you are now living is not your husband." It was a painful experience for her. No one likes to be told home truths, but it made her face the reality of her situation and accept responsibility. There is no other way to get life straightened out. We all have to say, "I am responsible for my own life. My behaviour or my misbehaviour, my action or my inaction are all my own choosing and my own doing. I am responsible for my life."

When we are young, this kind of responsibility does not concern us. Someone else makes the decisions on our behalf. Learning to make our own decisions and take charge of our own lives is part of the maturing process. Until we have learned how to do that we haven't grown up. We cannot go through life looking for alibis and for someone else to blame. As President Harry Truman said, "The buck stops here."

In accepting the truth about her own life, which Jesus revealed to her, the Samaritan woman was made to wonder if Jesus really was the Christ. The first thing she did was hurry back to the town to share her discovery with others. In fact, so strong was her desire to share, that she even forgot her water pot and left it at the well.

What about us? We maintain we know Christ. But are we just as eager as this woman to share our discovery with others? If we do, are we as convincing as this woman? Many believed in Jesus on the strength of her testimony. Is it true that we are 'Christians' for only an hour a week and our lifestyle does nothing to convince unbelievers that we are followers of Christ? If we want to do as Christ commands us, we have a duty to share the good news with others. We can't hoard Christ for ourselves.

St. Paul, too, was conscious of this when he wrote, "I am a debtor both to the Jew and the Greek, to the wise and the unwise." He realised the responsibility God had given Him of bringing Jesus to the whole world.

Now in order to share the life of Jesus we have to acknowledge our need of God's help. The Samaritan woman needed water and went to the well to draw it. There she met Jesus who said to her, "If you would ask Me, I would give you living water; and it would be in you a well of water springing up to eternal life." The word to stress is 'ask.' He was saying to the woman, "If you need Me and depend on Me, ask, I will add an eternal dimension to your life, helping you to lead a well ordered life." Some people find it very hard to ask Jesus for help. This could be for several reasons, pride, a sense of independence, fear of rejection or being misunderstood. Jesus makes the same offer to us as He did to the Samaritan woman, and like her, we need to take up His offer.

Lord Jesus, the story of this Samaritan woman tells us that we all have a need. The need is to lead a happy, well ordered life. The only one who can help us obtain this is You. You are waiting for us to ask for Your help. You will offer us eternal life, the living water. Once we've drawn from this well, You will help us share this water with others.

THE MIRACLES THAT TOOK PLACE AT JACOB'S WELL

Jn. 4:5-42

I shall never forget my visit to Jacob's well. It was a very special moment in my life – to stand in the very spot where Jesus stood talking to the Samaritan woman, and to read the story as recorded by St. John.

On their way from Jerusalem to Galilee, Jesus and His disciples were passing through Samaria. They stopped at Jacob's well for water. Jesus rested there while His disciples went into a nearby town to buy food. While He was alone there, a Samaritan woman came to draw water. Jesus asked her for a drink. She was amazed and asked, "What? You are a Jew and You ask me, a Samaritan for a drink?" The ensuing conversation was lengthy and full of surprises. Jesus suggested that He could give the woman "living water," and she responded, a bit sceptically, that she would welcome anything that kept her from having to come to the well for water. As they continued to talk, Jesus revealed His awareness of her chequered history with men. This revelation of her past surprised her and insisted he must be a "prophet." She said, "Our fathers worshipped on this mountain, while you say that Jerusalem is the place where one ought to worship." Jesus told her a day was coming when both Jews and Samaritans would worship "in spirit and in truth." She said, "I know that the Messiah is coming and He will explain everything to us." Jesus said, "I Who am speaking to you am He." Later she would say to her friends, "Come, see a man who told me everything I ever did! Could He be the Messiah?"

Have you ever discovered, to your surprise, that someone knew you in a way, and to a degree, that you would never have imagined? It may have been a friend, a parent, a colleague, or a spouse. You were astounded that this person understood you so completely, almost better than you knew yourself. It created a miraculous bond between you and this person. You had the joyful sense of being fully known. Someone had cared for you enough to look deeply into your soul and see the essential truth of your identity. Such intimate knowledge seems a miracle.

The enmity between the Jews and the Samaritans was intense. Jews saw Samaritans as "half-breeds." Years before, when great numbers of Jews had been taken into captivity, captives from other nations were relocated in Palestine to live among the remaining Jews. Intermarriage was inevitable. Samaritans were the progeny of Jewish intermarriage with foreigners. To mingle their pure Jewish blood with the blood of Gentiles was unforgiveable to Jews!

Samaritans lived in Samaria, an area between Galilee to the north and Judea to the south. Pious Jews travelling between Galilee and Judea would not pass through Samaria lest they come in contact with the Samaritans. This would add significant time and distance to their journey. Jesus, however, chose to pass through Samaria.

The woman at the well could not believe this Jewish teacher took such an interest in her. Neither could she believe the kindness of this Jew. He was not judgmental, even about her personal history. He reached across the chasm between Jew and Samaritan in everything He said. He accepted her for who she was. She concluded that He must be the Messiah.

To be loved and respected is a universal human need. Our personal sense of worth is greatly affected, one way or another, by how others relate to us. We have recently heard reports of "bullying" in our schools, some leading to the victim's suicide. On the other hand, acceptance by one's peers is a major source of self-esteem. If you have ever found acceptance where you expected it least and needed it most, you know what a miracle of grace it can be.

If the story from John 4 ended here, it would be sufficiently inspiring and satisfying. But there is more. The woman's claims to her town's folk struck them as the truth. Immediately they left the town and went to find Jesus. Meanwhile, the disciples had returned to Jesus. Now that they had food they encouraged Him to eat. But Jesus responded by saying, "I have food to eat that you know nothing about....My food is to do the will of the One who sent Me and to complete His work." Then He encouraged them to see how ripe the fields were for harvesting. They must have wondered what He meant. They did not know what miracle had already occurred at Jacob's well.

Another miracle was in progress. The Samaritans from the town arrived at the well. They already believed in Jesus because of the woman's testimony, and they implored Him to stay with them. He did, for two days, and their lives were changed. They said, "We know that He really is the Saviour of the world."

Miracles often begin when one person perceives the true nature and needs of another. Acceptance is an act of grace, in which someone is affirmed and loved despite their faults and failures. Reconciliation is the goal of Christ for us all, so that love reigns in the world. Such miracles happened once at Jacob's well.

Lord Jesus, help us not to be judgmental, but to accept people where they are and for You to help us to lead them to You.

FOURTH SUNDAY OF LENT YEAR A

(Five sermons)

WILL THE BLIND SEE?

Jn. 9:1-41

I think physical blindness is a terrible affliction, but is it worse than spiritual blindness? Today's Gospel touches on both kinds of blindness. Let us consider the following examples:

One man brushes his young daughter away when she wants to show him her artwork. "Don't disturb me! Can't you see I'm trying to watch Match of the Day".

Another father who is physically blind is so overwhelmed by his love for his daughter that he writes the song, "Isn't She Lovely" in her honour. His name is Stevie Wonder.

Which man truly sees his daughter? Which man is blind?

Here are two more examples. A man ignores his wife's pleas for attention. She wants to know if he still thinks she is attractive. She wants him to listen to her hopes and her hurts and share a greater intimacy with him. All he wants to know is has she washed his shirt for work.

Another husband, a blind man, who loves his wife so dearly writes her a love song, "You are so beautiful to me. You're everything I hoped for. You're everything I need. You are so beautiful to me." His name is Ray Charles.

Which man truly sees his wife? Which man is blind?

Our Gospel text features this very same irony concerning blindness in its various forms. A man is born blind, but is healed by Jesus. Pharisees are born sighted, but are spiritually blind. This text asks us, who is really blind? What kind of blindness is hardest to heal?

Notice first the man who was born blind. In the days of the Gospel, blindness from birth was considered the most difficult blindness to heal. The disciples are so overwhelmed by this man's predicament that they ask, "Who sinned, this man or his parents?" Surely, they thought, some terrible sin is behind such a severe punishment! Jesus brushes aside such idle speculation, and the theology behind it which assumes that all human suffering is the direct result of God's punishment for sin.

Jesus wants the man to see so He spits on the ground and with the mud makes a paste, smears it on his eyes. He tells the man to wash in the pool of Siloam. However, his healing is not complete. Jesus wants him to have insight, not just sight. He still must come to know about Jesus, the One who has given him sight. Only then will he become a witness for God, and learn to give God glory for his sight. By the end of the chapter, he truly sees.

The blind man had lived in a world of perpetual darkness. Never in his life had he seen the light of day. This gift of sight must have been an indescribably wonderful moment. Instead what should have been an occasion of joy became a storm centre of debate.

Now let us take a look at the Pharisees. These men were the respected holy men of the community. They tried to obey the Law of God to the letter. They studied and explained the scriptures. When the man who was born blind was healed, the crowd brought him to the Pharisees. They would surely be able to interpret this miracle. At first, the Pharisees were divided in their opinion. They genuinely struggled to understand the miracle. The man who was blind did not even know who had healed him, much less the significance of Jesus' call to faith. The Pharisees began their investigation by first interrogating the parents of the man. They wanted to see if the healing might be a hoax. The parents were afraid to get involved. If they showed any sign of siding with Jesus they could be expelled from the synagogue. They suggested questioning their son who had been healed. The man who now sees is not afraid to be honest with them. He says, "It is unheard of that anyone ever opened the eyes of a person born blind. If this man were not from God, he would not be able to do this thing." This made the Pharisees really angry. They were offended that a common man like Jesus could heal. They were also offended that a common man like the formerly blind man would dare to instruct them on the ways of God! Instead of conducting a serious search for truth, the Pharisees clung to their own version of the truth. By the end of the chapter, they were hurling insults at the man, shutting their ears to his testimony, and throwing him out of their presence. The Pharisees become increasingly blind throughout this story. By the end, they are clinging to their spiritual blindness, eyes tightly shut.

When Jesus heard what they had done to the man He found him. How pleased He was to hear this lonely man, after He had revealed to him whom He was profess, "I do believe, Lord." Then Jesus had the last word, "I came into this world for judgement, so that those who do not see might see, and those who do see might become blind."

All the signs were there that Jesus had given sight to this blind man and yet the Pharisees would not believe in Jesus. How true is the old adage, "There is none so blind as he who will not see." Surely the blindness of the Pharisees is the hardest blindness to heal. They just did not want to see!

Lord Jesus, because of our sins to some degree we are spiritually blind. Forgive us our sins and heal our spiritual blindness.

WHAT JESUS DID FOR THE BLIND MAN

Jn. 9:1-41

Most of us are blessed with reasonably good eyesight and we often take this for granted until we start having problems with our vision. What must it be like to be born blind like the man in the Gospel? He lived in darkness, never seeing a ray of light, let alone the bright sunshine. What did colour mean to him? How did he visualise shapes and sizes in God's created world – trees, birds, animals and, above all, people? Perpetual darkness prevented him from experiencing the fullness of reality.

What a pleasant shock it must have been in today's Gospel story for the man born blind to have his eyes opened by Jesus for the first time and to behold the world around him. We marvel at Jesus giving sight to the blind man, but we must not forget that John the evangelist wants us to appreciate the more spectacular cure that took place that in opening the man's eyes he recognised Jesus as the Messiah – the Anointed One. This is exactly what happened in our Baptism. We were born spiritually blind in the darkness of Original Sin. Just as the man's blindness in the Gospel story was not the result of his personal sin, so also the spiritual blindness with which we were born was not the consequence of any personal sin. We simply inherited it, and that is why it is called Original Sin. It was in Baptism that, for the first time we experienced the saving power of Christ. The spittle which Christ used to anoint the blind man in the story is a symbol of the Holy Spirit. Spittle is a fluid released from a person's mouth, and similarly when Jesus breathed His last from the Cross, the Holy Spirit was released on mankind. In Baptism, we were anointed by the same Holy Spirit who destroyed the darkness of Original Sin and opened our spiritual eyes to behold Christ, the light of the world, symbolised by the lighted candle.

The story of the Blind Man's encounter with Jesus has remarkable parallels with the story of the Samaritan woman's encounter with Jesus about which we heard in last Sunday's Gospel. The stories tell us the way Jesus brings people to believe in Him as the Lord, and they show us the steps which we also can use, as evangelising, to bring people to faith in Jesus.

Jesus meets the person at a wavelength which is tuned in to his/her particular need, rather than start talking about Him as the Messiah. Catholic missionaries in poor countries will agree that you have to fill people's stomachs first and then their souls. The Samaritan came to draw water so Jesus asks her for a drink of water. The blind man's immediate need was sight, so Jesus began by curing his blindness. Having thus gained an entry by reaching out to meet him in his physical need, He now gently moves from the physical to the spiritual plane, by turning his focus round on Himself. Here, we have beautiful turnaround: having asked the woman for water to quench His thirst, He then offers her living water to quench her spiritual thirst. Similarly, having anointed the blind man to open his physical eyes, Jesus then opens the man's spiritual eyes to recognise Him as the Anointed One.

The person's journey towards Jesus has now begun, and grace moves the person very gradually to make the final confession of faith in Jesus. During the course of the dialogue the Samaritan woman recognises Jesus first as a Jew, then as a Patriarch, then as a prophet and, finally as the Christ. Similarly, the Blind Man in the presence of his neighbours acknowledges Jesus first as His healer, then in the presence of Pharisees he acknowledges

Jesus as a prophet, then a second time before the Pharisees he declares Jesus to be His Master, and finally in the presence of Jesus Himself he acknowledges Him as the Son of Man and worships Him. In both cases, that faith journey is now complete.

The person who has come to faith in Jesus, now goes away joyfully and proclaims Jesus to other people by his/her own testimony. But here, sadly there is a difference between the postscripts of the two stories. Whereas, the Samaritan people were humble enough to listen to the woman's testimony and come to Jesus, the Jewish Pharisees were too proud to accept the Blind man's testimony and so refused to come to Jesus. The scene ends with Jesus's remark on this paradoxical irony: the man who was once physically blind now has spiritual vision; but the Pharisees who have physical vision are still spiritually blind. Pride blinds a person's spiritual eyes and prevents him from recognising Jesus.

Today, we reflect on the marvellous work which the Lord did for us at our Baptism when He cured our congenital spiritual blindness called 'Original Sin'. When we were anointed by the oil of catechumens and washed in the Baptismal waters, the Holy Spirit came down on us, opening our spiritual eyes to recognise and accept Jesus as our Lord and Christ. The light of Christ enables us to tell the good from the evil and so to live according to God's way.

However, as we go through life, the sins that we commit become like growths of cataract which obstruct our vision. That is why God has given us the Sacrament of Reconciliation. Our spiritual cataracts are regularly removed by the Holy Spirit in this Sacrament and we are healed by our Lenten practises of prayer, fasting and almsgiving.

Lord Jesus, give us the grace to keep our spiritual vision clear from the darkness of sin. And having had our vision restored, let us seek to bring others also to this light, by meeting them where they are and by accompanying them, step by step, on their journey to You.

THE PERILS OF A KNOW ALL

Jn. 9: 1-41

A familiar proverb says, "Knowledge is power". I'm sure we have all experienced the truth of this saying. If your car won't start and you don't know what the fault is, you are helpless. At this moment for you the 'strongest' man in town is the car mechanic. His knowledge is strength. The same is true in the medical profession. If you fall ill and can't help yourself, we hope a doctor who knows what is wrong and has the medicine will cure you. At that moment he is the strong one because of his knowledge.

It is true that knowledge is power. The more we know, the better prepared we are to cope with the problems and challenges of life. But there is another proverb given to us by William Shakespeare. "A little knowledge is a dangerous thing." His meaning is fairly obvious. A doctor who thinks he knows so much that he never questions his own diagnosis nor seeks the counsel of a colleague, poses a serious threat to the health of his patients.

It is important for us to know everything that we possibly can, but it is also imperative that we recognise the limitations of our knowledge. Today's Gospel reading tells us about a group of men who failed to make that distinction. They were knowledgeable, but they overestimated the extent of their knowledge. They had learned a little but assumed they knew everything. That erroneous assumption cost them dearly. It slammed the door of discovery in their faces and locked it tightly. They lived at the same time as Jesus, the greatest Teacher our world has and will ever know and they learned nothing from Him. They were too busy protecting their little store of knowledge to open their minds to any new insights. All they could do was to bicker about the proper observance of the Sabbath. As a result their lives were a tragedy.

Ignorance is not the primary hindrance of knowledge, arrogance is. People who are ignorant, and know it, can learn. People who know little and think they know much are almost impossible to teach. I smiled when I heard of the student who had completed his study of physics. One day, unknown to him he sat next to Albert Einstein, the greatest physicist of the twentieth century. He asked him what his profession was. Einstein said, "I teach physics." The student replied, "I finished that subject last year!" There was the great Einstein still learning more about his subject while this upstart had hardly scratched the surface.

St. Luke wrote of Jesus when He was 12 that He steadily grew in wisdom, age and grace before God. Obviously like any normal child He was still learning, still growing in wisdom. But I think that statement could have been said of Jesus at any point in His life. He never ceased to be a learner. Jesus involved His followers in on going formation. He taught them for as long as He lived, and when He left them He had this to say, "I have much more to tell you, but you cannot bear it now. When the Spirit of Truth comes, He will guide you into all truth". (Jn. 16: 12-13) Jesus clearly did not think that He had spoken the final word. He did not close the door of truth. He opened it and left it ajar. The only way that door can ever be closed again is for us to slam it in our faces, by the incredible arrogance of knowing too much. This is what the Pharisees did to themselves.

This attitude also destroyed their relationship with other people. They were so sure of their knowledge that they would not tolerate any opinion that differed from their own. The man who was born blind told them that Jesus had opened his eyes, and explained how He had done it. They should have praised and thanked God for such a miracle, instead all they could say was "This Man cannot be from God: He does not keep the Sabbath." The Pharisees were not prepared to accept what Jesus had done and so excluded the man who had been cured from the temple. That is precisely how an ignorant and arrogant person behaves.

Think of how many hearts have been broken and relationships ruined by that kind of dogmatic certainty. The father in a family makes his opinion known on a given subject. After that, no other opinion will be tolerated. Many a young person has left home too soon, because of that very attitude. An owner of a business has his own way of doing things, and is not open to improvements   Many a company has lost employees because of that attitude. Whatever our role in life may be, we should be careful of knowing too much. It could cost us the greatest knowledge of all – the privilege of really getting to know other people.

How true are the words of that Jewish prayer:

"From the cowardice that fears new truth,
From the laziness that settles for half-truth,
From the arrogance that thinks it knows all truth,
O God of Truth, deliver us."

LIGHT FOR THE BLIND

Jn. 9:1-41

The Feast of the Tabernacles is the last of the three great Jewish festivals and in Jesus' time involved a ceremony of lights. Giant candlesticks were erected in the temple's Court of the Women. The light was so bright that every courtyard in Jerusalem was said to be illumined. On this occasion Jesus declared, "I am the light of the world. Those who follow me will not walk in darkness, but will have the light of life." (Jn. 8:12)

Some people cannot bear to be wrong. When something bad happens, rather than examining their own possible culpability, they almost instinctively look for someone to blame. Blaming is for many a way of avoiding the truth about themselves.

Today's Gospel lesson centres around a man who was blind from birth. It was believed that the cause of human suffering was sin. Someone who was born with an affliction, therefore, presented a problem. The rabbis maintained that either the person's parents sinned, or unbelievably the person sinned in the mother's womb! When Jesus found the man born blind, the disciples asked him who was to blame for it. Jesus responded by saying neither was responsible, but that the man's blindness was an opportunity for the works of God to be seen.

Jesus' response may have had more than one meaning. First, since Jesus was clearly saying to His disciples that assessing blame for this man's blindness was inappropriate, isn't it possible that He was also saying that sin is not the only cause of suffering? Second, was Jesus suggesting to his disciples that locating blame was not the solution to every problem? The "blame game" remains a way of closing our eyes to the truth both about others and about ourselves.

Forty-five million people in the world are blind. The leading causes of blindness are age-related conditions (such as cataract, glaucoma, and macular degeneration) and uncontrolled diabetes. These causes are increasing. Blindness caused by infection, however, is decreasing. The World Health Organization estimates that three-fourths of all blindness can be prevented or treated. There is ever-increasing hope for those who suffer from one of humankind's most tragic plights.

On the other hand, physical blindness may not be the worst form of blindness. It is largely a practical problem. The eyes and the brain work together to create sight. Different parts of the eye function in unison to focus on light and images. The eyes then use special nerves to send what you see to your brain, and the brain processes and recognizes what you are seeing. All this happens almost instantly. When this marvellous system fails, however, all is not lost. With the loss of sight the other senses - - touch, hearing, smell, taste - - do their best to compensate. Today, in addition to Braille, there are devices that read out loud what is written on a page. With special equipment the sightless person can read almost anything. The blind, far from being denied self-realization, often out-achieve the sighted. They have excelled in music, the arts, and athletics. Some of the noblest and most gifted individuals in history were blind. Many of them saw things the rest of us have never seen.

Physical blindness, in many cases, is less serious and less of a handicap than the wilful blindness of those who will not to see the truth. Physical blindness does not necessarily limit a person's spiritual horizons or imagination or aspirations. But the blindness of ignorance, of bias, and of narcissism can be intractable and permanent without some kind of inner transformation. There are none so blind as those who will not see. This is a complex issue, and it is not simply a matter of spiritual sight or spiritual blindness. All of us, even the most open-minded of us, have blind spots, areas where we cannot or will not see objectively. Faithful followers of Christ must continually pray for clearer vision, and for a willingness to see the truth.

Jesus healed the man who was born blind. What followed, however, was a series of complications that almost drove the poor man out of his mind! Those who knew him would not believe he was the same person. Those who did not know him would not believe he had really been blind. And even his parents were afraid to vouch for him. In the end, when the authorities had cast the poor man out, Jesus found him and blessed his faith. "For judgment I have come into the world," said Jesus, "that those who are blind may see, and those who (claim to) see may become blind."

This entire episode rests on Jesus' claim to be "the light of the world." Christ's light does indeed reveal the truth to those who genuinely seek the truth, and Christ's light exposes the blindness of those who claim to possess the truth. Jesus makes this clear in his final words to the Pharisees, the blind ones who cannot see their own blindness!

Lord Jesus, sight, physical and spiritual, is a gift from God. Far from condemning the blind to remain in his condition, You took the initiative in giving both physical and spiritual illumination to a helpless victim who could not escape the darkness through his own efforts. The gift of sight is still available to those who confess their blindness and receive the true light, the Light of the world.

FIFTH SUNDAY OF LENT YEAR A

(Four sermons)

I AM THE RESURRECTION AND THE LIFE

Jn. 11: 1-45

Lazarus, the brother of Martha and Mary, and the friend of Jesus was sick. He must have been seriously sick for his sisters deciding it was necessary to call Jesus to come and see him. They found out where He was and through a friend conveyed this message to Him. You would have thought that Jesus would go immediately but He let two days go by. Instead He let valuable time go by, two valuable days. Jesus knew what He was doing. He was going to teach Martha and us that He was the Resurrection and the Life.

Martha and Mary were dreadfully upset that their brother had died and Jesus had not come immediately. In today's Gospel, apart from each other on different occasions, they both said the same words to Jesus, "If You had been here our brother would not have died." They knew Jesus had cured so many people at their request; He would surely have saved their brother, Lazarus, His friend. Why didn't He? Jesus obviously had something in mind.

Eventually Jesus approaches Bethany. Martha realises this and hurries to meet Him. Her first words to Him were, "If you had been here my brother would not have died." I think there is a hint of her reproaching Jesus for not coming sooner. Jesus did not pursue her train of thought for He wanted to elicit from her belief in the Resurrection. He said, "Your brother will rise to life." Then Jesus pronounced those immortal words, "I am the Resurrection. Anyone who believes in Me, even though that person dies, will live, and who lives and believes in Me will never die." Martha appreciated the depth and meaning of these words and made her tremendous act of faith, "I do believe that you are the Messiah, the Son of God, who was to come into the world." It was through the Holy Spirit that she was able to make this profession of faith.

After this Martha went to her home and calling Mary aside from the visitors who had come to mourn with her she said, "The Master is here and is asking for you." Jesus must have thought it strange that Mary had not rushed to meet Him. It was only then on hearing that Jesus was asking for her, she ran to meet Him. On meeting Him she said exactly the same words as her sister, "Lord, if you had been here my brother would not have died." She wept as she said these words and her grief so touched Jesus that He asked where Lazarus had been buried. The people who had followed Mary said, "Come and see." It was now that Jesus shed tears and the people remarked, "See how much He loved him." Others said, "He gave sight to the blind man, could He not have kept Lazarus from dying?"

When they arrived at the tomb Jesus told them to remove the stone from the entrance of the tomb. Martha never realised what Jesus was about to do for she said that the tomb would be smelling for Lazarus had been buried four days ago. Jesus reminded her, "Didn't I tell you that you would see God's glory if you believed?" Now Jesus thanked His Father for listening to Him. He said, "What I am about to say is for the people's sake that they may believe that you sent Me." He then cried out in a loud voice, "Lazarus come out." To the surprise of all Lazarus got up as if from a sleep and Jesus ordered the burial bands to be removed from him.

The Gospel story ends with the words, "Many of the people who had come to visit Mary (there is no mention of Martha) saw what Jesus did and they believed in Him.

Lord Jesus, we wish to conclude this wonderful story by using the very words of Martha, "Jesus, I do believe that you are the Messiah, the Son of God, who was to come into the world." May we all one day rise from the dead like Lazarus and share in Your risen life.

ONLY JESUS CAN BRING US TO LIFE

Jn. 11:1-45

Among the many amazing miracles of Jesus the raising of Lazarus ranks as the most astonishing and pre-eminent of all. The Jews believed that the soul of a dead person somehow remains in the body for three days, after which corruption sets in as it finally departs. This is why Martha objected to the opening of the tomb, "Lord, by now he will smell; this is the fourth day" (Jn. 11:39).

She is expressing the common view that this was now a hopeless situation. Is this the reason why Jesus delayed coming immediately? He wanted it to be a hopeless case! To raise a person back to life, who has already been dead four days and decaying, is as unthinkable as the prophet Ezekiel's vision in which the dry bones of the dead are miraculously restored to life.

For the early Christians the story of the raising of Lazarus was more than a reference to the resurrection of Jesus. For them this miracle is a challenge never to give up hope even in the hopeless situations in which they find themselves as individuals, as a church or as a nation. With God nothing is impossible. It is never too late for Him to intervene. God can bring about the impossible and so often He wants to use our co-operation in bringing this about.

The co-operation Jesus needed for this miracle was the faith of Martha, as is clear from His words to her were, "I am the resurrection and the life. If anyone believes in Me, even though he dies he will live, and whoever lives and believes in Me will never die. Do you believe this?" "Yes, Lord," she said, "I believe that you are the Christ, the Son of the living God, the One who was to come into the world."

Having been assured of her faith He now proceeds to perform the miracle. But we see that Jesus still needs more human cooperation. He issues three commands and all of them are obeyed to the letter. The first is, "Take the stone away" although Jesus had the power, by one word, to remove the heavy stone from the entrance of the tomb. Why didn't He? He wanted to elicit their faith, not only of Martha but also her friends.   If they did not believe they would not have co-operated. Their attitude could have been that we will not do this for the body is already in the process of decay and it is a waste of time. How right C. S. Lewis was when he wrote, "God seems to do nothing of Himself which He can possibly delegate to His creatures."

His second command is directed to the dead man, "Lazarus, here! Come out!" The dead man came out. Lazarus obeyed and with difficulty in the dark made his way to the entrance of the tomb, shuffling along for his body as well as his legs were bound with cloths.

The third command is addressed to the people, "Unbind him, and let him go." Even though Lazarus did his best to approach the entrance of the tomb, there was no way he could unbind himself. He needed the community to do that for him. By unbinding Lazarus and setting him free from the death bands the community is accepting Lazarus back as one of them.

Many Christian individuals and communities today have fallen victim to the death of sin. Many are already in the tomb of hopelessness and decay, in the bondage of sinful habits and attitudes. Nothing short of a miracle can bring them back to life in Christ. Jesus is ready to perform that miracle. He Himself said, "I have come that you may have life and have it to the full" (Jn. 10:10). Are we ready to co-operate with Jesus for a miracle? Are we ready to take away the stone that stands between us and the light of Christ's face? Are we ready to take the first step to come out of the place of death? Are we ready to unbind, that is forgive, one another and let them and us go free? These are the various ways we co-operate with God in the miracle of bringing us back to life and reviving us as individuals, as a church and as a nation.

Lord Jesus, just as you raised Lazarus from the dead, we ask you to forgive us all our sins and raise us to new life in You.

LAZARUS

It is a great thing to give living water to quench the thirst. It is an even greater thing to open the eyes of a man who was born blind. However, physically speaking, nothing can compare with opening the tomb of a dead man and raising him to new life, which is what Jesus did in today's Gospel story.

Death is the ultimate mystery before human wisdom and ingenuity bow in silent awe. It is the furthermost boundary of human experience beyond which the senses cannot penetrate. The grave, as a place of darkness, decay and smell, aptly symbolises all that death entails. Therefore, in reaching beyond the veil of death and bringing Lazarus to life, Jesus gives us the sign that he is the Lord of life. This was a prelude to the ultimate and definitive sign Jesus would give in His resurrection. The raising of Lazarus is thus seen to be a symbolic fulfilment of Ezekiel's prophecy that God will open the graves and raise the dead and is, in turn, a prophecy of Jesus' own impending resurrection and the eventual resurrection of all who die in Christ.

The story of Lazarus is certainly a spectacular miracle at the physical level, but it also speaks to us at the deeper, spiritual, level about what Baptism accomplishes in our lives. The power of Christ coming to us through Baptism, gives us a spiritual resurrection from the death of original sin to which we were all subject. This new life in Christ which began with our spiritual resurrection at baptism will be brought to fulfilment in the physical resurrection which is promised to us after our death, at the end of time.

Another purpose of the story is to tell us something about the identity of Jesus. This is expressed through the title which Jesus gives to Himself. To describe Himself, Jesus uses the prefix "I am" and appends to it the particular title which emerges from the theme of the story. Last Sunday, in the story of the cure of the man born bind, Jesus referred to Himself as "I am the light of the world." Today in the story of the raising of Lazarus, Jesus calls Himself "I am the resurrection." Now we know that "I am" was the sacred name by which God revealed Himself to Moses at the burning bush. Therefore, in applying the title, "I am the light of the world" and "I am the resurrection", Jesus is emphasising His status as God, whose different attributes are revealed by their various titles.

The stories we have heard in the Gospel over the past three Sundays also show how the people involved in each are led to make a personal confession of faith in Jesus. The Samaritan woman was led, step by step, to acknowledge Jesus as Messiah, that is, Christ; the man born blind, after his cure, finally worshipped Jesus as the Son of Man. In today's story, Martha, when questioned by Jesus whether she believed in Him, confesses her faith in Him as "the Christ, the Son of God, the One who was to come into this world." These stories invite us also, his disciples, who were washed, enlightened and raised to life in Baptism to make a personal testimony of belief or confession in Jesus.

This story includes one of the instances in the Gospel where Jesus openly expressed His emotions? We are told that Jesus wept; He was so overcome by distress at the death of His friend Lazarus and the sight of Mary's tears. He uttered a sigh which came from the depths of his heart. This is a symbolic expression of how passionately Jesus weeps for every person who is imprisoned in the tomb of sin. Then, just as He called Lazarus to come out, He calls the sinner to come out from his living death. Finally, He instructs the Church to unbind the sinner and let him/her go free, a task which the Church faithfully performs in his name through the Sacraments, especially Baptism and Penance.

As we reflect today on the raising of Lazarus, let us pray that we, too, may be released from whatever sins may imprison us. Let us be reassured that the Spirit of God which raised Jesus from the dead will raise us also to everlasting life, since the Spirit rests in our hearts through Baptism and the other Sacraments

WHY GOD'S WAYS ARE MYSTERIOUS TO US

Jn. 11:1-45

The most difficult question for any of us to answer is "Why?" A priest visited a young mother who had just received the doctor's diagnosis - she had leukaemia and was given two years to live. The mother looked at her three small children playing in the front room and simply said, "Father, why?"

Life is fraught with mystery. Everywhere the same question arises. Why war? Why starvation? Why disease? Why earthquakes? Why floods? Why is human suffering and heartbreak manifested in a thousand different ways?

Some of these things are under human control. War is the result of greed and hatred. There is no need for starvation if we share the resources that God has given us. He created a perfect world in which there was no hunger, disease nor conflict. These came into the world as a result of sin. So, if we want to eliminate these horrors from our world, we have the answer: just keep the Commandments of God!

But what about natural disasters beyond our control? Many people ask why God does not intervene to prevent such tragedies. Does He have the answers? Yes He has … but He's not telling us! It is something with which we have to live.

There is good and evil in the world. We should thank God for the good rather than wasting time questioning and complaining about the evil. Let us also remember that there is more to life than just this world. A perfect destiny awaits us after our probation in this world.

The friends of Jesus, Martha and Mary, also asked the question "Why?" They did not understand why Jesus did not come immediately, when they told Him that their brother, whom He loved, was sick.

One reason why we have trouble understanding is because God's timetable is different from ours. When Jesus heard that Lazarus was sick, He stayed where He was for two days. This confused Martha and Mary. They had sent Jesus an urgent appeal for help, believing that He could help and wanted to help, but He arrived too late. Their brother had died. They told Jesus, "Lord, if you had arrived sooner, our brother would not have died."

Have you noticed that when we pray for something, we not only make our request, but we set the delivery date? Is that right? Should we not leave God to deliver the goods when He sees fit? We must understand that Heaven's clock is different from ours. We operate in the realm of time; God operates in the realm of eternity. Simon Peter wrote, "One day with the Lord is as a thousand years and a thousand years as one day." God never has too little time. He is always right on time. So when we request something from God, we must be patient. Our prayer will always be answered, but always in God's way and that is not necessarily as we would want.

Another reason why we do not understand is because God thinks differently from the way we think. We can only see our way. God has a panoramic view of life. Spread out before Him is the total picture of history. If we fail to understand all God's ways it is because our human intelligence is finite and limited, so God's ways are bound to be mysterious to us. We experience life one event at a time. We must be patient and try to understand that God's thought processes are different from ours. He knows everything and sees everything in one glance.

Again, we do not understand because God's working methods are different from ours. When Jesus arrived in Bethany, Martha said to Him, "Lord, if you had been here my brother would not have died." She knew Jesus had the power to save him, so why waste time? But Jesus had something else in mind. He was not just intending to cure Lazarus - but to raise him from the dead.

Look at the loss to humanity if the Lord had accommodated Himself to Martha's method. Thousands of people have been able to face death because of these words Jesus spoke once Lazarus had died, "I am the Resurrection and the Life. He who believes in me, though he is dead, yet shall he live. And whoever lives and believes in me shall never die." In raising Lazarus from the dead Jesus demonstrated His power over life and death.

I remember a conversation a young boy had with his father. "Dad, I think God made some mistakes when He made the world." What made him say that, he asked. "Well, take for example this oak tree. It's big and strong and its fruit is a tiny acorn. Now look at that tiny plant, how frail it looks and its fruit is a huge marrow. You would have thought it would have made more sense if the marrow had been the fruit of the oak and the acorn the fruit of that frail plant." At that very moment a slight breeze stirred the oak tree and an acorn fell and hit the boy. He rubbed his head, smiled and said, "Dad, thank God, it wasn't a marrow!"

Lord Jesus, there is much we can learn from the story of the raising of Lazarus. It teaches us that You are in control. Although Your ways may seem mysterious to us, they make sense because You know everything and You know what is best for us. This is why we can confidently place our future in Your hands.

PALM SUNDAY

HOW FICKLE ARE WE

IN OUR COMMITMENT TO CHRIST?

There is a stark difference in today's two readings from Saint Mark: what happened that Jesus went from being hailed a King to the chants of "crucify Him" within just a few days? It is the story of how fickle people can be as the initial joy fades into the distance and they willingly followed Him on the death march to Calvary.

The first reading tells us about the joyful entry of Jesus into Jerusalem riding on a donkey. The people there are overjoyed and hail Him as their King. He gets the "red carpet" treatment with cloaks and palms jubilantly strewn in His path. We are given the opportunity of joining them, too, as we parade either around the Church or its grounds with our single palms and singing to our King.

Then in the reading of the Passion the mood changes. The King that we hailed is now degraded to the level of a criminal. The waving palms are replaced with whips, spitting and insults. The donkey is no longer there to support Him. He now has to carry a heavy cross that rubs through His skin and on to His shoulder bone, causing what Jesus told one saint was the most excruciating pain He physically felt in His Passion. The crowd are now leading Him out of Jerusalem to Golgotha, the place of execution.

The priest encourages the people to join in reading the Passion by saying the words of the people. Some do so vigorously shouting, "Crucify Him! Crucify Him!" The priest knows they don't mean it. They are play acting but He tries to imagine how those words must have affected Jesus when He first heard them. We wonder could this possibly have been the same crowd who had only five days earlier shouted, "Hosanna to the Son of David!" We know the Lord Jesus is always the same yesterday, today and forever, but this crowd's action shows how fickle people can be.

Today we begin the greatest week in Our Lord's life. If you and I really care for Jesus and want to thank Him for all He has done for us and is still doing, we will want to follow Him every step of this journey from His triumphant entry into Jerusalem to His rising from the dead. In this week we shall witness the deep suffering of Jesus which involves severe physical pain, keen emotional stress and acute depression. He accepted all this because He wanted to be obedient to His Heavenly Father and save every one of His sinful brothers and sisters who had strayed from God's love. He also wanted to fulfil the Will of His Father and be that Perfect Creature to love Him in return. It would be a tragedy if we could be in Church with Jesus during this week and we are not. Don't let the next time Jesus sees you in Church be on Easter Sunday. Be with Him all through the week in His greatest moments of love.

Holy Spirit, give me the wisdom to understand that the events in Jerusalem almost 2,000 years ago were the most important in human history, and inspire me to show my gratitude to Our Lord for what He accomplished by participating in the Church services of this Holy Week.

HOLY WEEK

THE MOST IMPORTANT WEEK IN OUR LORD'S LIFE

This is the most important week in Our Lord's life when He gave Himself to us in the Holy Eucharist and died for us so that we could live with Him forever in heaven. What part are you and I going to play in this week? Are we going to try and be as close to Jesus every moment of this week or is this week going to be just another ordinary week and the next time Jesus sees us in church will be next Sunday? On behalf of Jesus I am appealing to you to make this a HOLY week and not just an ordinary week?

Today we celebrate Palm Sunday when Jesus rode triumphantly as the Messiah into Jerusalem upon a donkey. I don't think Jesus ever rode upon a donkey. It was His custom to travel the length and breadth of Palestine on foot. Today, Palm Sunday, He showed unmistakably that He was the Messiah. He told His apostles to go to a village and there they would find an ass tied, on which no man had yet sat. They were to loosen it and bring it to Him. Jesus was doing this because the prophet Zechariah had written, "Rejoice, daughter of Zion! Shout with gladness, daughter of Jerusalem! See now, your king comes to you: he is victorious, he is triumphant, humble and riding on a donkey, on a colt, the foal of a donkey." (9.9) So when Jesus entered Jerusalem on a donkey He was symbolically indicating to the people He was the Messiah.

Spontaneously His disciples placed their garments on the donkey's back. Some even spread their cloaks on the road to show their reverence. Others cut down branches from trees to wave them in the air to express their joy and at the top of their voices they cried, "Hosanna! Blessings on the King of Israel." Hosanna in the Aramaic language means 'Save us!' They welcomed Him as a king, national liberator, but Jesus is not a political liberator. If He was He would be riding a horse, an animal of war, not a donkey, an animal of peace, docility and humility.

Today, we are amongst the crowd laying palms on the road and cheering Him with shouts of "Hosanna!"

But TOMORROW we witness Mary Magdalene anointing Him with ointment in preparation for this burial. We hear Jesus warning His friends, "You will not always have Me with you."

On TUESDAY Jesus acknowledges that two of His friends, Judas and Peter, the first will betray Him and the second will deny knowing Him.

On WEDNESDAY, which is called SPY WEDNESDAY, Judas negotiates with the Chief Priests a price for betraying Jesus.

On HOLY THURSDAY we are with Jesus at the Last Supper when He ordains His first priests and gives us the Blessed Sacrament as His parting gift. From the Last Supper we watch Him make His way to the Garden of Gethsemane and going through that mental torment of what He was to suffer the next day. He was afraid and prayed in anguish to His Father, 'Take this cup away from Me; nevertheless, let Your will be done, not Mine."

On GOOD FRIDAY we witness Him unjustly condemned to death. We join His mother Mary as He begins that painful journey to Calvary. We see Him stripped, nailed to His cross between two thieves. There He hung for three hours before He died. There He proved how much He loved us. "Greater love has no man than to lay down his life for his friend."

On HOLY SATURDAY we wait with Mary our Mother and long for the day of Resurrection, Jesus' triumph over Satan, sin and death. There is one ceremony we just can't miss, and so many do, and that is the Easter Vigil when we celebrate the Resurrection of the Lord. At this ceremony we want to congratulate Jesus and thank Him for all He did for us. It is sad to see how few attend this service. This is the greatest ceremony of the whole year in our Church.

Satan is going to be very busy very craftily tempting us not to come to Church this week. He will find very good excuses for us not to come to Church. When He does, just tell him to go back to hell because we want to be close to Jesus. By being close to Jesus this week, we can make this coming week not an ordinary week but a truly HOLY WEEK. Only then we shall be able to enter fully into the triumph of Easter Day.

HOLY WEEK

HOW FICKLE ARE WE

IN OUR COMMITMENT TO CHRIST?

Mk. 11:1-10 & 14:1-15,47

There is a stark difference in today's two readings from Saint Mark: what happened that Jesus went from being hailed a King to the chants of "crucify Him" within just a few days? It is the story of how fickle people can be as the initial joy fades into the distance and they willingly followed Him on the death march to Calvary.

The first reading tells us about the joyful entry of Jesus into Jerusalem riding on a donkey. The people there are overjoyed and hail Him as their King. He gets the "red carpet" treatment with cloaks and palms jubilantly strewn in His path. We are given the opportunity of joining them, too, as we parade either around the Church or its grounds with our single palms and singing to our King.

Then in the reading of the Passion the mood changes. The King that we hailed is now degraded to the level of a criminal. The waving palms are replaced with whips, spitting and insults. The donkey is no longer there to support Him. He now has to carry a heavy cross that rubs through His skin and on to His shoulder bone, causing what Jesus told one saint was the most excruciating pain He physically felt in His Passion. The crowd are now leading Him out of Jerusalem to Golgotha, the place of execution.

The priest encourages the people to join in reading the Passion by saying the words of the people. Some do so vigorously shouting, "Crucify Him! Crucify Him!" The priest knows they don't mean it. They are play acting but He tries to imagine how those words must have affected Jesus when He first heard them. We wonder could this possibly have been the same crowd who had only five days earlier shouted, "Hosanna to the Son of David!" We know the Lord Jesus is always the same yesterday, today and forever, but this crowd's action shows how fickle people can be.

Today we begin the greatest week in Our Lord's life. If you and I really care for Jesus and want to thank Him for all He has done for us and is still doing, we will want to follow Him every step of this journey from His triumphant entry into Jerusalem to His rising from the dead. In this week we shall witness the deep suffering of Jesus which involves severe physical pain, keen emotional stress and acute depression. He accepted all this because He wanted to be obedient to His Heavenly Father and save every one of His sinful brothers and sisters who had strayed from God's love. He also wanted to fulfil the Will of His Father and be that Perfect Creature to love Him in return. It would be a tragedy if we could be in Church with Jesus during this week and we are not. Don't let the next time Jesus sees you in Church be on Easter Sunday. Be with Him all through the week in His greatest moments of love.

Holy Spirit, give me the wisdom to understand that the events in Jerusalem almost 2,000 years ago were the most important in human history, and inspire me to show my gratitude to Our Lord for what He accomplished by participating in the Church services of this Holy Week.

EASTER

(Seven sermons)

THE LORD HAS TRULY RISEN

I find no difficulty in believing in the Resurrection. I think I can say I presume that by seeing so many of you in Church today, more than on any other Sunday in the year, you too believe that on Easter Sunday Jesus rose from the dead. We believe that on Good Friday Jesus was crucified, He died, He was buried and on Easter Sunday He rose from the dead. We have seen people die but we have never seen anyone rise from the dead, so what makes you and me believe in the Resurrection?

I find it hard to believe how anyone can disclaim the Resurrection of Christ. It is not only recorded in   the Bible it is mentioned in historical documents. We were not around when William the Conqueror invaded England in 1066, but we firmly believe this took place, simply because it is recorded in history books and that's good enough for us. Yet, there are still people who will not believe it.

I can't go along with the suggestion of some people who say that His followers made up the story of the Resurrection. It is true to say that His followers never expected Him to rise from the dead. Even though Jesus had told them not once but several times that He would be crucified, and He had always added, that on the third day He would rise. As soon as He started telling them about His suffering and death, they did not want to hear such talk and so they blocked their ears and did not listen to what followed that He would rise on the third day. They were like children whose parents tell them that one day they will die and then they will miss them. Children who love their parents don't like to hear them speak like that and so they block their ears. So we can say truly that the Apostles did not expect Jesus to rise. Nobody was more astonished than they were! The Crucifixion distressed and frightened them so much that they hid themselves in the Upper Room. Two of the women who loved Him so much brought spices to anoint His body after the Sabbath. Mary Magdalene who loved Him so much sobbed her heart out. She would have done anything to believe that He had risen from the dead. She thought someone had stolen His body. What about the Apostle Thomas? When the ten Apostles together told him that the Lord had risen, he would not believe. He had to see Him with his own eyes and touch Him with his hands. This was what he demanded and Jesus accommodated him. It was then that Thomas made his memorable act of faith, "My Lord and My God". That's how it all happened and how it is recorded in the New Testament.

So did Christ's disciples invent the story of the Resurrection? Why would they do that? Why would they spend the rest of their lives preaching something they didn't believe and eventually die for? It doesn't make sense. All I can say is that they must have been utter foolish men and women to spend their lives not only preaching about something that never happened but to die a martyr's death for it. In fact I think that one of the greatest proofs that Jesus had risen from the dead is the extraordinary transformation of Jesus' followers. From being frightened, timid men they became courageous and died for the cause of Christ.

Let us look at St. Paul who was the greatest preacher of the Resurrection. He was an enemy of Christianity. There was a time when he would have wiped out, from the face of the earth, everyone who followed Christ. What happened to him to make him travel the length and breadth of the known world preaching Christ crucified and Christ risen from the dead? Let him tell us himself in his own words. He wrote in his first letter to the Corinthians, (15:3-8) "Christ died for our sins…on the third day He was raised to life…He appeared to Cephas, and later to the twelve, and next to five hundred of the brothers at the same time, most of whom are still with us…then He appeared to James, and then to all the Apostles. Last of all He appeared to me." It was Paul who wrote, "If Christ be not risen, then our preaching is in vain." Surely this evidence alone is enough to make someone who doubts the Resurrection believe that Christ did rise from the dead? Yet people who know this still deny this historical fact. You could claim that there is no single historical event that is better documented than the Resurrection of Christ.

For many of us it was our parents and teachers who taught us that Christ rose from the dead. We loved and trusted them and believed that they would not lead us astray. Since then our reason has backed the faith we had in the Resurrection and is something we can never deny.

We cannot end these words without thanking Jesus today for all He suffered for us and for thanking the Father for raising Him from the dead. The Resurrection is the Father's approval of all His Son said and claimed. Let us conclude with an act of faith. "The Lord has truly risen. Alleluia."

THE NEED TO RENEW OUR FAITH

I never cease to be fascinated by John's account of the Resurrection of our Lord. To read it is to come away with the inescapable impression that it was written by an eyewitness. There is no laboured attempt at proof, just one man's version of what happened. The details are so graphic that it could only be told by someone who was there.

First, John remembers that Mary Magdalene came to him and Peter early on Sunday morning, just before dawn. She had been to the tomb. Obviously, she could not sleep. Sorrow can induce one of the worst forms of insomnia. When you're grieving in the middle of the night, it seems the day will never come; and you are not at all certain that you even want it to. So Mary got up before daylight and went to the grave. Not that that would do any good; that was just where she wanted to be. But on arrival at the grave she made a terrifying discovery. The tomb was open. The stone had been rolled away. Though Mary was frightened she got close enough to see, even in the darkness, that the body of Jesus was gone. Her immediate thought was that the body had been stolen. Someone, for some indescribably sick reason, has stolen the body of Jesus. At this point she hurried to tell the sad news to Peter and John.

Next, John remembers how he and Peter started out to run to the tomb. For a time they ran side by side; then John began to forge ahead. He was younger and probably in better condition and so got there first. He stood there in the half darkness, bent down, looked into the tomb and tried to figure out what happened. Then Peter arrived, and in typical fashion went straight into the tomb, and John followed him. There is no suggestion that they had a lantern; so by this time, there must have been enough light for them to see. Mary was right; the tomb was empty. Nothing was there but the grave clothes. That empty tomb and those grave clothes did something transforming to John. In one place, was the winding sheet, and in another was the cloth that had been about His head, neatly folded and laid aside. None of this gave the appearance of people in a hurry. If grave robbers had carried away the body of Jesus, why would they take the time to remove the sheet that enfolded Him? Why would they neatly fold the head cloth and lay it in another place? There was only one answer; Jesus had risen through the clothes. The robbery theory somehow didn't hold water.

At this point, John, speaking about himself said, "He saw and believed." This was the recorded profession of someone's belief that Jesus had risen from the dead. Some people find it easier to believe than others. John was one of those people. He had not yet seen the risen Lord nor talked with anyone who had. He did not even understand the scriptures that prophesied His rising. All he had was an empty tomb and some abandoned grave clothes. Yet, "He saw and believed."

Wrapped up in that four-word sentence is a world of meaning. It speaks of more than a conviction concerning the resurrection. John, obviously, is saying that standing there in that empty tomb, he arrived at the conclusion that Jesus had risen from the dead. But that is not the total story. For John to believe in Jesus was nothing new. At one point in his life, he had believed in Him so strongly that he forsook everything, his family, a secure job in order to follow Him. Then as the weeks and months went by, he had come to believe in Him more and more. The way that Jesus lived seemed right. The things that He taught made sense. The kind of Man that He was seemed the most real thing in all the world. John's total conviction about God, about life, and about himself had come to revolve around Jesus. In Him was the rhyme, the reason, the reality of everything. Jesus was more than just a friend. He was Truth in the midst of confusion. He was Light in the vast sea of darkness. He was the Eternal Life of God surrounded by human mortality. Then came that fatal day on Calvary, John's faith was dealt a mortal blow. When Jesus died, everything John believed in was shaken to the core.

Then standing there in that empty tomb, "He saw and believed." John is telling us that his faith in Jesus was validated and renewed. All of the things that he hoped for and believed in came rushing back. Life turned right side up again. He had not been misled after all.

That is precisely what you and I need this Easter morning – not simply to believe in the objective truth of the Resurrection, but to have our faith in Jesus and the things for which He stands renewed. This world has a way of playing havoc with the principles in which we try to believe. As one of our Christmas carols puts it, "Hate is strong, and mocks the song of peace on earth, good will toward men." How can one keep on believing in Christ in the kind of rat race that modern life represents? Everything that He stands for gets shoved aside, trampled on, crucified almost every day that we live.

Let's face it – most of the time we are afraid to trust Him, lest we make fools of ourselves in the process. He talked about loving our enemies, turning the other cheek, going the second mile. Where is the place for those kinds of things in this kind of world? The only thing that applies here is the law of the jungle, the survival of the fittest. Try to turn the other cheek in a business deal and see how far it gets you. This is a dog-eat-dog kind of world; and those who do not face that fact either get run over or left behind.

Let's be honest: isn't that how we really think most of the time? This world did to Christ the very worst it could. It rejected His Truth and nailed Him to a cross, but on the third day He overcame it all, even death. John saw and believed. That is what you and I need this Easter Sunday – a renewal of our faith.

CHRIST IS RISEN, ALLELUIA

If you were visiting Rome on Easter Sunday at 12 noon you would probably be among thousands of pilgrims in St. Peter's Square to receive the Easter blessing from the Pope and hear him proclaim the Easter message, 'Christ is risen, alleluia.' This message goes out on television and radio all over the world in many languages. The Pope is confirming the faith of those fortunate ones who are able to listen to him. This is precisely what Peter, his predecessor, did on that first Pentecost day in Jerusalem.

Peter was doing what the Lord had asked of him during the Last Supper when He said, "Simon, Satan will sift you like wheat; but I have prayed for you, that your faith may not fail, and once you have recovered, you in your turn must strengthen your brothers." (Lk. 22:31-32)

What faith Jesus had in Peter, especially when we remember how cowardly he behaved during His Passion! At the Last Supper Peter boldly said to Jesus, "Even if all the others should lose faith in You, I will never lose faith in You." To make an outburst like that in front of his fellow apostles showed how serious he was. He thought his friendship of Jesus was so strong that nothing would stop him standing up for Jesus no matter what others might do to Him. Within a couple of hours of making that bold statement Peter would show signs of his weakness. Jesus took Peter, James and John to be His companions in the Garden. He needed them to be close to Him as He faced the mental torture of what He would have to endure the following day. What comfort were they to Him? All they could do was sleep off a heavy meal. Jesus had to drink His cup of sorrow alone.

That was just the beginning of Peter's display of weakness. Later that night when Jesus was captured and was being tried before the High Priest, Peter was in the courtyard warming himself. Someone turned to him and said, "Aren't you one of His? Weren't you with Him in the Garden?" Peter denied he ever knew Jesus. Soon after this He couldn't even face a maid who challenged him that he was one of Jesus' followers. Three times that night he denied he had anything to do with Jesus. Then the cock crew. At that moment Jesus walked through the courtyard and looked at Peter. Peter realised just what he had done. He had denied His friend. In that look Peter knew he was still loved by Jesus and He had been forgiven for his weakness. Immediately he ran and ran until he could run no further, and wept bitter tears of sorrow.

That had to be the lowest point in his life. He had to face the fact that he was not the brave and strong man that he thought he was. He realised Jesus knew him only too well. That look of Jesus was indelibly printed on his mind. It told him how much Jesus still loved him and was convinced he had been forgiven. He knew Jesus always looked for the good in people and there was a better side to weak, fickle Peter. After the resurrection when Jesus asked him three times, "Do you love Me?" in front of his fellow apostles he was assured that Jesus had not regretted making him the leader of His apostles.

Yes, Peter was the rock on which Jesus had built His Church. Jesus prayers were heard because Peter was the one who was to strengthen the faith of his brothers. In the Upper

Room on the feast of Pentecost, where the Last Supper was held, we witness him acting as the leader and going forth and preaching that Christ had risen.

Peter has become a favourite saint for many a sinner. Like Peter we keep falling into sin and repenting. Every time we go to Confession we admit our sorrow and affirm with God's help we will not sin again, and yet we go on letting our Lord down time and time again. But as we hear the beautiful and most consoling words of forgiveness in Confession, let us try to visualise Jesus looking into our eyes as He looked at Peter, with love and forgiveness and compassion, and seeing the saint that He expects us to be and can be.

Lord Jesus, today has to be the greatest day of the year in the Church's calendar, so let us unite with all Catholics and Christians all over the world, being led by Pope Francis, and proclaim, "Christ is risen, alleluia."

PETER'S FIRST EASTER SUNDAY

My name is Peter, an Apostle of Jesus Christ. It is Easter Sunday afternoon and I am in the room where He had His last meal with us. I cannot believe so much has happened since then. I feel an utter failure. I have such mixed emotions.

When Jesus needed me and the rest of us, we let Him down. I did make some effort in the Garden when I cut off the ear of one of those who had come to apprehend Him but after that I was so scared. With John I followed Jesus as far as the court of the High priest. I was curious to know what they would do to our Master and would have liked to help but what good would I have been? There were so many of them and they were determined to eliminate Jesus. I was so weak. I cannot believe I even denied to a maid that I had no knowledge of Jesus! After my three denials a cock crew. He looked at me and I wept bitterly. But in that brief look I could see how much Jesus still loved me, and I knew He understood my weakness and was offering me forgiveness.

How Jesus endured all that suffering I shall never know. I could not believe my ears when I heard the crowd in Pilate's courtyard shout, "Crucify Him! Crucify Him!" Why didn't I defend Jesus at that moment? I did love Jesus, but I was so frightened. Jesus, as He stood before Pilate, was a broken Man. He had a crown of thorns on His head and a soldier's cloak around His shoulders. The soldiers must have mocked Him as a king. John related to me the events of the Passion. Jesus could hardly carry the heavy cross they laid on His shoulders. They had to force a man called Simon from the crowd to help Him carry the Cross to Calvary. In excruciating pain He hung for three hours before He died. How I wish I had been stronger like John and stood at the foot of the Cross to let Him know I cared and to bring some comfort to His mother. Since His death, I and the rest of the Apostles have lost all reason for living. He was our reason. For three years we followed Him day and night. We never let Him out of our sight. We hung upon His every word. Now what will we do without Him?

I spent Saturday evening with John. In the early hours of Sunday morning Mary of Magdala and another woman found us and told us the unbelievable news that the tomb was empty, and that they had seen an angel who said that Jesus had risen. John and I ran as fast as we could to the tomb. John got there before me but he let me enter the tomb first. It was just as the women had said.

The religious and Roman authorities had killed Jesus and now we will be their next target. I rallied the rest of the Apostles to the Upper Room, because I thought there will be safety in numbers. Here we are behind locked doors listening to every step on the stairway. All of us are here except Thomas and are wrapped in our thoughts. If only we could have Him here with us now! He would put new life into our hearts. He would bring us peace.

As Peter was having these thoughts he was startled. Jesus came through the locked doors. "Peace be with you!" We could not believe what we were seeing and hearing, and He greeted us again. "Peace be with you!" He then breathed on us. I could see what He was doing. Just as God at the beginning of creation breathed life in the Earth, Jesus was breathing life into us dead men. Then to assure us that He had not only forgiven us for the way we had treated Him, He also gave us the power to forgive others their sins. "Receive the Holy Spirit, whose sins you shall forgive they are forgiven; whose sins you shall retain they are retained."

Peace, the Holy Spirit and forgiveness of sins were Jesus' three Easter gifts to the Apostles, and they are the same gifts He gives us this Easter day. Like Peter there have been times when we have not lived up to the standards Jesus has set us. Like Peter we must trust that Jesus has forgiven us and on this day is giving us another chance to prove our love for Him.

Holy Father, may the peace of the Risen Christ and the friendship of the Holy Spirit envelop us today as we begin to celebrate the Easter season.

CHRIST OUR HOPE HAS RISEN

I love the way the Church unfolds the drama of Holy Week, the greatest week in the life of our Lord. Mary Magdalene, unknown to her, was anointing the feet of Jesus for His burial. Then follows the betrayal of Judas and the denial of Peter. On Holy Thursday we witness the Last Supper when Jesus washed the feet of His disciples, instituted the Holy Eucharist and ordained His first priests, and finally on Good Friday His Crucifixion and Death. On Holy Saturday the whole Church is in mourning and quietly awaits His Resurrection. The Church is bare, altars are stripped, the tabernacle is open and empty and before it is the crucifix telling all that Jesus is dead. Even the water fonts are dry. Because Christ is dead even the Sacraments of Reconciliation and of the Sick are not administered unless it is absolutely necessary. Then slowly the Church comes to life. Altars are covered, flowers decorate the church, the Paschal Candle take centre stage. At sunset or at midnight begins the Easter Vigil with the lighting of the fire and Paschal Candle and the deacon proclaims, "Christ the Light!"

There is one thing I can't stress enough at this point. Why is it taking years for people to appreciate that this ceremony is the most important one in the year and is so poorly attended in so many of our Churches? How I, and all priests, would love to see people making the effort to come and our churches being full to capacity.

It is however good to note that more people go to Mass on Easter Sunday than on any other day of the year. Some only go to church on Easter Sunday. It reminds me of a Vicar who would say at his Easter address. "I know I won't be seeing the majority of you until next Easter so I shall take this opportunity to wish you all a very Merry Christmas!"

It is sad that today there are many people who do not believe in the Resurrection of Christ. St. Paul says it all when he writes, "If Christ is not risen then our faith is in vain." Christ foretold that He would rise on the third day. "I shall destroy this temple and on the third day I shall raise it up." Of course the temple that He was referring to was His Body. If He had not risen He would be a fake and we would be fools to follow Him. His rising was proof that He was God. He already proved He had power over death by raising from the dead Jairus' daughter, the widow's only son at Naim and Lazarus. Before Lazarus was raised He told Martha. "I am the Resurrection." Having raised these three people from the dead why should we doubt that He could do the same for Himself. The Resurrection was the Father's stamp of approval of all His Son had done.

We all agree that the greatest mystery of our faith is the Blessed Trinity, Three Persons in one God. We also agree that high on the list of our beliefs is the fact of the Resurrection of Christ. Every Sunday together we recite, "On the third day He rose again" and we go on to say, "We look for the resurrection of the dead." We can all recite those words because we celebrate the Resurrection of Christ today.

Whenever I look at the crucifix I prefer to see the crucified Christ which reminds me of His love for us and how dreadfully we treated Him. But when I see in modern crucifixes the Risen Christ it says to us that Christ who died for us, conquered death and proved to us that He is God, our High Priest.

People we love die, but we know that it is not the end of them. I feel really sorry for those who say when our loved ones die it is the end. We won't see them again. I just can't imagine my parents just being a memory to me and nothing more. I am convinced that we are all immortal and that we will rise again and we shall meet again. When, please God, we get to Heaven, after the ecstatic joy of meeting the Blessed Trinity, Our Lady, the saints and the angels, it is my firm belief that we shall meet our parents. I, like you, can't wait for the loving squeeze I am going to give my Mum and Dad. We can talk like this because today we believe Jesus rose from the dead.

Today we can conclude by saying, "Thank you Heavenly Father for giving us Your Son and raising Him from the dead. Thank you Jesus for the example of Your life, for becoming Man, leaving yourself with us in the Holy Eucharist and for dying for us on the Cross."

Lord Jesus, may we never think lightly of our sins which crucified You and may we never forget what You did for us.

We also want to thank Mary, our blessed Mother, for the part she so generously played in our redemption. To see her Son suffer to the extent He did must have cost her dearly. It was that suffering that earned her the title, "Queen of Martyrs."

I wish you all the joys, peace and blessing of our Risen Lord.

SOME THINGS NEVER DIE

A man of sixty had gone back to visit his home town. One of the places he looked forward to seeing was the primary school he attended more than fifty years ago. While driving to the site, he planned his stroll down memory lane. He would start by finding his first classroom, where at the age five he had begun school and then work his way through the other classes.

But this sentimental journey never took place. When he arrived at the site, he discovered that his old school building was no longer there. It had been demolished, and a brand new one had been built in its place. He found himself thinking about the transient nature of life - how nothing ever stays the same. Communities change. Buildings are here today and gone tomorrow. People live and die. Even nations rise and fall.

Then he remembered how in that red-brick school house he had learned the multiplication tables. $2 \times 2 = 4$; $3 \times 3 = 9$; $4 \times 4 = 16$ and all of the rest. He had learned those when he was only a boy. But fifty years later, they were still true. And five thousand years into the future, they would still be true. Though the old school building was gone, there was at least part of what he had learned there remained. Simple arithmetic deals with ideas that are so basic that they never change. Time cannot erode them, and death cannot erase them. This means that in some ways we live in an eternal world right now. Generations will come and go. Empires will rise and fall. But in every one of them, 2×2 will always equal 4. They always have, and they always will. That simple little formula, which we all learned in childhood, belongs to a realm where death has no authority.

In a sense, that is the essence of our Easter faith. We are saying that Jesus lived the kind of life that transcended the power of death. His adversaries could kill him, which indeed they did, but they could not stop Him. As Peter said in his sermon in the house of Cornelius, "They killed Him, hanging Him on a tree, only to have God raise Him up on the third day." Our Gospel reading says, "Jesus had to rise from the dead." It was imperative. It was inevitable. He belonged to that eternal realm where death has no authority. Some things never die.

To think of death this way provides the only reasonable starting point for believing in immortality at all. If nothing in this world lasted, why should we think that anything in the next world will? But that is not a true picture of life here and now. Many of us have said a final earthly farewell to our fathers and mothers. Some of them have been dead and in their graves for years. But the love that they gave to us did not die with them. It is still a vital part of our lives. The love that we felt for them is not in the grave. We love them just as much today as we did when they were alive, perhaps even more. Love has an eternal quality. Death can take the lives of those we love, but it cannot touch our love. That belongs to a realm where death has no authority.

That is what we mean by our Easter celebration. We are not saying that death makes transient lives immortal. We are saying that what is eternal is eternal and for that, there is no death. This building, in which we are worshipping today, will someday be gone and completely forgotten. Not one trace of it will remain, but the one whom we worship here will always be the same. The quality that He gives to our lives will abide forever. It is a kind of living with which death has nothing to do. Some things never die.

To believe this is, of course, an act of faith. It cannot be proven, but it is a reasonable act of faith. If this is not the way life is, it is surely the way life ought to be. There should be something that death cannot destroy. There should be at least a few things that remain. Consider the alternative. If death was the end for our ancestors, then death will also be the end for you and me, and our children, and our children's children. Someday, the last generation will die and the earth itself will also die.

On that point, all of science is agreed. This earth is not eternal. It had a beginning, and it will have an end. Some think it will burn up, and others think it will freeze up, but all agree that it will come to an end. When that happens, this great human adventure will be over. What Bertrand Russell predicted will have come true, "All the labours of the ages, all the devotion, all the inspiration, all the noonday brightness of human genius are destined to extinction in the vast death of the solar system. And the whole temple of human achievement must inevitably be buried beneath the debris of a universe in ruins."

Is that where all of this and all of us are heading? Towards nothing? I cannot prove otherwise, but rational minds rebel against it. I find it hard to believe that faith was born only to be frustrated, that hope was born only to be mocked, and that love was born only to die. I find it hard to believe that nothing lasts except this endless process of not lasting. That could be true, I suppose. But it would not be the work of a rational universe. Something ought to last and the message of Easter is that something that will last forever.

We know that Jesus died. As Peter said: "They killed Him, hanging Him on a tree." But the nails that pierced His hands and feet did not pierce His truth. The spear that was thrust into His side did not extinguish His love. The final spasm of His body may have ended his earthly life but it did not end His soul. "They killed Him, only to have God raise Him up." And He is alive today. Yes, some things never die.

Lord Jesus, we live in a world of rapid change. Things come and go quickly that we feel uprooted. But Easter Sunday is a reminder that there are some things we can count on and that is that the truths of our faith never die.

THE FACTS ABOUT EASTER

1. Jn. 20 1-9

After Jesus had been crucified and buried in the tomb the Apostles were sad and dejected. They were missing their Master and Friend Who had been their Companion for three years. What saddened them was that when their Master needed them most they had failed Him. When they heard the news from the women that He had risen from the dead it came as a great surprise. It shouldn't have because on several occasions Jesus had told them that He would be handed over to His enemies, put to death and on the third day He would rise.

I'm sure you will agree with me that there was only person who expected Jesus rising from the dead and that was His Mother Mary. She believed the prediction of her Son. Although it is not recorded in the Gospels I firmly believe that when Jesus rose from the dead the first person He visited was His mother Mary, thanking her for all she endured with Him and for saying those words, "Behold the handmaid of the Lord, let what you have said be done to me." Those were the words brought Jesus into our world.

I think the reason why the Apostles failed to expect the resurrection of Jesus was because once Jesus told them of His dreadful plight they were heartbroken and did not want to hear what He was saying. They blocked their ears and in doing so they failed to hear what followed, 'on the third day I will rise again'.

When Jesus raised from the dead the three we know, Jairus' daughter, the only son of the widow of Nain and Lazarus He restored their life into their original bodies. But when He rose from the dead on Easter Sunday, He too had the same body but it was a glorified body with supernatural powers, a body that would never die, that would never need food and drink to be kept alive; a body that would never suffer and one that could travel as fast as thought and could pass through doors and walls.

People of all ages and beliefs have wondered what happens to our bodies when we die. The American Indians believed that their dead would arrive at a happy hunting ground and so when they buried their dead alongside their bodies they placed food and supplies for the journey. We all know that shrouds do not have pockets and that when we die we cannot take our possessions with us. The Egyptians may have believed that you could take your possessions with you into the next world for in 1922 when the excavators opened the tomb of Egyptian king Tutankhamen they found buried with him golden treasures. Why would they have buried these treasures if they were no good to him? Imagine the surprise the excavators got when they found that treasure! However, I think the greatest surprise ever to be found in a graveyard was the empty tomb of Jesus. It was a priceless find. Of all the treasures ever found, none can even begin to compare with the discovery of the empty tomb. If Jesus had not risen from the dead, our faith would be in vain. His Resurrection is the hope of our future life. Before the Resurrection of Jesus there was a deep chasm that separated our earthly and eternal life and that was death. Jesus by rising from the dead bridged that chasm. The tomb was no place for Jesus for He was now living. Jesus told His Apostles and us that He would be with us always. Now that He has risen from the dead we can believe that He will always be with us. He will never leave us.

Nowhere in the Bible will you find the word Easter. Yet that is the word we use to name the day of the Lord's Resurrection. The word "Easter" is of Anglo-Saxon origin. It is the word that has worked its way into our liturgy at a later date. It well reflects the spring celebration when nature is reawakened from its winter sleep to grow, bloom and make the world the beautiful place we know it. Jesus rose in conjunction with nature. As long as time will last, the story of the Resurrection will resoundingly echo from generation to generation and its hope-filled joy will reverberate from one century to the next. Jesus is our Hope and Resurrection.

Lord Jesus, we thank You for generously dying on the cross to save us. We thank our heavenly Father for His seal of approval on Your life and raising You from the dead through the power of the Holy Spirit. We thank too Our Blessed Mother Mary for the part she has played in our redemption.

ASCENSION

(Three sermons)

MEDITATING ON THIS MYSTERY OF THE HOLY ROSARY

The second Glorious Mystery of the Holy Rosary is the Ascension. Let us meditate on each Hail Mary of this decade?

First Hail Mary. Jesus, His Mother Mary, the Apostles and the disciples make their way to the Mount of the Ascension. On that mount stands a tiny mosque. On the occasion of my Silver Jubilee to the priesthood I was able to spend the whole of February in the Holy Land. I spent a whole morning just sitting there and thinking about Our Lord's Ascension into

Heaven. Two men were repointing the mosque and chipping away at the plaster. I asked them if they would let me do this for a few minutes so that I could say I helped to repoint this building!

What were the thoughts of Jesus' followers as they made this ascent? Jesus knew what He was doing. It was going to be His farewell to His mother and the friends He had these last three years. I am sure Jesus would have told His mother of His plans. Of course she would miss His physical presence. I don't think His friends knew exactly what was going to take place. Jesus was full of surprises. In a moment He would ascend into Heaven and He was longing to take His rightful place at the right hand seat of His Father. How the angels and saints would be longing and waiting for His presence. We would long to keep Him with us but we must not be selfish. He has left Himself with us in the Holy Eucharist. His work was done and now He deserves His reward. So He was not going to leave us. Where He has gone we must long to be.

Second Hail Mary. Matthew tells us, "When they saw Him they fell down before Him, but some hesitated." Wouldn't we like to be among those who fell down before Him and adored Him? Sadly, after all this time with His followers there were still some who hesitated to give their full belief that they were in the presence of the risen Lord.

Third Hail Mary. Jesus said, "All authority in heaven and on earth has been given to Me." We know that this authority He has invested in His Church. He has given to Peter and future popes the keys of the Kingdom of heaven. Whatever they bind on earth will be bound in heaven. We have that certainty that whenever the Pope teaches us on matters concerning faith and morals he can never lead us astray.

Fourth Hail Mary. "Go, therefore, make disciples of all the nations." These words were addressed not only to the gathering present but to all of Christ's followers. What are we doing to make disciples of all nations? In our own little way by our lives we must draw people to Jesus. We can pray for all those men and women who courageously devote their lives to be missionaries. We pray that their numbers increase.

Fifth Hail Mary. "Proclaim the Good News." What are the ways we can proclaim the Good News? By the way we live our lives at home, at school and at work. Does the way I speak ennoble people's minds or would people never know that Jesus is my Lord and Saviour? Do we miss opportunities of spreading the faith when the occasions arise?

Sixth Hail Mary. "Baptise them in the name of the Father, and of the Son and of the Holy Spirit." I thank God that he has given me the gift of the priesthood and that I have been able to baptise people. I pray for the Capuchin priest who baptised me and was instrumental in giving me the gift of faith. I pray for my parents who brought me to the baptismal font and for the part my godparents played in my life. I pray for all those I have baptised and pray that one day we shall all meet again in Heaven. I ask God to give the gift of faith to my non-Catholic friends, in fact to all unbelievers.

Seventh Hail Mary. "Teach them to observe all that I have commanded you." I pray to the Holy Spirit to help me to be a good preacher and teacher of the faith, that my words will inspire my hearers to lead good Christian lives. I pray for all Christian parents and teachers to enjoy the privilege of handing on the one true faith to their children.

Eighth Hail Mary. "And know that I am with you always; yes, to the end of time." Jesus could not have given us more assuring words that He would never leave us. We can believe that He is with us in the Holy Sacrament of the altar; in the words of the Bible and whenever we are gathered together in prayer. We need never fear that we are on our own or we are lonely because on this day He said, "And know that I am with you always; yes, to the end of time."

Ninth Hail Mary. The Lord ascends into heaven. I like to picture Our Lady and that gathering watching Jesus ascend into heaven. What were their thoughts? Were they sad at His leaving them? In fact they should have been glad to see Jesus going to His well deserved reward. It would be selfish of us to want to keep Jesus here with us. He has done His task on earth perfectly and it is only right that He should be in His rightful place with His Father and the Holy Spirit.

Tenth Hail Mary. He now sits at the right hand of His Father pleading our cause. He is still working for our salvation, wanting us to make a success of our lives and to join Him one day in the home His Father has prepared for us. May a day never go by without us looking up to Heaven and longing to be where Jesus is.

Lord Jesus, when we meditate and pray the Rosary in this manner we can never say that the Rosary is a boring prayer. It unites us with You and our mother Mary and is a powerful force of bringing peace in the world and keeping Satan away from us.

THE END OF A PERFECT EARTHLY LIFE

Lk. 24:46-53

The beginning and end of Jesus' life on Earth was full of incidents. Apart from those three days when He was separated from His mother and foster father how we would love to know how He spent those quiet years of His life. As far as we know the years were uneventful. Today we concentrate on His Ascension into Heaven.

The final three years had been extremely busy. In that period I would love to know how many miles He travelled on foot. I am sure walking those long distances with His Apostles was not a waste of time but used profitably. He was able to have His Apostles all to Himself and He was able to teach them all they needed to know. There was so much they had to learn from Him.

Now He was returning to His Father and they were to take over His work. The success of His Mission depended on how well He had taught them although, of course, all that He had taught them would be confirmed and consolidated by the Holy Spirit, soon to be sent to His fledgling Church.

On the day of the Ascension Jesus, His mother Mary and His followers walked from the centre of Jerusalem to the hill from which He would ascend into Heaven. The majority of those disciples adored Him as their God, but there were still some who hesitated about giving Him full credence. When they reached the top of the hill Jesus had just a few moments left with them. He thought of His loving Mother who would miss His physical presence tremendously. He looked at the 11 Apostles, who would also miss Him. He had to leave them for His work was done.

Now it was for them to continue His very work, to baptise, to teach and lead people to Heaven. He began by telling them, "All authority in Heaven and on Earth has been given to Me. Go, therefore, make disciples of all the nations; baptise them in the name of the Father and of the Son and of the Holy Spirit, and teach them to observe all the commands I gave you. And know that I am with you always; yes, to the end of time." He added, "Stay in the city then, until you are clothed with the power of the Holy Spirit."

When He had finished talking to them He slowly ascended into the sky. They watched Him intently. They had seen Him do many marvellous things, but never this. Then a fleecy white cloud appeared and hid Him from their sight. How did they feel? I am sure there was a tear in Mary's eyes. When would she be reunited with Her Son in Heaven? The Apostles felt that they would be at a loss now that their Master had gone. Those last 40 days had been so strange.

Jesus was with them for a moment and then He would be gone. He would come back unannounced, and again He would disappear. Those days I suppose prepared them for the final time that He would leave them. How we would love to talk to Mary and each Apostle to ask them how they really felt. They would have loved, of course, to have Jesus remain with them. But Jesus' work was done and it was only right that He should receive the reward of a life well spent, returning to His Father in Heaven to be at His Father's right hand. There He continues to be active, pleading our cause, for our sins to be forgiven and waiting for us to join Him. He was still working for our world.

Now Mary, the Apostles and the rest of His disciples had to return to Jerusalem to await the coming of the Holy Spirit, the Spirit of love, who would recall to their minds everything that Jesus had taught them. The Holy Spirit now would be their constant Companion - guiding, strengthening and loving them. Although they were unable to see Him, He would inspire them as Jesus had inspired them.

Those nine days before Pentecost were very important days. They were to look forward to His coming. The more eagerly they desired His presence the more impact He would have on their lives. During that time Peter showed himself their leader, the position Jesus had given Him. He recalled the scriptures and told them that someone was to take the place of Judas. The first election in the Church was held and Matthias became the twelfth Apostle.

During those nine days, they prayed and prayed and prayed. They longed for this Holy Spirit that Jesus had spoken about to come and transform their lives. Their whole attitude could be summed up in words they did not speak but which are so familiar to us, "Come, Holy Spirit, fill the hearts of Your faithful and enkindle in them the fire of Your love."

At this moment in the Church's year we are like them. We have witnessed the Ascension of Jesus into Heaven and now we are awaiting the coming of the Holy Spirit in a fresh way. The Father and His Son Jesus will surely send Him to us. Like the Apostles, if He is to have an impact on our lives, we have to await His coming eagerly. We have to say over and over again, "Come, Holy Spirit. Come to each one of us. Transform us, change us, and mould us to be other Christs." We must all long for His coming.

Lord Jesus, the more eagerly I look forward to the coming of the Holy Spirit, the greater the impact He will have on my life.

UNFINISHED BUSINESS

Mt. 28:16-20

Why didn't Jesus ascend into Heaven on the day of His Resurrection? Why should He wait forty days? Evidently He still had a number of tasks to perform.

He had to be quite certain that the disciples fully understood what they had experienced. If He had left this world on Easter Sunday, their recollection of the event would be hazy. They would wonder afterwards whether they had imagined it all. For example, how many of us remember all that happened on our wedding day or the day of our ordination? Unless we have a video to record it, a lot of the details are very blurred in our memory. We may remember some of the guests who were present, but can we recall the words of the vows we made? It was such an important day in our life, yet we couldn't take everything in. Jesus knew that this was how the disciples would feel at the Resurrection. They would need time to let the full significance of this event sink into their minds. Jesus gave them this extra time so that they could strengthen their conviction and be powerful witnesses.

After His Resurrection He used those forty days profitably doing much unfinished business. He met some of the disciples on the shore of the Sea of Galilee. When they returned from a fishing trip, they found Him cooking breakfast and He greeted them with the words, "Come and eat." He shared the meal with them to prove that He was no ghost.

During those forty days Jesus gave special, individual attention to some of His friends and disciples. He spoke to two of them on the road to Emmaus, firmly convincing them that the Messiah had to die and rise again, as the Old Testament had prophesied. He sealed this truth by revealing His identity in the breaking of bread.

On the very day of His Resurrection, Jesus met His friend Mary Magdalene in the garden. She was grieving over His death, and the disappearance of His body. He knew that her heart was broken and she needed comfort and reassurance that He had truly risen from the dead. Some translations of the Gospel record Jesus' words to Mary as, "Do not touch Me, for I have not yet ascended to My Father." What He was actually saying was, "Stop clinging to Me, as if you want to chain Me to the earth. I'm not going to ascend immediately. We still have some time to spend together." As always, Jesus was being gentle and patient with His friends.

There was unfinished business with Peter. His confidence had taken a hammering. Having boasted before his fellow apostles that he would never desert Jesus, he denied Him three times, and fled from the scene of the crucifixion. How embarrassed and ashamed he must have felt. Jesus especially appeared to Peter not to reproach him, but to heal all his guilt and confirm his position as the rock on which His Church was to be built. Three times He invited him to say, "I love you" and prepared Peter for his future role when He said, "Feed My sheep."

Thomas, too, needed special encouragement. He had been absent when Jesus appeared to the other disciples in the Upper Room, and he just could not believe that Jesus had risen from death. Jesus gave him the very evidence he wanted, to be able to see Him and place his hands in the wounds. Without this personal encounter, Thomas would not have believed in the Resurrection and would never have been able to be a persuasive witness to others.

The forty days were a time of preparation and further instruction for all the disciples, so that they would know what to do once Jesus had left them and returned to His Father. He told them, for example, that they would be able to do the things He had done during His time on earth: healing, reconciling, preaching. They were to remain in Jerusalem and wait for the coming of the Holy Spirit. The Spirit would be their Advocate recalling to their minds everything He had taught them and strengthening them to be His witnesses.

Having completed His teaching, Jesus gathered His disciples around Him and went to the Mount of Ascension. He bade farewell to them with the final command, "Go and make disciples of all nations, teaching and baptizing them." He assured them that even though He would be taken from their sight in a few moments, He would still be with them and always remain with them.

How can Jesus leave us and at the same time remain with us? It's true that He has left this earth and returned to be with His Father but He is no longer subject to the restrictions of a physical body, He can be anywhere and everywhere. As He promised, He remains with us in the Eucharist. He is with us in the words of Scripture and He is with us when we pray together.

Lord Jesus, the Ascension is a proud day in the history of mankind, a day for great rejoicing. For on this day You, our own flesh and blood, took the most exalted place in heaven at the right hand of Your Father pleading our cause.

TRINITY SUNDAY

(Three sermons)

THE CENTRAL MYSTERY OF OUR FAITH

The first Christians were Jews. They were staunchly monotheistic. They believed in one God, but this one God had touched their lives in three different ways. Gradually their understanding of this doctrine grew and developed, that in this one God there are three Persons.

At first they saw God in the natural order of things. The first four words in the Bible are, "In the beginning God." That is the basic assumption of the Church's faith. Everything started with God. He is the One and only eternal Being in the entire universe. His initial act was to create. The earth on which we live was made by Him. The air we breathe, the water we drink, and the food we eat were all made by Him. The stars that shine above us are His handiwork. He also made us. We can see His fingerprints on all of creation, but we can't help but raise some questions, for nature is very diverse.

It includes gentle rains that cause the crops to grow. It also includes floods that can devastate the lives of people. It also includes severe droughts that lay waste the land, and leave people starving. It includes beautiful sunsets and devastating earthquakes. It includes the playful dolphin and the great white shark, which, if given a chance, will devour a person. Small wonder that when primitive people looked through the lens of nature, they saw many gods, some good and some evil. The glory of the Hebrew people is that they saw one God over all creation. For centuries, they recited it in what is called "the Shema". Recorded in Deuteronomy 5:4 it says, "Hear, O Israel, the Lord our God is one Lord." While nations around them recognised many deities, the Hebrews affirmed their faith in the one true God. He was the Creator and Sustainer of all things. He alone was to be worshipped and obeyed.

The fishermen of Galilee had been brought up in this faith. Gradually their understanding of the one true God changed forever when they met a Man named Jesus of Nazareth. He was a man like themselves. He wore the same clothes and spoke with the same accent as other Galileans. But He was different from all other men in that the power of His words and the impact of His personality were almost beyond belief. He was a carpenter by trade and had no more formal education than they did. They had never known anyone like this man. They were drawn to Him. When He said, "Follow Me," they did so unreservedly and left their families and occupations to be with Him.

For three years, He was their constant companion. They observed Him in all kinds of situations. The more they saw of Him, the more they were astounded. When others were small minded, He did not descend to their level. When the people wanted to crown Him king, He rose above personal ambition. When influential people plotted to get rid of Him, He didn't seem to be in the least frightened or embittered. He fascinated them when first they met and as the days went by that fascination only increased. Sometimes they would talk among themselves and wonder aloud, "Who is this Man?"

They became convinced that He had to be the Messiah, the promised Redeemer of Israel. Others who had witnessed the wonderful things He had said and done thought He may be a prophet, but to them He was more than that. One day, Simon Peter spoke on their behalf, "You are the Christ, the Son of the living God." They had become sure of that, but were much less sure of what it meant. Their hopes seemed to be set on some kind of earthly kingdom. When He was arrested and crucified their dreams and hopes were shattered.

Fuller understanding of Who He really was did not come until after His Resurrection. For forty days, He appeared to them over and over again. Slowly, the truth dawned upon them that this Man was more than a man. The one and only true God had laid aside His sovereignty to share their human lot. It was almost more than their minds could grasp. They were soon to discover that there was more to this mystery.

Before Jesus died He had promised them another "Comforter" who would take His place in their lives. He would be with them everywhere and forever. This new Companion was a Person. Jesus told them He would "guide them into all truth." (Jn. 16:13) The promise did not claim their attention at first. As long as Jesus was visibly present with them, that was enough. Once He had ascended into Heaven this almost forgotten promise took on new urgency. They thought of little else. Absorbed in prayer together, they awaited the coming of the Holy Spirit.

He came on the day of Pentecost. His coming came with a mighty wind and tongues of fire that rested on them. The promise was being fulfilled. They knew now that God was living within them. They could all go their separate ways, while God stayed with all of them. Their monotheistic faith was still unchanged. They believed there was one God. They still recited the Shema, "Hear, O Israel, the Lord our God is one Lord." But their understanding of that faith had undergone a profound change. The God who had created and sustained the universe had walked among them. And this God who had once walked among them now lived with them. They now believed that in the One God there were Three Persons, Father, Son and Holy Spirit.

So the early church came to pray, "Glory be to God the Father, God the Son, and God the Holy Spirit."

It is the central mystery of our faith. The Church has taught us to begin and end all our prayers with the words, "In the name of the Father and of the Son and of the Holy Spirit." To remind ourselves of the Three Persons living within us we should cross ourselves not with just our index finger of our right hand, but with three of our fingers.

Let us close with one of the ancient blessing of the Church. Paul wrote it to the Corinthians centuries ago. "May the grace of the Lord Jesus Christ, and the love of God and the fellowship of the Holy Spirit be with you all." Amen.

THE BEST NEWS

Mt. 28:16-20

I was singing in the Galleries in Wigan for the starving in the world and a Muslim approached me. He said, "Is it true that you believe that in God there are three Persons?" I said to him, "You are right in saying that." He said, "Impossible, three into one doesn't go." I said to him, "You're right again, for three into one does not go. But I still maintain in God there are three Persons. I, and all other Christians, can believe that because God has given us the gift of faith. It is the greatest mystery of our faith which we can't understand, nor explain." I am sure he went away thinking that we Catholics are crazy!

I have always loved and admired characters like Abraham, Moses and King David. They believed that in God there was only one Person. God did not reveal to them this intimate detail of His family life. In their days polytheism was rife. If God had revealed to them that there were three Persons in God, pagans would surely think these Jews believed in three gods.

The Apostles were Jews. They had believed from childhood that there was only one Person in God. They had grown up with stories of Creation, the flood, the call of Abraham, the Exodus, the giving of the Law and their forefathers entering the Promised Land. They could look back and see the hand of God in history.

They looked around and saw God in nature. Their view of the natural order was prescientific and far different from ours. They could see God everywhere. When it rained, God was watering the earth. When there was drought, God was punishing His people for their sins. A bountiful harvest was a sure sign of God's favour; a skimpy one showed His displeasure, and a total failure proclaimed His wrath. They could see God in the stars. They knew the Psalm that said, "The Heavens declare the glory of God and the firmament proclaims the work of His hands." Many times in the warm weather at night they had laid on their backs and gazed up at the stars and wondered about God who had created them.

That is how the Apostles first came to know God. Through their own experiences, through the writings of the prophets, they had learned to see His hand in everything. He was back there in history. He was up there in the Heavens. He was in the moral law. He was the Creator and Sustainer of all things.

Then one day their concept of God took on another dimension when they met a Man named Jesus. At first they saw Him only as a Man, but there was something that captivated them so that they wanted to be His followers. For three years they lived with Him. They listened to the things He said. He spoke with authority and conviction and all that He said made sense.

They watched how He lived and the way He related to people. He had such compassion for the downtrodden. He was concerned for the hungry and the health of the sick. He was kind to everybody. When anyone was rude or insulting to Him, He did not fire back in anger. Whenever He saw others being abused, His anger could burn white hot. He lived His life on a high moral plain, but showed sympathy and understanding for those who were stained and scarred by sin. He was so gentle and happy that children loved to be around Him. He was also so strong and confident that He could walk through the midst of an angry mob without being touched.

The more they listened to Him teach, and the longer they watched Him live, the more they were convinced that He wasn't just a Man. He spoke to them about His Father who was God and that He was the Son of God. Then one day Jesus asked them who He was. Peter spoke with the conviction of all their hearts, when He said, "You are the Christ, the Son of the living God."

Finally, they saw Him die, and they had never seen anything like it. But then they saw Him alive again, and knew He had conquered death and the grave. By this time, it was impossible for them to think or talk about God without thinking and talking about Jesus. They had come to know God their Father through His Son. Then the day came when He was taken up out of their midst, and they stood watching Him go. They did what He said and went back into Jerusalem to await the coming of the Comforter. This Comforter came upon them nine days later and they believed that He was the Third Person of God. He was the Holy Spirit Who became such a force in their lives. He gave them strength to spread the Good News that Jesus had taught them. He enabled them to live as Jesus lived. It was they who handed on to us this mystery that in one God there are Three Persons.

I like to think that the first time God revealed this truth of there being Three Persons in one God was to Mary, the virgin of Nazareth. It was in response to Mary's question of how she could bear a Child and yet be a virgin. The archangel Gabriel said to her, "The Holy Spirit (the Third Person) will come upon you, and the power of the Most High (the First Person) will cover you with its shadow. And so the Child (the Second Person) will be holy and will be called the Son of God." I am sure that you will agree with me that it was fitting that Mary should be the first one to know that in God there are Three Persons.

Let us thank God that we Christians and Catholics believe in this Most Holy Mystery of the Blessed Trinity, and we pray that He will give this precious gift of faith to the Muslim who spoke to me in Wigan and his fellow believers. May Almighty God, the Father, Son and Holy Spirit bless you and remain with you forever.

OUR LOVE FOR THE THREE PERSONS IN ONE GOD

Have you ever asked yourself the question, "Do I pray correctly?"

There is a right and a wrong way of praying. I must admit that for many years I could say I went about saying my prayers in the wrong way. I always addressed my prayers to Jesus. Jesus would be the first one to say, "No. I would like you to address your prayers to My heavenly Father." He would continue, "Don't you remember that when I taught My apostles to pray, I did not tell them to pray, 'Dear Jesus,' but 'Our Father.' So strictly speaking all our prayers should be addressed to God Our Father. Where does Jesus fit in? He tells us that we are to go to our Father through Him. "Ask the Father anything in My name and He will grant will grant it to you. "Where does the Holy Spirit fit in? He is the One who motivates us. So we pray correctly when we address our prayers to the Father, through Jesus, His Son, and by the power of the Holy Spirit. Now we know that our prayers aren't just centred around Jesus, but the Three Persons of the Blessed Trinity. Our prayers are not just Christocentric, but Trinitarian. By following Jesus' instructions as to how we pray we cannot go wrong. Jesus tells us, "I am the Way." In other words, "Give Me your hand and I will lead you to the Father."

This approach does not belittle any Person of the Blessed Trinity, but acknowledges their position in the Godhead. We are confirming that the Father is the principal and origin of the Blessed Trinity, that Jesus Christ is His Son and equal to Him, and that the Holy Spirit is also God, equal to both of them. We believe that Jesus was sent by the Father and Holy Spirit to become man, and so make the Godhead visible to us. We believe that the Holy Spirit was sent by the Father and the Son to dwell in us; to sanctify us and draw us to the Father through the Son.

I am sure we all agree that the person who prayed perfectly was Mary our Mother. Jesus, in the thirty years He had spent in her company, must have taught her her unique relationship with the Father. How cooperative she was to the Holy Spirit who motivated her every thought and action. So we can always approach Our Blessed Mother and ask her to teach us how to pray as God wishes.

A lovely habit to form is on awakening every morning to say just two words, "Our Father." Should you have an anxious, hard, worrying day ahead of you, you can leave all your worries in the capable hands of our loving Father. If He cannot look after us, no one can.

Today, without a doubt can be described as the loveliest feast in the Church's calendar. It is wonderful to think that we are temples of God; that the three Persons of the Blessed Trinity live in each one of us. We could literally kneel before another person and pray to God in them. It also means that God lives in me and that is why it is of prime importance that I should give time every day to be alone with and converse with the Blessed Trinity within me. I can remind myself of their presence by making the Sign of the Cross often, especially on awakening first thing in the morning and on retiring to bed last thing at night. I can ask myself, with what respect do I make the sign of the cross? Is it done in a slap dash and hurried fashion or with great love and respect? When I make the Sign of the Cross with my right hand I should use the three fingers, not just the index finger, to remind myself of the Three Persons of the Blessed Trinity Who live in me. It is of prime importance that I should give time every day to be alone with and converse with the Blessed Trinity within me. I can remind myself of their presence by making the Sign of the Cross often, especially on awakening first thing in the morning and on retiring to bed last thing at night. I can ask myself, with what respect do I make the Sign of the Cross? Is it done in a slap dash and hurried fashion or with great love and respect? We can also glorify the Blessed Trinity whenever we say the "Glory be."

It is sad that one beautiful custom has almost disappeared from the Church and that is to ask a priest's blessing whenever he is in your home. Next time a priest comes to your home, don't let him leave without first saying, "Father, may I have your blessing".

I would like to end by giving you that blessing. "May the blessing of Almighty God, Father, Son and Holy Spirit come down upon you and remain with you forever."

CORPUS CHRISTI

(Three sermons)

ALLOWING CHRIST TO LIVE THROUGH US

We want to lead good lives with a desire to be genuinely Christian in a real and practical sense - but doing that requires such strenuous effort that we sometimes get tired of trying. If only there was some way to be spontaneously at our best! But it is often easier to be small-minded, mean and selfish instead of being big-hearted, kind and generous.

We see others struggling as well. Think of some of the Christians we have known. Their lives show the unmistakable signs of stress and strain. They are like a vocalist singing a song that is beyond his range, straining to reach the high notes. They are obsessed with the things they must and must not do.

Happily, however, we have known Christians who seem to practise their faith with such ease. Watching them live is like watching Lesley Garrett when the audience are lost in the joy of her performance. Jesus was like that. Read the stories of His life. He never gave the impression that He was trying to be good. He simply was good. What if there was a way to be more like Him.

Perhaps there is. In today's Gospel reading, Jesus spoke of Himself as "the living bread come down from Heaven". Then He said, "He who eats My Flesh and drinks My blood lives in Me, and I in him." Perhaps that is the answer. We cannot become more Christ-like by just attempting to keep the rules. We cannot become genuinely Christian by willing ourselves to do better. We have tried that, and with some degree of success, but if we allow Him to live His life in and through us, then we can live in a close relationship with Christ and become like Him.

That experience is not as far-fetched as at first it might seem. Most of the finest qualities in our character we caught them from someone else! In Florence you will find Michelangelo's statue of David. It is a beautiful figure, with a physique and posture that are almost perfect. The attendants of the museum say that it is interesting to watch the visitors. Those that stand and gaze for a while at the statue begin to respond. They stand a little straighter. They hold their heads a little higher. Most of them are not even aware that they are doing it. They are simply demonstrating one of the basic laws of life - that we tend to become like the people with whom we associate.

Observe a husband and wife who have had a good marriage for 50 years and more. They love each other very much, and know each other very well. They have also influenced each other very profoundly. Their values, and their feelings, and their thought patterns, are very much alike. Sometimes they finish each other's sentences! When we care about people and admire them, we tend to become like them.

It is not our wills that shape our lives so much as it is our friendships. Make a mental list of the qualities in your life with which you are pleased. Then divide those qualities into two groups - those that you gained by forcing yourself and those that you learnt from your family and friends. Is there any doubt which list will be longer? All of our lives we have been living with other people, and those relationships have been making us what we are. Those people have actually become a part of our lives.

A child who was reared by ill-tempered parents is, more often than not, ill-tempered himself. It will be almost useless to exhort him to control his temper. He is probably already trying as hard as he can to do that, but put him under the influence of someone with a gentle spirit. Let him live in that relationship day after day and without even realising it, he will begin to gain better control of his temper. It is true that we tend to become like the people with whom we associate.

Do you remember George Eliot's story called "Silas Marner"? It was about a hard-hearted, greedy old miser who became a gentle and loving man. It was not because he tried. He had no desire to change but, one day, someone left a child on his doorstep. He brought that child into his home. The little one worked her way into his heart and the child-like qualities of trust and gentleness began to take shape in the old miser's life. He lived in a new relationship and was changed.

We are not likely to have a child left on our doorstep, but we can expect Christ at the door of our hearts. He is there day after day, waiting for nothing more than a welcome. He comes to us through the pages of the New Testament, through the worship of the church, through the Eucharist. If we are tired of trying to live the Christian life, and failing, maybe we need to change our approach. We can enter into a vital relationship with Christ, and allow Him to live His life through us.

Lord Jesus, every time we come to Holy Communion, let us take to heart Your words, "He who eats My Flesh and drinks My blood lives in Me, and I in him." Just trying hard to be good is not enough. It is only by eating Your Body and drinking Your Blood that we will live with You and so become more and more like You and be the good persons we want to be.

HOLY COMMUNION SHOULD BE A FORETASTE OF HEAVEN

What does the feast of Corpus Christi mean to you? It tells me just one thing - how Jesus must love us. Who is Jesus? He is the Second Person of the Blessed Trinity - God. He reigns supreme in Heaven with His Father and the Holy Spirit and yet at the same time it is His ardent wish to live with us and be the food of our souls in Holy Communion. Have we fully realised that truth? That God wants to live with sinful us.

At the Last Supper Jesus said to His Apostles, "I have longed to have this meal with you. "His attitude has not changed. Those words He says to each one of us every time we come to Mass. Our reception of Holy Communion should be the highlight of our week, unless we go to Mass daily and it is the highlight of our day. Today we have to ask ourselves how ardently do we look forward to receiving Jesus in Holy Communion? How fervent are our thanksgivings after Holy Communion?

Another marvel of the Holy Eucharist is that Jesus makes Himself our prisoner day and night all the time. He waits there patiently for you and me to visit Him. Listen to a poem my father used to recite to me. How relevant it is for us today! It is called 'Where were you?' and captures how much Jesus, in the tabernacle, longs for us to visit Him.

I have not seen your face today.

Where were you?

A hundred others came to pray.

Where were you?

From out my prison I have gazed

At thousands who have kneeling prayed.

I wanted you.

I wanted you, you did not come.

Where were you?

I waited there in silence dumb.

Where were you?

Ah, could you not one moment spare.

Ah, surely you have a little care.

I wanted you.

You had no time, ah, so you said.

Where were you?

Where my sad heart in silence bled.

Where were you?

Among your friends long hours you spent

While I my loving heart was rent in solitude.

Tomorrow you will surely come.

Remember I am helpless, dumb, uncomforted.

Think of how excited we are when we plan to see someone we love. And how we treasure the moments we are with them. Is there anyone who is more desirable than Jesus? We will only be able to gauge our love for Jesus by the love we have for Him in the Holy Eucharist. If I hardly visit Him in Church, can I say I really love Him?

We all long to get to Heaven, and please God with His help we will. We shall see Jesus and realise just how lovely and wonderful He is. It is then I think that all of us will regret not having loved Him more on this Earth by spending time before Him in the tabernacle. Let us grow to enjoy Jesus' presence in the Blessed Sacrament. It will make a tremendous difference in our lives and put the pursuit of material things and everything else in perspective.

Lord Jesus, may we make every Holy Communion a foretaste of Heaven and look upon each as if it were to be the last Communion we receive on this Earth. In this way we shall make it our best. You love to hear us say 'I love You' when we have received You in Communion. So many people come and pour out all their troubles, problems and anxieties, but many forget to say to You, 'Jesus, I love You.' May we never forget to say these words to you.

RESPECT FOR THE BLESSED SACRAMENT

What is the greatest treasure our world possesses and the one most neglected and least appreciated? It has to be the Holy Eucharist. For most of the time Jesus makes Himself a prisoner. Patiently He waits for us to use Him or visit Him when we please.

Just listen to the words Jesus said to St. Margaret Mary as she prayed before the Blessed Sacrament. In the Host He showed her His Sacred Heart and said, 'Behold this Heart that has so loved men that it has spared nothing and in return I receive from most men only ingratitude, by their irreverences and sacrileges, and by the coldness and contempt which they show me in this Sacrament of Love. I have a burning thirst to be loved by men in the Blessed Sacrament and I hardly find anyone who strives according to my desire to quench My thirst, by making some return.'

Jesus severely reproached the saint for her lack of respect and attention when she was in the presence of the Blessed Sacrament when she recited the Divine Office and made her meditation. He asked her to render constant homage to Him in the Blessed Sacrament to make up for the hearts which dishonour Him and He told her that He 'desires to be treated as a king in the palace of a king.'

What humility and tremendous love is shown by Jesus that He is entirely contained in this small host which can be carried about by His priest and His Eucharistic ministers. How wonderful it is that Jesus in the Eucharist places Himself completely in the hands of us human beings. At Christmas we marvel at the thought of God the Son becoming man and beginning His human existence in the womb of His mother Mary. We can in some sense compare ourselves to Mary. For whenever we receive Holy Communion we carry the Risen Lord within us. Isn't that a wonderful thought? Yes, when we receive Jesus in our hands, we can say God puts Himself entirely in our hands.

A man, who was not a Catholic, once asked me, "How do Catholics look upon the Eucharist?" I said we believe that Jesus Christ, who is true God and true man is present in what looks like a wafer of bread and wine. He said, "If you Catholics really believed that, you should never get off your knees in Church." How right he was.

I can't remember where it is, but there is a Catholic Church in Britain which is open 24 hours of the day. Priest and parishioners got together and decided to organise a rota so that there are always two people in Church adoring Jesus in the Blessed Sacrament. That's a real demonstration of devotion to Jesus. When you think of it, if we really believe that Jesus is present in the Blessed Sacrament we would want to keep Him company all of the time. How I would love to see that practice in every Church. I would like to be a part of it. Wouldn't you? It could be done. It would only mean giving up, say, half an hour of your time during the day or an hour at night. If there were sufficient dedicated people each one's turn would come around once or twice a week. Is that a lot to give to Jesus who gives us Himself entirely and all His time?

What does it all come down to? Faith. The stronger our belief in the Eucharistic Presence, the stronger will be our love and the more time we will want to spend with Jesus.

Has the stark reality of Jesus in the Blessed Sacrament hit us? That God the Son, the Second Person of the Blessed Trinity, takes on the appearances of bread and wine and lives with us. When we receive Our Lord in Holy Communion we are one with Jesus. Physically the species of bread and wine are absorbed into our blood-stream. Spiritually we share in His divinity. We are in Him and He is in us. When we eat a potato, that potato becomes us, but when we eat Jesus in Holy Communion we are meant to become like Him. We are meant to take on all His characteristics of love and goodness.

Sadly, through lack of instruction, this next bit of information has to be said. Namely, that there are times we are not permitted to receive Holy Communion. When we have committed grievous sin or have not kept the hour fast.

Nowadays you have to spell out what mortal or serious sins are. Let me give a few examples. To miss Mass deliberately on a Sunday is a serious sin. There are some who are surprised when you say this. But a little thought shows just how serious it is. Supposing you were to say to me, "Father, I would love to invite you to an evening meal. Will you come tomorrow at 8?" I looked happy and said, "Delighted, I'd love to come." You really went to town and put on a magnificent meal for me. Wine, cheese, liqueurs, the lot. Nothing was spared. 8 o'clock came and I did not turn up. 9 o'clock, still no Father Francis. You were so disappointed after all the trouble and expense you had gone through. You met me the next day and said, "Father, what about last night, 8 o'clock?" And I said, "O yeah! The meal you invited me to. That's right I didn't make it." No apology, no explanation! I'm sure you would not believe how ungrateful I could be. You would be really hurt.

That's what happens in human relationships. You would have every right to be hurt and expect an apology. Now when we miss Mass what happens? Every Sunday our heavenly Father invites us to a party, the Mass, and the food He gives us is His Son. If, deliberately, we do not attend this party, haven't we hurt Him and doesn't He expect an apology in the confessional? That is why we can't go to Holy Communion without first going to Confession.

Other mortal sins are when we offend our parents or our neighbour in a serious manner. When we have committed adultery, fornication or sins of self-abuse. When we have stolen the equivalent to a person's daily wage. These are just a few examples of many. Just because we come to Mass that doesn't entitle us to receive Holy Communion. We have to try and be as worthy as we can.

Again it needs to be said that we cannot receive Holy Communion in a church of a different faith from ours and neither can a member of another Church receive Holy Communion in our Church. To do so would mean we would have to accept all that their faith teaches. This we cannot do, and neither can they, for the simple reason that Holy Communion is the ultimate expression of one's faith. So you and I cannot receive Holy Communion in an Anglican Church. If we did, we would have to accept that the Queen is the Head of the Church in England and we can't, because we know the Holy Father is.

Lord Jesus, we began by saying that the greatest treasure we possess is the Holy Eucharist, may we all give It the love and respect that is Its due.

PENTECOST

(Three sermons)

RECOGNIZING the voice of God, and RESPONDING to that voice.

After the Ascension where did Our Blessed Mother and the Apostles go to? They went back to Jerusalem to prepare for the coming of the Holy Spirit. In the next nine days they were wrapt in prayer asking the Holy Spirit to come down upon them. Jesus had told them the Holy Spirit would comfort and befriend them. He would recall to their minds everything Jesus had tried to teach them in the last three years. Among His last instructions Jesus said, "And now I am sending down to you what the Father has promised. Stay in the city then, until you are clothed with the Power from on high". (Lk. 24:49) It was important that they should prepare for the coming of the Holy Spirit. The Holy Spirit would have a greater effect on their lives if they longed for His Coming.

Since the feast of the Ascension how well have we prepared for His Coming? Have we come to Church today and been told is the feast of the Holy Spirit and we have not looked forward to it or prepared for it? If that is the case our response to His Coming to us today will have less effect than if we had prayed to Him several times a day since Ascension Thursday and longed for His Coming. Isn't this true if we are going on a holiday? Looking forward to it and planning for it helps us to enjoy the holiday even more.

Let me tell you a story. At a military base the following words appeared on a notice board, "A telegraph specialist - someone specialized in Morse Code is needed. Those interested in the job report to the Captain's office tomorrow at 09 hours."

At 9 a.m. the next day, soldiers had already filled the Captain's waiting room. There were so many that the room was filled to capacity. The job they were all seeking was a very desirable one. They all wanted it! They waited. Some of them read magazines. Some listened to music through their headsets. Some carried on conversations among themselves. There was a cough here, a laugh there, the deep sighs of boredom, the low steady hum of voices. Just the quiet buzz of cooped-up humanity. Then suddenly there was also the sound of dots and dashes coming from a telegraph machine somewhere. As a result a soldier stood up, walked across the room, opened the door to the Captain's office, and disappeared behind the closed door.

The Captain welcomed the soldier, and said, "Sit down, soldier. What made you come in here?"

The soldier replied, "Sir, I heard a Morse Coded message that said 'This is your Captain. If you're reading this message, come into my office immediately.'"

"That's exactly right," said the Captain. "You were listening, you heard, you knew the message was for you and you responded. Excellent, soldier. The job is yours."

That story has a good message for us today. If we aren't careful, we can get caught up in the noise of the world all around us - like the soldiers waiting to enter the Captain's office. If that happens we will completely miss the fact that the "Captain" who is the Holy Spirit is speaking to us. God is speaking to us all the time and how many of us are listening?

All of us through our Baptism and Confirmation are temples of the Holy Spirit, but is He lying dormant within us? The Holy Spirit wants to make us more like Christ, but it is up to us to activate Him. Today He wants to inspire, guide and teach us, but like that soldier are we listening? Or are we like the other soldiers who were wrapped up in themselves and their own world?

Today calls us to a new beginning – the day when our Blessed Lady and the first disciples were given the spectacular gift of the indwelling of the Spirit of God. The Holy Spirit changed the disciples from being weaklings into brave witnesses for Christ. He fired them to bring people to Christ.

It is no less spectacular for us – we have been given the same gift and we are called to LISTEN, to hear, to know the message and it is for us TO RESPOND in obedience to what we hear.

A day should never go by without us praying to the Holy Spirit in our morning and evening prayers. Every morning we could say a prayer like this, "Holy Spirit, today, I want You to be a part of my every thought, word or deed. I want to be aware of You every moment of the day. I never want You to leave me." At night we could say, "Holy Spirit, how did we get on?" Not just, "How did I get on?" We should be constantly thanking the Holy Spirit for any good we do for we cannot even take the first small step towards Heaven without His Help, as St Paul says, "You cannot say the name of Jesus without the help of the Holy Spirit".

Today, how important it is that we should spend some time in quiet prayer, thinking and loving the Holy Spirit for He is the God of Love. If we want to know how to love, the Holy Spirit is the one to teach us. Such quiet reflection is time well spent and not a waste of time.

Heavenly Father and Jesus Your Son we thank for the gift of the Holy Spirit. May we listen to His still small voice within us -- and respond to what we hear.

'IS THE HOLY SPIRIT ACTIVE OR DORMANT IN MY LIFE?'

Today is Pentecost, the feast day of the Holy Spirit. Let us acknowledge this fact and invite Him into our lives. This is what Our Blessed Lady, the Apostles and the early disciples of Jesus did on that first Pentecost almost 2,000 years ago.

He made His presence felt with a mighty wind that rushed through the room in which they were, and with tongues of fire that rested on each of their heads. For nine days since Ascension Thursday, at Jesus' request, they had been pleading with Him to come among them. When He did He changed them forever.

His coming made them completely different people. Before that fateful day the Apostles would have been considered as cowards, uncertain about their future, lacking direction and inspiration. Once the Holy Spirit had entered their hearts and minds, at their invitation, they became fearless, enthusiastic for the cause of Christ, with a mission and a message.

Their one desire was to preach about Christ who had been crucified and was now risen from the dead. Now they realised that those three years they had spent in His company had all come together and what they had seen and heard made sense. They regarded themselves as the most blessed of men. The world was at their feet and their one desire was to conquer it for Christ. During that day there were 3,000 converts and the Catholic Church was born. The Holy Spirit had given them all the strength, the zest and the hope they needed to continue the work that Christ had started. They were completely under the control of the Holy Spirit - their words were His words. They not only heard God's words but spoke them to those who needed to hear them in the languages they could understand.

It is easy to be carried away by what happened on that particular day long ago ... but what about now? What does it mean for us to be filled with the Holy Spirit? His coming at Pentecost was not a one-off occasion. This was just the start of His permanent presence in the Catholic Church.

The Holy Spirit came to each of us at our Baptism and our Confirmation. If only we could realise just how close He is to us still! What a difference He could make in our lives. What a mistake it is for us to allow Him to remain dormant within us.

If our prayer life is tepid or the bare minimum, if we are not making headway in our relationships with God the Father, Jesus and the Holy Spirit, it means just one thing.

And if we are drifting through life without purpose or direction, if there is no joy nor peace in our lives, if there is frequent impatience or anger, inability to control the tongue and delight in gossiping, it means just one thing.

And if we are selfish, lacking in care for others, if I cannot control my senses and seek to dally with pornography on the internet, it means just one thing ... that the Holy Spirit is dormant within us, His presence ignored, as we go on our own tragic way.

Can we not hear the Holy Spirit saying, 'Come to Me. Open your heart and let Me change you to lead a fulfilled and exciting life. Let Me grow in you. Let My love, joy, peace, patience, goodness, generosity, trustfulness, gentleness and self-control be with you'?

On this Pentecost Sunday let each one of us make a resolution to wake up to His presence within us. Let us begin by first thanking God the Father and His Son Jesus for giving us God the Holy Spirit. Let us admit our sorrow to the Holy Spirit for not letting Him be effective in our lives. Let us ask Him to make us aware of His beautiful presence in us and at the beginning of every day to say this prayer, 'Give me the strength Holy Spirit to do the work of this day, and grant that at its close, I am found worthy of Your trust in me.' And at the end of each day to ask, 'Holy Spirit, how did we get on?' … the 'we' being the Holy Spirit and ourselves. For if I forgot Him and went it alone, my day has failed to live up to His expectations.

Come Holy Spirit, Creator come

From Thy bright heavenly throne,

Come, take possession of our souls,

And make them all Thy own.

Make them all Thy own.

CONTINUING WHAT JESUS STARTED

Acts 2:1-11; I Cor.l2:3-7,12-13; Jn. 20:19-23

The story of Pentecost, as told in the Book of Acts, confronts us with things that are not easy to understand. The Holy Spirit made His presence felt with a strong wind. This demonstrates for me the power of the Holy Spirit. Then we are told, "Tongues as of fire appeared which parted and came to rest on each of them." I think the fire demonstrates the love the Holy Spirit was imparting on the Apostles. Next we are told that "they began to express themselves in foreign tongues as the Spirit prompted them." Was it a miraculous ability to speak languages they had never learned? Or did they speak in their own language but their hearers understood them in theirs? That first Pentecost confronts you and me with much mystery.

Our Gospel reading has some of the same. Jesus suddenly appeared in a room where all the doors were locked. Obviously, His resurrected body could do things that His natural body could not. Once in the room, we are told that He breathed on the disciples and said, "Receive the Holy Spirit." That too raises questions. Was the Spirit given on the day of Pentecost, fifty days after the resurrection or was the Spirit given on the evening of the first Easter? Maybe it was both.

I do not know exactly the when and the how of the coming of God's Spirit upon His church, but I think I know the why. The risen Christ first said, "As the Father has sent Me, so I send you." Then He breathed on them and said, "Receive the Holy Spirit." It means that we are to continue what Jesus started and we are endowed with God's Spirit to help us do precisely that. Our mission is a continuation of Christ's mission and we are enabled to do it by the power of the Holy Spirit.

Now there are certain things Jesus did which are beyond our capabilities. All of the Gospels attribute some things to Him that we can never do. Matthew tells us He walked on water. We can't do that. Mark tells us He restored the sight of a blind man. Again we can't do that.

Luke tells us He stilled a storm with just the sound of His voice. We can't do that. John tells us He called back to life a man who had been dead for four days. We can't do that.

If we take the New Testament literally, the life and work of Jesus is out of our reach. What then is the meaning of this statement, "As the Father has sent Me, so I send you."? I am going to mention three things that Jesus did, which everyone of us can continue.

First, He treated all people with respect. Every person was important to Him. A rich man, who was a Pharisee, invited Jesus to dinner and He went. These people, as a whole, were rather hostile toward Jesus, but He honoured the man's invitation. He treated him with respect. At that dinner, a prostitute entered the room and washed Jesus' feet with her tears and dried them with her hair. He was no different to the rich Pharisee than He was to the poor prostitute. Jesus treated them both with respect. We can do the same.

To someone, this may seem like a watering down of Pentecost. After all, when the Holy Spirit came upon the church, He gave them great power. He enabled them to preach the gospel and to heal the sick. Why are we talking about so mundane a matter as treating people with respect? The most convincing sermon to be preached in this community will not be from this pulpit. It will be out there on the streets, in the homes, and in the stores, where Christian people treat each other with respect. I can think of nothing that would be more healing in our society than showing respect to each other on a daily basis. "As the Father has sent me, so I send you."

Another thing that Jesus did was give preference to the wayward and the weak. He once told a story about a shepherd who had a hundred sheep but one was lost. The shepherd left the ninety-nine and went looking for the lost one. That's what Jesus did. He reached out to the people who existed on the margins of society. He cared for everybody, but especially for those who needed Him most. We can do that. It won't be easy for we tend to care for those who are nice and won't give us any hassle. We are not very keen to help people at the bottom of the heap who are of not much use to us. They cannot recommend us for a job or a promotion. They cannot buy our products. They cannot bolster our egos. Why bother with them? Jesus was not like that. His chief concern was not the people who could help Him, but the people whom He could help. By the power of the Holy Spirit, like Jesus, we can be like the shepherd looking for the lost one. "As the Father has sent me, so I send you."

A third thing that Jesus did was forgive. He forgave a woman who was caught in the act of adultery. He called Judas "friend", knowing all the while of his betrayal. He forgave those who nailed Him to the cross. He forgave His disciples for forsaking Him in His hour of need. Jesus was always ready to offer forgiveness. In our reading, He commissioned His church and His apostles to become agents of forgiveness. Do you know of anything our world needs more than that? Forgiveness puts us at right with God and brings us together.

Lord Jesus, Pentecost marks the coming of the Holy Spirit upon the church. May we by Your Holy Spirit, be empowered to continue what You started - to treat all people with respect, to care for those who cannot care for themselves, and to forgive those who have wronged us. "As the Father has sent Me, so I send you."

SECOND SUNDAY OF EASTER

THE NEED TO RENEW OUR FAITH

Jn. 20:1-9

I never cease to be fascinated by John's account of the Resurrection of our Lord. To read it is to come away with the inescapable impression that it was written by an eyewitness. There is no laboured attempt at proof, just one man's version of what happened. The details are so graphic that it could only be told by someone who was there.

First, John remembers that Mary Magdalene came to him and Peter early on Sunday morning, just before dawn. She had been to the tomb. Obviously, she could not sleep. Sorrow can induce one of the worst forms of insomnia. When you're grieving in the middle of the night, it seems the day will never come; and you are not at all certain that you even want it to. So Mary got up before daylight and went to the grave. Not that that would do any good; that was just where she wanted to be. But on arrival at the grave she made a terrifying discovery. The tomb was open. The stone had been rolled away. Though Mary was frightened she got close enough to see, even in the darkness, that the body of Jesus was gone. Her immediate thought was that the body had been stolen. Someone, for some indescribably sick reason, has stolen the body of Jesus. At this point she hurried to tell the sad news to Peter and John.

Next, John remembers how he and Peter started out to run to the tomb. For a time they ran side by side; then John began to forge ahead. He was younger and probably in better condition and so got there first. He stood there in the half darkness, bent down, looked into the tomb and tried to figure out what happened. Then Peter arrived, and in typical fashion went straight into the tomb, and John followed him. There is no suggestion that they had a lantern; so by this time, there must have been enough light for them to see. Mary was right; the tomb was empty. Nothing was there but the grave clothes. That empty tomb and those grave clothes did something transforming to John. In one place, was the winding sheet, and in another was the cloth that had been about His head, neatly folded and laid aside. None of this gave the appearance of people in a hurry. If grave robbers had carried away the body of Jesus, why would they take the time to remove the sheet that enfolded Him? Why would they neatly fold the head cloth and lay it in another place? There was only one answer; Jesus had risen through the clothes. The robbery theory somehow didn't hold water.

At this point, John, speaking about himself said, "He saw and believed." This was the recorded profession of someone's belief that Jesus had risen from the dead. Some people find it easier to believe than others. John was one of those people. He had not yet seen the risen Lord nor talked with anyone who had. He did not even understand the scriptures that prophesied His rising. All he had was an empty tomb and some abandoned grave clothes. Yet, "He saw and believed."

Wrapped up in that four-word sentence is a world of meaning. It speaks of more than a conviction concerning the resurrection. John, obviously, is saying that standing there in that empty tomb, he arrived at the conclusion that Jesus had risen from the dead. But that is not the total story. For John to believe in Jesus was nothing new. At one point in his life, he had believed in Him so strongly that he forsook everything, his family, a secure job in order to follow Him. Then as the weeks and months went by, he had come to believe in Him more and more. The way that Jesus lived seemed right. The things that He taught made sense. The kind of Man that He was seemed the most real thing in all the world. John's total conviction about God, about life, and about himself had come to revolve around Jesus. In Him was the rhyme, the reason, the reality of everything. Jesus was more than just a friend. He was Truth in the midst of confusion. He was Light in the vast sea of darkness. He was the Eternal Life of God surrounded by human mortality. Then came that fatal day on Calvary, John's faith was dealt a mortal blow. When Jesus died, everything John believed in was shaken to the core.

Then standing there in that empty tomb, "He saw and believed." John is telling us that his faith in Jesus was validated and renewed. All of the things that he hoped for and believed in came rushing back. Life turned right side up again. He had not been misled after all.

That is precisely what you and I need this Easter morning – not simply to believe in the objective truth of the Resurrection, but to have our faith in Jesus and the things for which He stands renewed. This world has a way of playing havoc with the principles in which we try to believe. As one of our Christmas carols puts it, "Hate is strong, and mocks the song of peace on earth, good will toward men." How can one keep on believing in Christ in the kind of rat race that modern life represents? Everything that He stands for gets shoved aside, trampled on, crucified almost every day that we live.

Let's face it – most of the time we are afraid to trust Him, lest we make fools of ourselves in the process. He talked about loving our enemies, turning the other cheek, going the second mile. Where is the place for those kinds of things in this kind of world? The only thing that applies here is the law of the jungle, the survival of the fittest. Try to turn the other cheek in a business deal and see how far it gets you. This is a dog-eat-dog kind of world; and those who do not face that fact either get run over or left behind.

Let's be honest: isn't that how we really think most of the time? This world did to Christ the very worst it could. It rejected His Truth and nailed Him to a cross, but on the third day He overcame it all, even death. John saw and believed. That is what you and I need this Easter Sunday – a renewal of our faith.

IMMACULATE CONCEPTION

HOW IMPORTANT MARY WAS TO GOD AND US

I have some exciting news for you today. So much news we hear and read is bad and depressing. Today is a very special and important day for all men and women. Let me tell you why.

It was always the will of the Father, the Son and Holy Spirit to be loved perfectly by one of His creatures. But how was this possible? His Son, who was begotten of the Father from all eternity, not created, was at a moment in time to become man. He would need a mother who from the first moment of her existence and right throughout her life was sinless. That person was to be Mary, the girl from the village of Nazareth. Her parents were Anne and Joachim. They were to be the only mother and father to conceive a daughter who was immaculate, sinless. This had to be, for it would just not be fitting that God the Father's Son should have a mother who was in any way, or for any moment of time under the dominion of

Satan. So Mary was conceived immaculate and also to be given the unique privilege of being sinless all her life.

Now in today's Gospel this truth is revealed to us. The archangel Gabriel, not just an angel, is sent by God to Mary, a virgin in the village of Nazareth. She addressed her in these words, "Hail, full of grace." That can only mean one thing, that Mary was conceived immaculate, and sin had never touched her. These words greatly disturbed Mary and she was afraid to be addressed in such glowing terms. Of course Mary was humble. She knew in comparison to God she was nothing. He was all that mattered. All that she had she knew had been given to her from God. All praise should be given to Him. The spotlight should only be on God. Now she was seeing that some of that light was being diverted in her direction. Later on Mary was to say, "He looked upon the lowliness of His handmaid, from henceforth all generations will call me blessed."

Gabriel could see how fearful Mary was and so he said, "Mary, do not be afraid you have won God's favour. You are to conceive and bear a Son and you must name Him Jesus. He will be great and will be called the Son of the Most High." This got Mary thinking. She was saying to herself, "It is my intention to be a virgin. How is it possible at the same time that I can be a mother?" So Mary said to the angel, "But how can this come about, since I am a virgin?" Gabriel now was to reveal for the first time that in God there are Three Person, Father, Son and Holy Spirit. Up to this moment the Jews, who had a close relationship with God, believed that God is just One Person. How fitting it should be that this family information of God should be first revealed to Mary, the greatest human person who walked our earth. Jesus is not a human Person. He is a divine Person who through Mary took to Himself our human nature. So let's listen to Gabriel's revelation of the Blessed Trinity and in doing so God reveals He is not going to take away Mary's virginity. "The Holy Spirit (the Third Person of the Blessed Trinity) will come upon you and the power of the Most High (the First Person of the Blessed Trinity) will cover you with its shadow. And so the Child (the Second Person of the Blessed Trinity) will be holy and will be called the Son of God." Yes, I repeat, how fitting it is that this revelation of there being Three Persons in One God should have been first revealed to Mary.

God never forces anyone. He has given each one of us free will. His plan hinged upon Mary's consent. If she said 'No' His plan would be dashed. It was at this moment that not only Gabriel, but all Heaven and earth breathlessly awaited Mary's response. Mary who loved God so much, as no other creature did, could make only one response. Beautifully, humbly and so willingly she said, "I am the handmaid of the Lord, let what you have said be done to me.' Those are the greatest words recorded in the Bible. If Mary had said 'no' there would have been no Jesus and no salvation for us. And so the Word, the Second Person of the Blessed Trinity became flesh and lived among us. That, my friends, is the exciting news Holy Mother Church has for us today.

Heavenly Father, we thank you for the tremendous love You have for us Your children; that Your Son loves us so much that from all eternity He wanted to become one of us. Mary we thank you for the generous part you played in our redemption. We can truly say that had there been no Mary there would have been no Jesus. You are so important to God and us.

O Mary conceived without sin, pray for us who have recourse to thee.

ANNUNCIATION

THE MOST BEAUTIFUL LOVE STORY

The young couple, Mary and Joseph, were in love with each other and looking forward to being married. They also had a great love for God. As the story unfolds, we learn about an even greater love, the infinite love which God has for every human being.

For many, many years mankind was separated from God through the sin of our first parents. God was waiting for the appropriate moment to bridge the gap between Himself and us. The only way God wanted it to come about was for His Son to become one of us. Now His Son, the perfect God man, could say to His Father "On behalf of my sinful brothers and sisters I apologise for the wrong done." This day, the feast of the Annunciation of the Lord, was the day that God chose to put His plan into action.

This love of God was revealed to Mary in the words of an archangel. Mary was the highly favoured woman who was to give birth to God's Son. Mary was at first very disturbed by this news, and she could not understand how such a conception could take place. The angel gave her the explanation she needed. "The Holy Spirit will come upon you and the power of the Most High will cover you with its shadow. And so the Child will be holy and will be called the Son of God." In these words God announced for the first time that in Him there are three Persons, Father, Son and Holy Spirit. Before this moment, the Jews had believed that there was only one Person in God. Even great men like Abraham, Moses, King David and the prophets had no knowledge of the Blessed Trinity. How fitting it was that this intimate detail of God's life should have been first revealed to Mary, who was to bear His Son.

Each Person of the Blessed Trinity loved us and wanted to play a part in saving us. The Father was giving His Son, the Son was humbling Himself to become one of us, and this would be achieved by the love and power of the Holy Spirit. Now, only one more thing was needed, the love and co-operation of Mary. Mary was free to say yes or no to God. Our salvation depended on her answer. Because she loved God so much there was only one answer she could give, and that was, "I am the handmaid of the Lord. Let what you have said be done to me."

All the persons in our story fully gave their love. What is God asking of us? He wants our love. Because we are sinners, we cannot love Him perfectly, as He loves us, but we can try our best. This is a love story which will never end, because it will continue into eternity.

(Today's feast has a message for those who practice and believe in abortion. Life is sacred and begins at the moment of conception, not after 20, 22 or 24 weeks as some would have us believe.)

Let us end on a note of thanks. We thank each Person of the Blessed Trinity and Mary and Joseph for the part they played in our redemption.

ASSUMPTION

RESPECT FOR OUR BODIES

"Mary, the immaculate and ever-virgin Mother of God, when the course of her earthly life was over, was taken up, body and soul, into heavenly glory." With these words, Pope Pius X11 declared in 1950, the doctrine of our Blessed Lady's Assumption into Heaven was an essential truth of the Catholic faith. Many of you will recall the event. You may remember the outcry and the protests which it provoked. Many Christians of other denominations were angry and distressed that the Pope had placed yet another formidable obstacle across the path leading to Christian unity. Sadly, too, there were many Catholics who wondered whether a solemn definition in this matter was either necessary or wise. They have all been proved wrong. History has shown that from that moment, Christian unity began to be taken seriously and was given fresh impetus.

Some have asked the question "Is the doctrine of Our Lady's Assumption really that important?" For nineteen hundred years the Church got on perfectly well without insisting that everyone should believe that Our Lady is already glorified in her body, like Jesus her Son. What point was there in making so contentious an issue an article of faith in 1950? They thought, surely Christians in a pagan world have much more urgent problems to worry about?

We have to consider what makes our present times so different from all the preceding centuries in the history of the world. May I suggest two things. First, never in human history has there been such appalling bloodshed, cruelty and torture as in the first fifty years of the 20th century. In Europe alone, sixty million men, women and children lost their lives in two World Wars. Just mention names like Hiroshima, Nagasaki, Auschwitz and other concentration camps and we're reminded that never before on such a large scale have human beings shown such utter contempt for the human body.

The second feature which distinguishes our own age from all the preceding centuries can also be summed up in one word; let us label it "glamour". "Glamour" sums up the idolization and worship of the beautiful human body and particularly the beauty of a young woman's body. In the majority of films and television shows, the character of the person is secondary, the primary importance is how they look. A whole industry has been built on that word "glamour."

There you have the first half of the 20th century at its most distinctive. Never has the human body been so debased. It has been treated as an object, a thing. On one side it is treated with contempt, and on the other side, it is idolized. Pope Pius XII's solemn proclamation of the doctrine of the Assumption of Our Lady was a cry to the Church and the world that both these ways of looking at the body are intolerably wrong. Our bodies are neither to be despised nor to be worshipped. They are to be treated at all times with reverence and respect, because they are a part of a person who is created in the image of God. And that is the importance of Our Blessed Lady's Assumption.

Our final destiny also is to enjoy the resurrection of the body, when we too are cleansed from all sin. In the meantime our bodies are to be used in the service of God and our neighbour. They may be ugly, they may be old, they may be crippled; that doesn't matter. Nor does it matter whether or not they are handsome, young, healthy and strong. All that matters is the person inside.

We must never belittle the body. For each one of us, the body is an essential part of what makes you uniquely you and me uniquely me, and therefore, we look forward to the resurrection of the body and life everlasting.

If the doctrine of the Assumption was relevant to the Church and society at large in 1950 it is just as relevant to our world today. The body is still despised through bloodshed, an increase in abortions, and the acceptance of euthanasia. It is also worshipped through the blatant and unashamed display of pornography, exploitation and child abuse.

May the purity of Mary be a beacon attracting us all to have the correct attitude to our bodies, which enshrine our souls and form the complete human person.

EXALTATION OF THE HOLY CROSS

BY THE HOLY CROSS YOU HAVE REDEEMED THE WORLD Jn. 3:13-17

What should have been the end of an itinerant preacher from a small corner of a vast empire was the beginning of a world religion that has swept the face of the Earth - Christianity is the only religion that has grown out of the death of its founder. The Cross is to the Church what the flag is to every country. It is with this sign that we bless ourselves, other people and various objects.

There was a time when the cross was one of the world's most hated signs, similar to the electric chair, the gas chamber, the guillotine, the firing squad or the hangman's rope. Death, by crucifixion, was regarded as the cruellest form of capital punishment. Cicero, the Roman Senator, said, 'No cross should ever come near a Roman soldier.' What originally was a sign of punishment and death now symbolises abundant life.

Some people wear crosses as jewellery because of its Christian symbolism but for many it has lost much of its original significance. Yet they would not dream of sporting a miniature electric chair or gallows around their neck. The cross should evoke an even greater sense of horror since it was the instrument by which the Son of God made man was executed.

When the early Christians first began to honour the Cross, because of its association with Jesus, the non-Christians were scandalized. St Paul called it an obstacle to the Jews, and madness to the Greeks and Romans. It represents the price, of course, of victory and salvation. Jesus had to be nailed to His Cross before He could receive His crown from His Father for reopening the gates of Heaven by atoning for the sins of the world. His crucifixion appeared to be a defeat.

How is it possible that the Cross of Christ could turn defeat into victory and death into life? It was the Father's will that His Son should give Himself up to the forces of destruction - Satan and all his powers - and defeat them by dying on the Cross and rising from the dead. "God so loved the world that He gave His only Son, that whoever believes in Him may have eternal life." What generosity!

How many human parents would sacrifice their child to save others? Just as the Hebrews of old looked at the bronze serpent to save them from death, so we look at the Cross of Jesus to save us from sin, eternal death and hell. St Francis said the Cross was his meditation book: how often do we look at the crucifix and think of what Jesus did for us and what our sins did to Him? If we did this frequently we would most definitely sin less.

The words of the Preface of the Mass sum up the whole meaning of today's feast: "The tree of man's defeat became his tree of victory. Where life was lost, there life has been restored through Christ our Lord." Jesus turned the sign of death into a triumph over evil.

May we never fail to appreciate the words, 'We adore You, O Christ, and we praise You, because of Your holy Cross, You have redeemed the world."

ALL SAINTS

LIVING THE BEATITUDES

I love the feast 'All Saints'. It tells me that all the good people who tried their best to love God and their neighbour are now enjoying the bliss of heaven. I believe that my parents who did lead saintly lives are now in heaven and are praying for me to join them. I'm sure there are many of you who feel the same way about your parents.

Ask most people what brings them happiness. Some would say money and plenty of money, an annual holiday, a comfortable life, a good marriage, a stable job and so on. Jesus would say the truly blessed are those who are poor in spirit, those who mourn, the meek, the persecuted. Jesus says these are the things that bring happiness. Jesus' values in the eight Beatitudes turn the values of the world upside down and His values show us the way to true happiness. Whenever I read the Beatitudes I think I am reading a thumb nail autobiography of Jesus. He was all those things.

To be poor in spirit means that we see our utter poverty, and how reliant we are on our Father in heaven. We recognise we depend upon Him for the air we breathe, our next heart beat, for our nourishment. Knowing that He will look after us and never let us down, brings us so much peace and happiness. When we mourn for our sins and those of the world, we are appealing to God's love and forgiveness. We know He does listen and does forgive. To be meek doesn't mean that we lack backbone. It means that we are truly humble and we live our lives with gentleness and self control.

What wonderful promises for those who live the Beatitudes. It doesn't bring them the material happiness the world hungers for, but entry into the kingdom of heaven. They will be satisfied, they will see God and be called children of God. The saints who have gone before us lived their lives this way. They are the ones we remember today.

Lord Jesus, Your ways are so different from those of the world. The Saints, whose feast day we keep today, are saints precisely because they followed Your way. As a result their lives involved much conflict and sacrifice, but ultimately it brought them real happiness. May we follow in their footsteps.

LONGING FOR HEAVEN

We are all on a journey – a journey to heaven, I hope. I hate the thought of one person being in hell. I often pray for people like Judas, Henry VIII, Hitler and Stalin and I hope, before they took their last breath, they prayed for forgiveness. The thought of anyone being in hell abhors me. To be separated from a loving God, from our blessed Lady and all the lovely saints I have known and our loved ones would be insufferable. How happy I would be if I could help save one soul from hell.

Every day I pray for this intention with the prayer, "Eternal Father, do not consider what we truly deserve but lead us all to heaven there to be happy with You forever."

Today is All Saints day and let's talk about heaven – this happy and perfect place that our heavenly Father has prepared for those who love Him. I think how long more I have for this life? If I live till 90 I have ten years of my life left. How true were my Mum's words, "The older you get, the quicker the years will fly by." I am so glad I am posted to Pantasaph, my burial place. The next ten years, should I live that long, are going to fly by and then I hope I shall be going to heaven via purgatory. What bliss God has prepared for us! Is there any greater joy than to gaze into the faces of Jesus and Mary knowing how much they love me; to meet our heavenly Father and the Holy Spirit? One of the joys of heaven that I am looking forward to is having a hug from our blessed Lady; to meet St. Joseph and all my favourite saints, my Guardian Angel, St. Francis of Assisi, St. Marcellus, Padre Pio, Leopold of Mendic, Maria Goretti, Bernadette, Charles Borromeo, John Vianney, Gertrude, John Fisher and Thomas More just to mention a few; to meet my Mum and Dad and my eldest brother and my second eldest who I feel sure are in heaven. I tell you, I can't wait. Heaven is going to be one perfect eternal wow! I know if I repent of all my sins and daily look forward to what God has prepared for me surely He is going to give me heaven.

I say these words to encourage you to long every day for your heavenly home where we will enjoy eternal bliss.

Heavenly Father, may all of us present, in fact everyone who is living on this earth now live with You, Your Son Jesus, the Holy Spirit, our blessed Lady and all our loved ones.

HOW TO HONOUR THE SAINTS

Rev. 7:2-4, 9-14; 1 Jn. 3:1-3; Mt. 5:1-12

Since the year 610, November 1 has been designated as the day we honour all the saints. What is the best way we can honour them?

We could, of course, speak of them in glowing terms and sing their praises. All this would be very appropriate but I am not at all sure that the saints would feel highly honoured by that. Remember we are thinking now of the greatest men and women who ever lived. Flattery means nothing to truly great people. They are not concerned about what others may think of them, but what God thinks of them.

In our first reading from the Book of Revelation, Saint John relates his vision of the saints in Heaven. "They have washed their robes white again in the blood of the Lamb." That is a symbolic way of saying that their sins have been forgiven through the sacrificial death of Jesus. In other words, before they were saints, they were sinners like the rest of us. They, no less than we, needed forgiveness and cleansing. Their access to the throne of God is based, not on personal merit, but on divine grace. This is a truth that needs to be emphasised. It seems obvious enough, but we tend to forget that the saints were just as human as we are. So, while paying tribute to these giants of our faith, we should keep that truth clearly in mind.

We also honour the saints by learning from them. They thought of themselves as sons and daughters of God, and wanted to be like Him. They wanted to live in such a way as to please their heavenly Father, achieving all that He wanted them to do. Their faith told them of the wonderful future He had in store for them. All these sentiments are summed up by John in the second reading, "We are already the children of God but what we are to be in the future has not yet been revealed; all we know is, that when it is revealed we shall be like Him because we shall see Him as He really is." We are all the sons and daughters of God. We have the potential to become saints. Those who are already saints, we can be certain, are praying that we will all realise our highest possibilities.

Another way we can honour the saints is by continuing the work which they started. Suppose you were a keen gardener. You cultivated the most beautiful roses imaginable. You were assiduous in watering, feeding and pruning these plants. When you are dead and gone, and can no longer look after them, how happy it would make you to know that there was someone else who was to take the same care of them as you did. One of the best ways of honouring your memory would be for someone to take care of the things which meant so much to you. So it is, too, with the saints.

These noble men and women of our faith lived unselfish lives. They devoted their lives to the service of others - feeding the hungry, nursing the sick, teaching the poor and underprivileged, and spreading the Gospel in foreign countries as missionaries. The examples are too numerous to mention. Many of them died heroic deaths for what they believed, being prepared to go to the scaffold rather than deny their faith and the authority of the Pope. What does our faith mean to us? What does the Pope mean to us? What does the Mass mean to us?

When we see such examples of dedication can we be casual about these things? We honour the saints when we love the things which meant so much to them and to which they devoted their lives.

That, I am convinced, is what the saints would ask of us. The causes for which they lived and died have not yet come to completion. That is always true of all great people. They give themselves to projects, too big to be finished in one lifetime. If their work is ever completed, it will be done by succeeding generations.

Lord Jesus, the unfinished work of Your Father's kingdom on Earth has been entrusted to us. We will not finish it, but we can carry it forward. Our small efforts in furthering the causes they believed in will surely honour all the saints of all the ages.

SS PETER AND PAUL

JESUS FINDS THE BEST IN US

Mt. 16:13-19

In every one of us there is more than one person. In his well-known story of "Dr. Jekyll and Mr. Hyde" Robert Louis Stevenson said, "All of us have a bright side to our nature, but we also have a dark side as well, and there is a constant battle between these two selves as to which one we put on show." Within all of us there is tremendous potential for good and for evil. The important challenge we face is how to bring out the best that is in us.

Today we honour the memory of two men who succeeded in doing that. The names given to them at birth were Simon and Saul, but the world remembers them as Peter and Paul. They were both leaders in the early Church but it would be difficult to find two more different individuals. Peter was a fisherman; Paul a Pharisee. Peter was married; Paul was single. Peter had a limited education; Paul was a scholar. Peter was an ordinary practising Jew; Paul practised his faith with fanaticism. Peter was a founder member of the original Church; Paul hated that Church and did his best to destroy it until Christ changed him. The only things these men had in common were their Jewish heritage and their devotion to Christ, and that they made themselves available to the Lord Who brought the best out of them.

Peter was with Him from the beginning. Paul met Him later on the road to Damascus. Having fallen under the spell of His friendship both of them walked with Him for the rest of their lives. Slowly they changed from being self-centred to being Christ centred. It was their devotion to Jesus that made them the men whose memory we honour. The moment we too make Christ the desire of our hearts and the centre of our lives, we will find that little by little, we unconsciously become like Him Whom we admire and love.

Jesus always wanted to bring the best out of people by challenging them. In our Gospel reading He gave Simon his new name, "You are Peter." At that moment, Peter seemed anything but rock-like. He was vacillating, impetuous and unstable, but deep inside him was the potential to be the foundation stone of Christ's church. With His help that is what he became. Jesus challenges all of us by saying, "You must be perfect as your heavenly Father is perfect." That's a goal we will never reach in this life but we must strive towards it. By telling us we are the salt of the earth, and the light of the world, He shows His confidence in us. This makes us realise He believes in us, and therefore we should believe in ourselves.

We all know people who bring the best out of us, and we also know people who bring out the worst in us. Surely, Jesus was someone who brought the best out of people. We can think of many who were changed by Him: the apostles, Mary Magdalene, the centurion, Zacchaeus, and others. He made them feel special, giving them self-respect because He showed them how much God loved them. We cannot imagine Jesus missing an opportunity to encourage people, but there was one person who He was unable to influence and that was Herod, to whom He never spoke one word. This must have been because Herod had hardened his heart to Him, and Jesus knew all His wisdom would fall on deaf ears. Why should He throw His pearls before such a swine? Jesus can draw the best out of us only if we open our hearts to Him and want to change.

If Jesus could bring the best out of an ordinary fisherman like Peter and a religious fanatic like Paul, could He not do the same for us?

THE NATIVITY OF JOHN THE BAPTIST

THE LESSON JOHN THE BAPTIST TEACHES US

Today's feast day has an all important lesson to teach us. John the Baptist was obsessed with the person of his cousin Jesus. His whole life was focused on preparing people for His coming. So today he gives us the opportunity to ask him to help us make Jesus the centre of our lives.

The Church sees the importance of John the Baptist for he is the only person, apart from Jesus and His mother Mary, whose birth we celebrate. Should his birthday fall on a Sunday, his birthday takes precedence over the Sunday liturgy.

The circumstances of John's birth were unusual. God sent His archangel Gabriel to announce to Zachary, an old man whose wife Elizabeth was well past child bearing age, that his wife was to bear him a boy and he was to call him John. They had long given up hope of ever having a child. How they would have loved one. It was the desire of every couple to have a child. To be childless was a stigma. When told this news by Gabriel Zachary doubted him and for this God struck him dumb.

During Elizabeth's pregnancy Mary, who was carrying Jesus, came to visit her cousin Elizabeth, and, as God promised Elizabeth was filled with the Holy Spirit and John was washed clean of original sin. He is the only person, apart from Jesus and Mary, who was born without original sin.

John was well aware of his mission. He was to prepare the people of Israel for the coming of Jesus, the Messiah. This he did by spending years in the wilderness in prayer and fasting. There in the desert he had nothing to distract him. When the time was right he came to the river Jordan and began inviting people to repent of their sins and be baptised. People of every station in life flocked to listen to him - priests, Pharisees, soldiers, tax collectors and ordinary folk. They repented of their sins and were baptised.

One day Jesus came to be baptised and John would not hear of it. He felt he should be baptised by Jesus, but Jesus gently persuaded him to baptise Him and he responded. For doing this John was rewarded by the presence of the Blessed Trinity and hearing the voice of the Father saying, 'This is My beloved Son.'

Now his mission was completed. He wanted to wean his disciples away from him and join their allegiance to Jesus. He did this by telling them, 'Look, there is the Lamb of God who takes away the sins of the world.' John had become so popular. He did not want the limelight for himself. His attitude to Jesus could be summed up in his words, "He must increase and I must decrease."

John the Baptist was the first martyr of Jesus. He pointed out to Herod that he was leading a sinful life. It was wrong for him to take Herodias who was the wife of another man. This infuriated Herodias and so she plotted his death. And so John gave his life for the truth.

Surely the greatest proof we have of the importance of John the Baptist is the fact that Jesus who is God said, 'Of all men born of women there is none greater than John the Baptist.' Praise indeed coming from the lips of Jesus!

Now what is John the Baptist's message to you and me? It would be the same as the message he gave to the people of Israel. 'Repent of your sins.' Jesus shows us how this is done. He has given us the beautiful Sacrament of Reconciliation and sadly there are so many Catholics who make little or no use of this Sacrament. They come to Communion every Sunday but it has been years since they have gone to Jesus in this Sacrament to receive His forgiveness and cement their friendship with Him. If you don't believe me listen to the words of St. Pope John Paul II. He said, 'If you do not go to Confession once a month you are not taking your spiritual life seriously.'

So our prayer today can be, "Lord Jesus, may we learn from John the Baptist to love you passionately, to make You the centre of our lives and to remain close to You by the means You have provided, the Sacrament of Reconciliation."

MOTHER OF GOD

Today our hearts should jump with joy at the thought that at the very beginning of a New Year we are keeping the feast of Mary, Mother of God. I think the reason why the Church has done this is so very obvious. We know that God is everything, and that everything else compared to Him is nothing. But among that nothing there is someone who shines out brilliantly. That person is Mary. In her humility she was able to recognise this. "He looked upon the nothingness of His handmaid, from this day all generations will call me blessed."

We know that it was always the intention of God to be loved perfectly by one of His creatures. This could only come about if His Son was to take to Himself our human nature. That would mean that He would have to find a perfect mother. It would just not be fitting if even for a split second Satan should have any dominion over her. The person He chose was Mary, the girl from Nazareth. She was therefore conceived immaculate and also given the unique privilege of being sinless all her life.

Mary was not forced into making this commitment. God's plan depended upon Mary's choice. He sent one of His highest ranked angels, Gabriel, to reveal His plan that she had been chosen to be the mother of His Son. We must remember that Mary's love for God increased with every moment of her life. Because she loved God so much how could she ever contemplate not fulfilling His plans? At the Annunciation I can just picture her bowing her head and joining her hands in reverence and saying with all the love in her heart, "Behold the handmaid of the Lord, let what you said be done to me." From that moment she became the Mother of God. From that moment she became the cause of salvation for herself and the whole human race. We can definitely say that when Jesus became Man He found Heaven in His mother Mary and that when He lived on this earth He was happiest when He was in her presence. We can express in wonder and love, "What a mother! What a lady!"

Mary always points the way to Jesus, never to her own glory. At the wedding feast of Cana, she told the servants, "Do whatever He tells you. It is significant that these should be the last recorded words of Mary in the Gospel. She continues to give the same message to us, "Do whatever He tells you".

Isn't it wonderful that we too can claim Mary as our mother? Jesus had done all He could for us. He gave us a Church in which we could find our salvation. He had given us the example of His life and His message was there in the Gospels. But as He hung on the Cross there was still one last treasure He had for us and that was His mother, when He said to us in the person of John, "Behold your Mother."

If only we could appreciate how much Mary loves us as a mother. When God wanted to tell us how much He loved us and how He would never desert us He used the image of a mother. "If a mother should forget the child of her womb, I shall never forget you." Could Mary, our mother, ever forget any one of us?

She has all the beautiful natural instincts our own mothers had for us. There have been times I have been in a home where there is a new born baby and the mother has heard her child crying in another room and I haven't heard a thing. The very cry can tell a mother whether it is a cry of hunger, discomfort or pain. I couldn't even hear the cry and if I did it would just be a cry calling for its mother's attention. We can always take our fears, our tears of unhappiness and pain to Mary, our mother, and she will comfort us, as no one else will.

No loving mother will ever forsake or abandon her child. I shall never forget that lovely story we witnessed on television some years back when there was that dreadful earthquake in Armenia. A mother and a daughter had been buried in the rubble for eight days. The rescuers had given up all hope of finding anyone alive. Yet, after that period, they dragged them alive from the rubble. The mother had kept her baby alive by cutting her finger and allowing her to drink the blood that flowed from it. That to me is a perfect picture of the lengths to which our blessed mother Mary would go to prove her love for us.

Is there anything Mary, our mother, would like to see in all of us? I think I can enumerate three things. Firstly, when she looks at each one of us, she would like to see something of her Son in us…the enthusiasm her Jesus had for doing the will of His Father, all His characteristics such as His caring nature, His gentleness and kindness. Secondly, she would love all of us to be united and loving one another. How it must break her heart to see her own countrymen and women in the Holy Land fighting and killing each other! Thirdly, she longs for us to be united with the Blessed Trinity and her one day in Heaven. It breaks her heart if any one of her children through malice should separate themselves from God and her.

Today then we ask the Holy Spirit to give us a tender and attentive love for God's holy mother and our heavenly mother and that we would never do anything to hurt or break her loving heart.

We end on a note of thanks. Thank you Jesus for giving Mary to us to be our mother, and thank you Mary for all the love and attention you give us.

LITTLE GIRL OF GALILEE

Little girl of Galilee, growing up so happily

Down by the lake, walking in the sand

Not knowing yet what God has planned, Mary.

What's it like to be so highly favoured Mary,

That nothing can stop God's love flowing in you

Like an ocean filling a drop of dew, Mary.

The night was black as death.

The whole world holding its breath.

How can I imagine your joy when you gave birth to a baby Boy, Mary.

Lulalulalu, lullalulalu

Rock Him gently but hold Him tight.

He's someone precious; He's our Light, Mary.

He must grow to man, be as strong as He can.

Some day He will have to bear, things that we are too weak to share, Mary.

Thank you is all I can say for showing us the way.

For giving to us the eternal Son.

For saying so firmly, "Thy Will be done", Mary.

Ref D9 B4b 290620-87544 145 Arial 11 PP VM F